52 Week Devotional
For Boys Ages 10-12

An imprint of Rose Publishing, Inc.
Carson, CA
www.Rose-Publishing.com

52 Week Devotional
for Boys Ages 10-12

H. Michael Brewer

Janet Neff Brewer

Jeannette Dall

Linda Washington

Compiled from Gotta Have God One-Year Devotional for Boys Ages 10-12, series, vols. 1-3 (Carson, CA: Rose Publishing ©2012-2015)

Gotta Have God! 52 Week Devotional for Boys 10-12 Compilation ©2016 Rose Publishing, Inc.

ISBN 10: 1-58411-176-3
ISBN 13: 978-1-58411-176-4
RoseKidz® reorder# L46972
JUVENILE NONFICTION/Religion/Devotion & Prayer

RoseKidz®
An imprint of Rose Publishing, Inc.
17909 Adria Maru Lane
Carson, CA 90746
www.Rose-Publishing.com

Cover and interior design by Nancy L. Haskins
Interior illustrations by Aline Heiser, Dave Carlson and Brie Spangler

Printed in South Korea   01   04.2016.APC

Contents

Contents

Your Best Friend

Hey, guys! Do you know Jesus wants to be your best friend?

It's true! There's no one He loves more than you. You probably have some questions about your life, and God has the answers. No matter what you are going through, He can help. And as you discover more and more about God, you'll wonder how you ever got along without Him. The good news is that you don't have to worry. God is on your side.

In this book, you'll enjoy 52 weeks of devotions and hands-on activities. That's a whole year's worth of exploring God and you. Each week you get to do five devotions and two activities to help you get closer to God. Puzzle answers are at the end of this book.

Work on one page a day. Find a quiet place where you can concentrate and not be disturbed. Take time to talk to God in prayer as you go through the book. Start today and learn why **you gotta have God!**

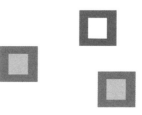

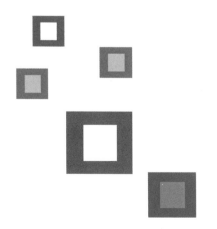

You Are God's Child

I have summoned you by name; you are mine.
– Isaiah 43:1

A Special Name

Robert Samuels was reading an article about famous sports people of the 1900s. "Listen to these neat names," he said to his dad. "Air Jordan. Slammin' Sammy. Big Mac. Crazy Legs. The Greatest. I wish I had a special name."

His sister had some suggestions. "How about Boring Bob? Or Recap Robert because you say everything twice?"

Robert glared at Tammy. "We'll call you Tattletale Tammy."

"Okay, enough already. Name calling is off limits." Dad paused. "Robert, you were named for your great-grandfather, the first mayor of this town. But you're forgetting your best identity. You are God's child because you believe in Jesus."

Your Turn

1. What is special about your name?
2. What is special about being called God's child? What does it mean to you?

_____

_____

_____

_____

Prayer

God, thank You for making me Your child. Help me always be proud of following You. Amen.

You Are God's Child

I have summoned you by name; you are mine.
– Isaiah 43:1

Created in God's Image

The Hernandez family arrived at the annual family picnic. A woman ran up and hugged Mrs. Hernandez. "Ellen, I'm so glad you came!" She saw Hector. "Your son sure looks like you—same freckles, same hair. Catch ya later."

"Cousin Rosie," Mrs. Hernandez explained to her son.

A man shook Mr. Hernandez's hand. "Welcome, Bill! Good to see you." He looked at Hector and said, "You sure look like your dad—same eyes, same nose."

"That's your Uncle Ben," Mr. Hernandez explained to Hector.

At noon, Hector took his loaded plate and sat next to Grandpa. "I'm sure getting tired of people saying I look like Mom or Dad. I'm me!"

Grandpa gave a hearty laugh. "Sure, but you're also a little bit of your mom and dad. You even have some of me in you. All the relatives here are alike in some way. We're from the same family." Grandpa took a bite. "Actually, all the people in the world are alike in one way. We're made in the image of God. That means we share His nature. We can love, be wise, be truthful, and enjoy the wacky relatives He gives us."

Your Turn

1. Who do people say you look like?
2. Why is it important that you are made in the "image of God"?

_____

_____

_____

Prayer

God, help me remind people of You when they see how I act and hear what I say. Amen.

You Are God's Child

I have summoned you by name; you are mine.
– Isaiah 43:1

Remember Who You Are

Andy slammed his locker shut and set off for home. At the school door, a group of boys caught up with him. They were laughing and joking.

"Hey, Andy!" one of the boys said. "Want to come over to Jerry's house?"

"We're watching a really cool movie—Main Street Murders," Jerry said. "My brother told me to return it, but we're going to watch it first."

"Bet there's a lot of blood, gore, and sex," said Scott. "Hurry! Just tell your parents you had to stay after school."

Remember who you are! Remember who you are! The words screamed in Andy's brain. He said, "I can't go with you. That's lying and disobeying my parents. Count me out." Then he headed home. He told his mom what had happened.

"Good for you!" his mother said. "It took courage to do that."

"I remembered what Dad said," Andy replied. "'When you face a problem, remember who you are.' I am part of the Reilly family and God's family. We don't lie or disobey."

Your Turn

1. Why might Andy want to go with the boys?
2. How do you think he felt after he said no to the boys?

_____

_____

_____

_____

Prayer

Dear God, help me always remember who I am—Your child. Amen.

You Are God's Child

I have summoned you by name; you are mine.
– Isaiah 43:1

Gifted by God

"You shoulda seen me today!" Rick O'Neal yelled as he ran into the house. "I pitched a no-hitter!"

"All right!" his father slapped hands with him.

"Nobody could touch me! I told Austin Campbell I could do it. I'm a better pitcher than he is any day."

"Well, Mr. Cool, I'm sure you've heard of the word 'sportsmanship.'"

"Yeah, yeah. But you gotta admit, Dad, I'm a better pitcher than Austin."

"Well, I'd like you to admit something too." said dad.

"What?"

"That God is the One who gave you that talent. Knowing that God is the One who gives us good gifts and talents will help keep us from…" his father cleared his throat, "…from getting big heads."

"Aw, Dad, can't I brag a little?"

"You can be happy about doing something well. But boasting about it isn't cool. Would you like it if someone told you he's a better pitcher than you are?"

"Well, I'd know he was lying," Rick said with a grin.

His dad grabbed him in a light headlock.

Rick laughed and said, "Uncle!"

Your Turn

1. What abilities do you have?
2. How can you use your abilities for God?

_____

_____

Prayer

God, help me appreciate the gifts and talents You have given me. Amen.

You Are God's Child

I have summoned you by name; you are mine.
– Isaiah 43:1

No Gift or Ability Is Better Than Another

The Sunday-school class was setting up for a skit. The boys volunteered to build the stage backdrop, but they didn't want the girls to help.

"What can girls do?" Ryan sneered.

"We can do anything you can do," Stephanie said. "Anyway, I'd rather paint the backdrop."

"Building is more important. I bet you can't hammer a nail straight."

"Oh? What do you know?"

"I know I'm hoping I'm not hearing you two arguing over which job is better," Mr. Simmons said. "This is supposed to be fun. When we all work together, no job is more important than another. Just like no ability God gives someone is better than an ability He gave to someone else. Isn't that right?"

"I was just teasing, I suppose the set wouldn't look good without paint," Ryan said.

Stephanie picked up her hammer while handing a paintbrush to Ryan and said, "How about I help you build the set and you can help me paint. Deal? "

Ryan smiled and said, "Deal!"

Your Turn

1. Think about the talents you have. How do you view those abilities? (Circle one.)
   - I'm better than anyone else at what I do.
   - I'm no better than anyone else.
   - I haven't thought about it much.
2. How do you think God wants you to see your abilities?

_____

Prayer

LORD, help me see my abilities the way You do. Amen.

You Are God's Child

Family Coat of Arms

Year ago, families had "coats of arms." These were shown on shields and tunics worn by soldiers. A coat of arms let everyone know about the person's family or who the soldier was fighting for. A coat of arms showed the family name, a motto or family saying, and some symbols that revealed the family's business or what the family was known for.

Create a coat of arms for your family. Your last name goes in the center. Think of a short motto for your family and write it down. Add some symbols that tell about your family. For example, the cross of Jesus, a pile of books, an animal, a heart (love), a baseball and bat.

Prayer

LORD, thank You for my family. When I think about being made in Your image, I am reminded of just how special my family is. Amen.

You Are God's Child

Men of God

God used the gifts and talents of many people. Can you find these names in the word search puzzle? The answers will be found across, down, diagonally, and backward. In this puzzle, "John" and "John Mark" are two separate answers.

Aaron
Abraham
David
Ezra

Isaiah
James
John
John Mark

Jonathan
Joseph
Josiah
Matthew

Moses
Nathan
Noah
Paul

Peter
Philip

```
P  I  L  I  H  P  E  S  O  J
J  N  U  E  S  V  J  B  A  O
O  D  A  T  K  A  W  H  B  N
S  I  P  T  M  E  I  A  R  A
I  V  A  E  H  N  Z  A  A  T
A  A  S  T  T  A  I  R  H  H
H  D  T  J  I  E  N  O  A  A
H  A  O  N  T  X  R  N  M  N
M  H  R  M  O  S  E  S  V  O
N  K  R  A  M  N  H  O  J  Q
```

Prayer

Dear LORD, I love to read about the mighty men of God in Your Word, the Bible. They teach me how You want me to be. Amen.

God Gave You Your Family and Friends

Be devoted to one another in brotherly love.
– Romans 12:10

Little Brother

"And stay *outta* my room!" Kent yelled just before he slammed the door. That'll teach him! he thought. *Little brothers—what a pain!* This was the third time that week Kent had caught his six-year-old brother in his room.

Suddenly Kent's glance took in a folded piece of blue construction paper on his pillow. He picked it up and read, "My big brother is kool." Petey had misspelled "cool." Kent smiled. He opened the card. "I know you are sad about your bad grade. I hope you feel better."

Kent shook his head. He had been in a foul mood because of the bad grade he'd received on a science quiz. He suddenly felt sad that he had gotten so angry at Petey. Petey was a pain sometimes, but he did like to do things to cheer up others.

Kent threw open his door. "Hey, Petey!" he called. He stepped out and searched for his brother. He found Petey playing with a construction set on the floor in his bedroom. "I'm sorry I yelled at you," he said. "Wanna play a computer game with me?"

Petey's face brightened. "Yes!"

Kent breathed a silent prayer, *Thank You, God, for my little brother.*

Your Turn

1. In what ways are you thankful for the people in your family?
2. Write at least three ways you could tell your family members how important they are to you.

_____

_____

Prayer

Thank You, God, for my family. Amen.

God Gave You Your Family and Friends

Be devoted to one another in brotherly love.
– Romans 12:10

Miss Velma

"Tyrice, get ready. I want you to go with me to Miss Velma's," Mrs. Robinson said.

Tyrice groaned. "Do I have to, Mom? She always calls me Bernard." Bernard was his brother.

"You know she likes to see young people in her house. She gets lonely."

"She's old. And she smells funny."

"We're all the family Miss Velma has. She was my grandmother's best friend. Miss Velma's like a grandmother to me. I'm grateful to God we still have her with us. You know she thinks the world of you. She's done some nice things for you, hasn't she?"

Tyrice didn't want to admit that. Miss Velma never forgot to send him a birthday or Christmas present. Yet he always grumbled when his mother made him give her a card. Suddenly he felt ashamed. "Hey, Mom, can we swing by the grocery store? I wanna get Miss Velma a plant." he asked. Will three bucks do that?"

Mrs. Robinson smiled and hugged Tyrice before he could escape.

Your Turn

1. Name someone you feel close to in your neighborhood or at church.
2. How can you let that person know that he or she is special to you?

_____

_____

_____

Prayer

Thank You, LORD, for giving me so many people to care about and who care about me. Amen.

God Gave You Your Family and Friends

Be devoted to one another in brotherly love.
– Romans 12:10

Respect

Rodney knew he was in for it when he saw his uncle's face.

"Rodney, what's this I hear about you yelling at your basketball coach?" Uncle James asked when he met his nephew after practice.

"Football and basketball players on TV do it all the time," Rodney said.

"You know better than to talk back to your coach. I just had a long talk with him. He's ready to put you on the bench for pulling a stunt like that."

"He just doesn't like me!" Rodney burst out. "He never says anything bad about anyone else. Just me. He got mad at me because I wouldn't pass the ball to his son. His son can't shoot!"

"Rod, I know you've been having some trouble with your coach. But do you remember what we've been talking about at Bible study? God gives people authority over us. That means they deserve our respect. You know what that means, don't you?"

Rodney had some idea, but he wanted to play dumb. "No."

"You owe your coach an apology."

Rodney groaned, but he knew his uncle wouldn't allow him to refuse for long. Besides, he knew his uncle was right.

Your Turn

1. Who are the leaders in your life?
2. Why is it important to show respect to those in authority?

_____

_____

Prayer

LORD, I need Your help to respect and obey the leaders in my life. Amen.

God Gave You Your Family and Friends

Be devoted to one another in brotherly love.
– Romans 12:10

God Wants You to Be Kind

Chris sighed. He'd heard it all before.

"Why do you never invite the boy next door to do anything with you?" his mom said.

Blah, blah, he thought. Could he help it if Reginald wasn't cool? It wasn't his decision. The other kids in the sixth grade had decided it. Chris was just going along with how everyone felt about Reginald.

If only Reginald were better at sports. He couldn't dribble a basketball to save his life. And baseball? Well, just forget that! Chris was good at both. He was also, if he said so himself, liked by his classmates.

Yeah, too bad about Reginald. Chris ignored the nagging feeling in the back of his mind. He tried to tune out the voice in his head that said he ought to make an effort to be kinder to Reginald. Lately, those things had been getting stronger and stronger. Whenever Chris thought about God and what God had done for him, he noticed that bad feeling about Reginald rising to the surface.

Your Turn

1. What do you think Chris could do to be kinder to Reginald?
2. What's a way you can be kind to him?

_____

_____

_____

_____

Prayer

Dear God, show me how to be kind to everyone I meet. Amen.

God Gave You Your Family and Friends

Be devoted to one another in brotherly love.
– Romans 12:10

Smells and Howls

Sam and Jordan were surprised to see their dad sitting on the back-porch steps when they biked up the driveway. Their dog, Skipper, was sitting next to him. The cat was curled up enjoying the sun.

"Hi, Dad, Skipper, and Cleo," said Sam, nodding to each one.

Skipper wagged his tail, Cleo ignored them, and Dad stood up. "When I walked in the back door, I was met with bad smells and loud howls."

"Oops!" said Sam. "I was late getting ready for school. I forgot to feed Cleo and Skipper."

"I hate taking out the garbage," said Jordan. "I decided to wait until the can was full."

Dad told the boys to wait right there. He returned with an alarm clock and asked Sam to set the time.

Sam did, but the second hand didn't move.

When Jordan opened the back, they discovered the battery was missing.

"This clock is like our family," their father explained. "When some family members don't do their parts, it affects the rest of us." He produced the missing battery.

The boys put it in, and the clock started ticking.

Your Turn

1. How could the boys' neglect affect the family?
2. How is your family affected if you don't do your jobs?

Prayer

Heavenly Father, thank You for putting me in a family. Help me do my part in building good family relationships. Amen.

God Gave You Your Family and Friends

Job Jar

What family chore do you dislike the most? Probably everyone in your family, including your mom and dad, has a job they really hate doing. Try making a "Job Jar" so you can trade responsibilities for a week.

What You Need

- Large glass jar with a lid
- Index card
- Stickers
- Markers
- Clear tape
- Slips of paper
- Pencils

What to Do

1. Clean a large glass jar and lid.
2. Write "Job Jar" on the index card in large letters. Use the markers to decorate the label. Tape the label to the jar. The rest of the jar and the lid can be decorated with stickers.
3. Give each family member two or three slips of paper and ask them to write one job they dislike on each slip. Fold the papers in half and put them in the Job Jar.
4. Once a week, have each family member pick a job from the jar. If you get your own, put it back and choose a different one. Do the job you picked for one week. You may find you like doing a job someone else hates.

Prayer

Dear LORD, even when I don't look forward to doing a chore, help me do the work with a cheerful attitude. Amen.

God Gave You Your Family and Friends

Your Mission

Your mission, should you choose to accept it, is to show concern for others. Cross out the X's, Q's, and D's to find out how you can do this.

DBQXEDFXQADXQIDRQ

XDBQXEDXHDQOXNXQEDQXSDTX

QSXDHDXQODXQWXQMXEDRQXDCXY

XDHXQEXDQLXPXDODTXQHXQEQXRXDS

_____

_____

_____

_____

Prayer

Dear God, please help me remember to always show kindness and concern for others. Amen.

God Wants You to Be a Peacemaker

How good and pleasant it is when brothers live together in unity.
– Psalm 133:1

Out of Tune

The Benson home was seldom quiet with four kids, two cats, one dog, and a bird. Talking, laughing, music, and ringing phones were all familiar, pleasant parts of their daily family life. But sometimes not-so-pleasant sounds were also heard. Jack poked Jeff. Jeff poked back harder. Greg teased Linda, and Linda yelled, "Mom, Greg's bugging me!" Greg thought he could do whatever Jack did, even though Jack was two years older. And the boys thought Linda got everything her way because she was a girl.

The Benson family loved playing music. Mom played piano, Dad played the clarinet, and each of the kids played some kind of instrument. One night, Dad said, "Let's have a family concert." He handed out the music. It was a familiar song. Everyone tooted and plunked along harmoniously. They turned their pages…and kept playing. Everyone was now playing a different song.

Everyone stopped. What a horrible racket! Even the dog ran from the room.

"Not much harmony," said Mr. Benson. "Everyone was doing their own thing instead of playing together." He handed out new music. As they played in harmony again, the kids got the point of their dad's demonstration.

Your Turn

1. What was causing disharmony in the Benson family?
2. How does your family resolve arguments and fights?

Prayer

God of Peace, help me live in harmony with my family and friends. Amen.

God Wants You to Be a Peacemaker

How good and pleasant it is when brothers live together in unity.
– Psalm 133:1

Good Friends Include Each Other

Troy hesitated. He knew he should ask Kenny to come on the family ski trip. His aunt said he could ask a friend, and Kenny was his best friend. But Kenny was a terrible skier. He always asked a lot of questions and fell down a lot. Troy, on the other hand, was a great skier. He loved to ski! He didn't like having to coach Kenny all the time. *This is gonna be a drag with Kenny,* he thought as he stared at the phone. He dreaded calling his friend.

"I sure wish my friend Carol could be with us on this trip," his aunt suddenly said.

Troy turned. He hadn't realized she'd come into the room.

"I sure miss being with her," Troy's aunt said with a sigh.

Troy remembered how sad his aunt had been when her friend died. He suddenly felt bad that he hadn't wanted Kenny to come. He picked up the phone and dialed Kenny's number. He was soon so busy talking that he didn't see his aunt smile.

Your Turn

1. Who encouraged Troy to ask his friend to go on the trip? How?
2. How do you include your friends?
3. How do your friends include you?

_____

_____

_____

Prayer

Lord, show me how to include my friends. Amen.

24

God Wants You to Be a Peacemaker

How good and pleasant it is when brothers live together in unity.
– Psalm 133:1

True Friends Never Abandon Each Other

Jake couldn't believe it. Austin had invited him to a pool party at his house! Everybody in the sixth grade wanted to go. Practically the whole sixth grade was invited…except Max. To some of the sixth graders, Max was a major geek.

Just as Jake celebrated the good news, Max called. "My dad's taking me to the movies on Saturday," Max said. "Want to come?"

Jake felt terrible. "Uh…I've been invited to Austin's."

Max groaned. "You too? Guess that means you don't want to be my friend anymore."

"That's not true!"

"Yeah, sure." Max said. "Bye." He hung up.

Jake decided to ask God what to do. He didn't want to lose Max as a friend. When Saturday came, Jake went to the party. He only stayed for half an hour. It turned out to be boring. He decided to go with Max to the movie.

"I'm sorry I got mad at you," Max said when Jake arrived. "I should have known you still wanted to be my friend."

Your Turn

1. If you were Jake, would you have gone to the party?
2. Why is it important to never abandon a friend?

_____

_____

_____

Prayer

LORD, I want to stick with my friends. I can do that with Your help. Amen.

God Wants You to Be a Peacemaker

How good and pleasant it is when brothers live together in unity.
– Psalm 133:1

One Happy Family

We're all one big happy family, Sherman thought sarcastically. He didn't feel like he belonged at this church. His family had recently started coming, and he didn't like it. He also hadn't made any friends.

Now the fifth- and sixth-grade class wanted to do something for the church's anniversary. "Let's do a skit or something," someone suggested.

Why should I even care what happens? Sherman thought. But as ideas were discussed, Sherman suddenly had a great idea for a skit. He wouldn't have said anything, but someone suddenly asked him if he had any ideas. In a small voice, Sherman shared his idea.

"Hey, cool!" someone said. Other kids spoke up excitedly. "I can help work on your skit," one boy said. "I can help too," another one said.

My skit? Sherman thought. Suddenly he remembered that boy's name was Jason.

Others volunteered too. Before Sherman knew it, class was over. For the first time since he'd started coming to this church, he felt like he belonged.

Your Turn

1. In God's family, everyone has a place. What is yours?
2. What has someone at church done to help you feel you belong?

_____

_____

_____

_____

Prayer

Jesus, I want to be a caring member of Your family. Amen.

God Wants You to Be a Peacemaker

How good and pleasant it is when brothers live together in unity.
– Psalm 133:1

What's Special About Andrew?

Andrew listened to his brother singing in his room. Even though he'd just told his brother he sounded like a walrus, his brother had a great voice. He was often asked to sing at church. *Nobody asks me to sing,* Andrew thought, even though he knew his voice was best used in the shower. *Nothing special about me,* he decided.

"Andy!" his father called from the kitchen. "I need your help, buddy."

"Okay, Dad!" Andrew went to see what his father wanted.

"Set the table, please. Dinner is almost ready."

While Andrew got forks and knives and spoons, he asked, "What am I good at, Dad? Everybody around here gets asked to do stuff at church, but nobody ever asks me. I'm just Billy's brother."

"That's not true. Just the other Sunday your teacher told me how much she enjoys having you in her class."

"Really?"

Mr. Cornell nodded. "You bet. Do you know why?"

Andrew shrugged.

"Because you're helpful with the other kids. I've always known that about you. Another reason you're special is that God made you Andrew Cornell."

Your Turn

1. What was special about Andrew?
2. What is special about you? (Think of at least two things.)

_____

_____

Prayer

God, thanks for reminding me that I am special. Amen.

God Wants You to Be a Peacemaker

Prayer for a Friend

One of the best ways to help a friend is to pray for him or her. Maybe there's a need that you can't meet for a friend, but God can do everything! Use the prayer list below to write down who you will pray for and what you will pray for them. Don't forget to list how God answers!

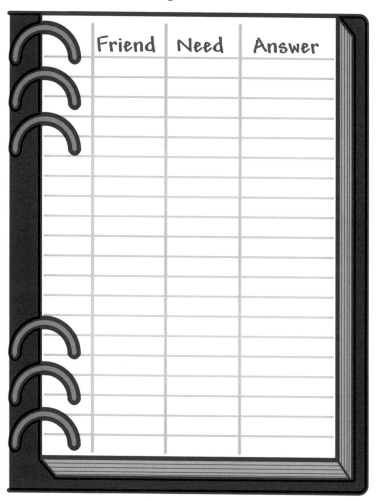

Friend	Need	Answer

Prayer

Dear Lord, I want to pray every day for my friends and family. Please remind me and help me find time each day to pray. Thank You. Amen.

God Wants You to Be a Peacemaker

A Message from a Friend

The puzzle below is a message from your Best Friend. Your friend's words are recorded in John 15:14. Put the letters below each column in the boxes above that column. The letters may not be listed in the order they appear in the column. Mark off the used letters to help you keep track. A letter will only be used once. Words may continue from one line to the next. The black boxes in the puzzle separate words.

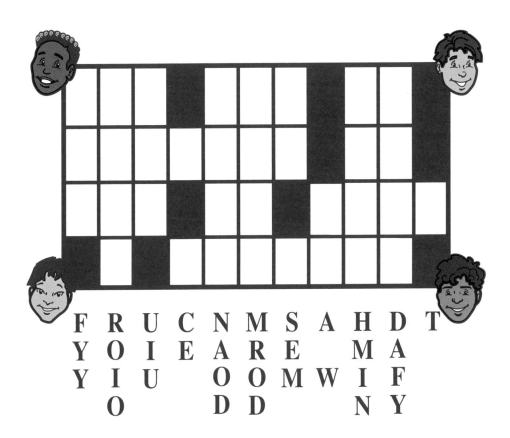

```
F R U C N M S A H D T
Y O I E A R E   M A
Y I U   O O M W I F
  O     D D     N Y
```

Prayer

Jesus, just as You are a friend to me, I want to be a good friend to others. Amen.

God Helps You Face Your Fears

Do not fear, for I am with you....
I will strengthen you and help you.
– Isaiah 41:10

Kevin's Fear

I don't have to be afraid. I don't have to be afraid, Kevin repeated. Yet he was. He made a face as he thought about it. He was worried about making his Little League team look bad. His teammates had gotten angry the last time he'd struck out. He thought about next Saturday's game. *What if I strike out again?* His stomach hurt.

"Why are you looking like that?" his brother asked. "Are you worried about Saturday's game?"

"How did you know?" Kevin asked.

"You've been quiet ever since the last game."

"I don't want to strike out." Kevin felt a little better just admitting it.

"Why don't you pray about it?" Derek asked. "I'm not saying ask God to help you not strike out. I'm saying ask God to help you not be afraid and to do your best. I've done that lots of times."

Kevin grinned. "You're pretty smart! Thanks."

Your Turn

1. What was Kevin afraid of? How will his brother's advice help?
2. What are you afraid of? How can you follow Derek's advice?

_____

_____

_____

_____

Prayer

LORD, when I'm afraid, give me Your strength and peace. Amen.

God Helps You Face Your Fears

Do not fear, for I am with you....
I will strengthen you and help you.
– Isaiah 41:10

God Is with You!

Shawn James looked at the elevator down the hall from the apartment he lived in. The gang that hung around the building had marked it with graffiti. Shawn shook his head. Some of the members of the "Red Dogs" gang had asked him to join them a week ago. So far, Shawn had avoided running into them. But how long would it be before they asked him again?

That horrible feeling of fear clutched at him. Shawn's friend Trey had been beaten up for not joining the gang. Shawn and Trey had both become Christians at the church near where they lived. Would Shawn be the next person to get beaten up? He had prayed many times for God's help. Would He answer?

"Hey, Shawn," Ross, another friend, said as he left his apartment. "Good news, man. Police arrested most of the Dogs yesterday. Caught 'em stealing stuff out of Mrs. Grey's apartment."

Shawn sighed with relief. His fear was gone too.

Your Turn

1. What do you usually do when you're afraid?
2. Who can you ask for help? Don't forget to talk to God!

_____

_____

_____

_____

Prayer

LORD, give me the courage to face my fears. Amen.

God Helps You Face Your Fears

Do not fear, for I am with you....
I will strengthen you and help you.
– Isaiah 41:10

Quick to Anger

"Why are you so mad?" Steve asked. He grinned at his big sister, Wendy, knowing that a grin would make her even madder.

"Because you make me sick sometimes!" Wendy yelled. "I know you have my tablet. You're always taking my tablet. You dropped it last week and now there's a crack on the screen!"

"I didn't take anything this time," Steve said.

"Wendy!" their mother called. "Come here, please."

Steve trailed after Wendy. He knew that sound in their mother's voice. Mrs. Hiller held up a tablet when they walked in. "This yours?"

Wendy looked embarrassed. "Where did you find it?"

"That's not as important as the fact that you keep losing your temper. I heard you all the way in here. Remember what I told you about that?"

"Yes," Wendy acknowledged.

Steve had been grinning at Wendy's discomfort. His mom's gaze fell on him. "That goes for you too."

Your Turn

1. Have you ever been quick to get angry at someone? What happened?
2. Why be quick to listen, slow to speak and slow to become angry?

_____

_____

_____

_____

Prayer

Lord, when I get mad, help me stop and talk to You about it. Amen.

God Helps You Face Your Fears

Do not fear, for I am with you....
I will strengthen you and help you.
— **Isaiah 41:10**

Don't Hold a Grudge

"Why are you so happy?" Jason asked his friend Colin.

"I'm finally the team captain in street hockey," Colin said. "I can get back at Bruce for choosing me last when he was team captain."

"What are you going to do?" Jason asked.

"Not choose him. I told Alex, the other team captain, to wait 'til everybody else has been chosen and then pick him if he wants. Bruce is gonna look stupid."

"Man, you know that's not right," Jason said.

Colin rolled his eyes. "Here we go."

"What?" Jason asked.

"You're gonna talk about religion. I just know it."

Jason sighed. He'd invited Colin to Sunday school several times. Sometimes Colin went and sometimes he didn't. Jason also knew Colin was one to hold a grudge. "I know you're still mad at Bruce," Jason said, "but what's getting back at him going to do? You won't feel better."

Colin gave Jason a look. "Later," he said.

Jason sighed again. *I know I did the right thing in telling him.*

Your Turn

1. Was Colin right to get even? Why or why not?
2. What happens when you try to get even with someone?

_____

_____

_____

Prayer

God, help me do the right thing. Amen.

God Helps You Face Your Fears

Do not fear, for I am with you....
I will strengthen you and help you.
– Isaiah 41:10

Missing Gramps

Jared sat scrunched up, his head in his hands. He was so upset he didn't hear his mother come into the room. She put a big box next to him.

"I went to Gramps' house today," she said gently. "I brought home some things I thought you might like to have. You can look at them when you feel like it." Then she left.

I'll never feel like it! Jared thought. He sobbed as he thought about Gramps' sudden death from a heart attack. One day his grandfather was laughing and joking, and the next day he was dead.

After a while, Jared glanced at the box. The Chinese checkerboard and jar of marbles were sticking out. When his mom came in with a snack, she found Jared holding the marble jar.

"It helps me feel better to hold these," Jared whispered. "They help me remember all the games Gramps and I played. I miss him so much."

His mom hugged Jared. "I know. And it's okay to cry and feel sad. You loved Gramps a lot. But you know what? Things have changed for Gramps too. He's in heaven with Jesus now."

Thinking of Gramps happy in heaven helped Jared smile a bit.

Your Turn

1. Has anyone you loved died? How did you feel?
2. What do you think heaven will be like?

_____

_____

_____

Prayer

LORD, comfort me when I'm sad. Let me help people who are sad. Amen.

God Helps You Face Your Fears

Get It? God It? Good!

Instead of getting even with someone who makes you mad, here are some things to "get" instead. Look up the Bible verses to see what God has to say.

Get:
* wisdom
  (James 1:5)
*with God in
  prayer
  (Matthew 6:13)
*rid of thoughts
  of revenge
  (Hebrews 10:30-31)

Prayer

Lord, I want to do what You want me to do. Please help me do the right thing in every situation. Amen.

God Helps You Face Your Fears

Heaven Is a Wonderful Place

No one knows for sure what heaven will be like. Think of the most beautiful or perfect place you've ever been. Then think of the place where you feel the happiest. Heaven will be a thousand times better than either of those places! Draw a picture or write about your ideas regarding heaven.

Heaven

Prayer

Dear LORD, I know that one day I will be in heaven with You, and it will be perfect. Amen.

God Helps You Overcome Sadness

[There is] a time to weep and a time to laugh.
– Ecclesiastes 3:4

Feeling Miserable

Scott slammed the kitchen door so hard that his mother jumped and the cat went running. After dumping his backpack on a chair, Scott stomped upstairs and flung himself across the bed. He covered his face with his pillow.

His mom came into his room. "I take it you had a bad day." All she heard was a muffled grunt. "Do you want to talk about it?"

Scott removed the pillow. "It was a rotten afternoon. I'll never be able to face my class and coach again." He took a deep breath. "We had a basketball game against Edison Middle School. We were ahead by two points. Then I got the ball, raced down the court, and made a perfect lay up. Everybody was yelling. I thought they were cheering for me."

"That's bad?" Mom asked.

"Yes. I put the ball in the wrong basket! How could I be so dumb?"

"I can see why you're miserable," said his mom. "You may feel sad for a while, but you'll be happy again. When I'm sad, it helps me to help someone else so I forget about me. Your brother would love to learn how to shoot baskets."

At least I won't mess that up, Scott thought as he went to find Jimmy.

Your Turn

1. How do you get over feeling sad?
2. How can God help you when you're sad?

_____

_____

Prayer

God, thanks for being with me all the time—even when I'm miserable. Amen.

God Helps You Overcome Sadness

[There is] a time to weep and a time to laugh.
– Ecclesiastes 3:4

Divorce Worry

"So what do you worry about?" Sid asked during a break in his turn at the joystick. He waited while the game reset.

"I worry about not getting a turn," his brother Carl said.

"I'm serious." Sid surrendered the joystick. "I heard Mom and Dad fighting yesterday. They must've thought we couldn't hear them. Do you ever worry that they'll get a divorce?"

Carl glanced at him. "They've fought before."

"Lamar's parents are getting a divorce." Lamar lived two doors away.

"Oh." Carl paused. "Well, I've heard Lamar's parents fighting. They never seemed to even like each other." He concentrated on the game for a bit before he spoke again. "Mom and Dad aren't like that."

"Yeah, I guess…"

"Maybe you should talk to them instead of worrying about it."

Sid stared at Carl. What his brother said made sense. He had heard that God sometimes spoke through people, but he never expected God to speak through his brother.

Your Turn

1. What worries you right now?
2. What do you usually do when you're worried? Do you need to do something different?

_____

_____

Prayer

God, I'm worried about _____ (fill in your worry). I'm not sure what to do. Please help me know what You want me to do. Amen.

God Helps You Overcome Sadness

[There is] a time to weep and a time to laugh.
– Ecclesiastes 3:4

Best Friend Worry

"Jan, why are you still staring at the wall?" Michael asked. "Earth to Jan! Houston, we've got a problem."

"Funny." Jan didn't feel like laughing. "Christine's mad at me again."

"So what else is new?" Michael chuckled. Michael stopped laughing when he saw how worried his sister looked. "She's never been a good friend. You don't need her."

"She's my best friend. Or was." Jan looked close to tears.

Michael leaned against the wall. "What exactly are you worried about?"

Jan shrugged. "I don't know what I did wrong this time."

"What are you really worried about? "There's got to be more to it."

"Christine's popular. If I'm not friends with her…" Jan's voice trailed off.

Michael waved his hand. "Don't worry."

"Easy for you to say," Jan countered.

"Easier to do than worry. What about trusting that God is in control? Didn't you tell me that just last week?" Michael grinned at Jan.

Your Turn

1. What was Jan really worried about?
2. Have you ever had a worry like that? What did you do?

_____

_____

_____

Prayer

Thank You, God, for being in control of my life. Amen.

God Helps You Overcome Sadness

[There is] a time to weep and a time to laugh.
– Ecclesiastes 3:4

Learning to Lean

"I can't do this!" Philip Franklin yelled. "This report stinks. That means I'll get another bad grade!"

"What's wrong?" his father asked.

"I don't know if my report on Saturn is good enough."

Mr. Franklin put his hand on Philip's shoulder as he read what was on the computer screen. "I know you've done your best."

"I've been studying, Dad. I thought I was doing better." Philip felt almost ready to cry in frustration. He'd been getting extra help at school, so now everyone knew he had a problem learning. He worried that the problem would last forever.

"I don't think your report is as bad as you think," Mr. Franklin said. "Your teacher will understand. Your grades have gotten better. But this isn't something to worry yourself sick over. I wish you didn't have to go through this, son. Your mother and I pray for you every day. We know God is helping you right now. He wants you to lean on Him."

"Thanks, Dad." Philip wasn't always sure that God cared about his problems. But right then, he felt better.

Your Turn

1. Is there a problem that worries you right now?
2. Who can help when you have a problem?

_____

_____

_____

Prayer

LORD, instead of worrying, help me trust You. Amen.

God Helps You Overcome Sadness

[There is] a time to weep and a time to laugh.
– Ecclesiastes 3:4

Live One Day at a Time

"I'm dead," Kiyoshi said.

"You look alive to me," his friend Wanda said. She'd come over to play games on Kiyoshi's computer.

Kiyoshi looked at her for a second. "Mr. Fletcher wants to see Mom and me in his office tomorrow." Mr. Fletcher was the principal of their school.

"What did you do this time?" Kiyoshi was famous for practical jokes.

Kiyoshi shrugged. "I don't know. Mom says she received a letter in the mail. She wouldn't tell me anything. She said we'd find out tomorrow."

"You think it's something bad?"

"Got to be. But what? I can't stop worrying about it."

Wanda shrugged. "My mom always tells me not to worry about stuff. 'Live one day at a time,' she says." Wanda was good at imitating her mother. "Anyway, that's what God wants us to do."

"But what's that supposed to mean? What do I do right now?"

"It means don't worry about what could happen tomorrow."

Your Turn

1. What worried Kiyoshi?
2. Why is it better to trust God one day at a time, instead of worrying about tomorrow?

_____

_____

_____

Prayer

Lord, help me not worry about what could happen tomorrow. Amen.

God Helps You Overcome Sadness

Happy/Sad

Fit these happy and sad words into the puzzle.

DOWN

EXCITED
GROAN
LAUGHING
MOPE
MOURN
SAD
SOB
WHIMPER

ACROSS

CRYING
GIGGLE
GLAD
HAPPY
JOYFUL
MISERABLE
POUT
SINGING
SMILE

God Helps You Overcome Sadness

Zap Those Worries

Wouldn't it be great if you could zap your worries as easily as you zap space aliens in a game? With God's Word, you can cut your worries down to size. Check out the worries on the left. Are any of these your worries? Which of the verses from the power grid would you use to defeat those worries? Look up the verses and then draw a line from the worry to the Scripture that will help eliminate it.

Prayer

God, thank You for Your promises that help me to trust instead of worry. Amen

God Wants You to Be Humble

All those who exalt themselves will be humbled, and those who humble themselves will be exalted.
– Luke 14:11

The Math King

"So, Kiyoshi, what happened in Mr. Fletcher's office?" Wanda asked. Kiyoshi grinned. "He wants me to take advanced math."

"Cool! And you thought you were in trouble. So maybe you can help me with my pre-algebra homework? I brought it with me."

Kiyoshi looked at the problems Wanda pointed out. "You mean you can't do this? This stuff is easy."

"Kiyoshi, I know you're smart, but don't act like a jerk."

Kiyoshi figured out the first problem. "See? The answer is n=6(2)." He buffed his fingernails against his shirt. "I'm the math king."

"Glad you're so humble about it," Wanda said. She looked at the paper. "Hey, math king, I think something's wrong. You said n=6(2) is the answer, but 14 can't be divided by 6 evenly."

Kiyoshi snatched the paper. "Oops!"

Wanda laughed. "Looks like the math king just lost his crown."

Your Turn

1. What does it mean to be humble?

_____

_____

2. On a scale of 1 to 10, how important is it for you to be humble? Circle your choice.

1   2   3   4   5   6   7   8   9   10

(Not much)   (A lot)

Prayer

LORD, I need Your help to be humble. Amen.

44

God Wants You to Be Humble

*All those who exalt themselves will be humbled, and
those who humble themselves will be exalted.*
– Luke 14:11

Depend on God

"Why do you think he said that?"

David looked at his father. "Said what? Oh, the stuff about thanking God for making it possible for him to be the MVP (the most valuable player)? I don't know."

"Take a guess."

David was silent for a moment. "Maybe his father made him do it!" A couch pillow suddenly sailed toward his head. "Okay," he said as he ducked, "maybe he just thought it was a nice thing to do."

"Was he saying he depended on God more than on his own ability?"

David shrugged. "Yes, but he's good, Dad. Nobody pitches like him."

"True. But who gave him that ability in the first place? And anything could have happened to him. He could've been injured during the season."

"I guess…I never thought about that. I…I guess I kinda depend on God too."

"Kinda?" his dad repeated with a grin.

Your Turn

1. What talents do you have?
2. Why is it important to thank God for what you can do?

_____

_____

_____

_____

Prayer

Lord, thank You for giving me the abilities I have. Amen.

God Wants You to Be Humble

*All those who exalt themselves will be humbled, and
those who humble themselves will be exalted.*
– Luke 14:11

God Helps You Love

Brent Carlson slowly walked down the stairs, hoping that his mother had changed her mind. She hadn't. They were still going to visit Grandpa Joe. He sighed as he followed his mother to the garage.

"He always acts like he doesn't like kids," he declared while buckling himself in.

"I know." His mother started the car.

"So why do I have to go?" Brent asked.

"Because he's your grandfather. Because he's in the hospital." Mrs. Carlson backed out of the garage.

Brent grunted. He thought his grandfather was mean and grouchy. He never seemed to have a kind word to say to anyone.

"I know your grandfather doesn't act very loving sometimes. But that doesn't give us the right to treat him the same way. God helps us love those we have a hard time loving."

Brent grunted again. *That's Grandpa for sure!* he thought.

Your Turn

1. Think of someone you have a hard time loving. How do you usually respond to that person?
2. What do you think God wants you to do?

_____

_____

_____

Prayer

Lord, when it comes to loving some people, I have a hard time. Help me love those I can't love on my own. Amen.

God Wants You to Be Humble

All those who exalt themselves will be humbled, and
those who humble themselves will be exalted.
– Luke 14:11

The Doormat

"I'm sick of being the new kid!" Wesley threw down his backpack as he came in the back door.

His older sister, Stephanie, laughed. "Is that why you've been letting your so-called friends take advantage of you?" A seventh grader, Stephanie thought she knew a lot more than Wesley, a mere fifth grader.

"What do you mean?" Wesley asked.

"I saw you at the park today letting that creep Simon ride your new skateboard. He also wrecked it and didn't even say he was sorry. He just threw it back at you and went off with his friends. You should think better of yourself than to let people treat you that way."

"What do you know?" Wesley asked.

"I know that I don't want friends like that because that's not the kind of friend I am. I like myself better than that."

"I can tell," Wesley said with a grin. He ran before Stephanie could get him in a headlock.

Your Turn

1. Why is it important to love yourself as well as love your neighbor?
2. Can you love yourself too much? Why or why not?
3. What are some ways you can show love to your neighbor?
   To your family? To yourself?

_____

_____

_____

Prayer

LORD, You tell me to love my neighbors as I love myself. That's what I want to do. Amen.

God Wants You to Be Humble

All those who exalt themselves will be humbled, and
those who humble themselves will be exalted.
– Luke 14:11

The Man on the Corner

"Look, Karen. He's here again." Stuart nudged his cousin and nodded to a man begging on the street corner. Stuart fished around in his pocket for some change to give to him.

"Don't give him anything!" Karen hissed. "He looks homeless, but he might not be. My dad says some people just don't want to work."

"Yes, that might be true for some of them," Stuart acknowledged. "I've seen that man here for the past week, since the weather turned warm." Stuart gave his money to the man.

The man nodded and smiled.

"Humph!" Karen said. "You just threw your money away. He'll just buy alcohol or something else unhealthy."

Stuart shrugged. "There's nothing wrong with helping people. That's what my heavenly Father said. We're only responsible for what we do, not for what others do. As a Christian, I want to help people. If that man gets drunk with the money I gave him, that's between God and him. Get it?"

"Maybe you're right," Karen said.

Your Turn

1. Do you agree with what Stuart said? Why or why not?
2. What person or problem stirs your compassion?

_____

_____

_____

Prayer

When I help someone, let them see Your compassion in me. Amen.

God Wants You to Be Humble

Who's Number One?

If you're a sports fan, how do you show which team is number one with you? Buy a hat? Wear a T-shirt? How would you tell the world that God is number one in your life? Use the T-shirt and pennant to draw or write some slogans that honor God.

Prayer

LORD, I depend on You because Your Word says You are my strength. Thank You for always being here with me. Amen.

God Wants You to Be Humble

Love Tester

Do you think love is just some ooey-gooey feeling? Think again. Use the Love Tester to see where you stand on the subject of love. On a scale of 1 to 10, how important is it…

to forgive someone who has wronged you?

1   2   3   4   5   6   7   8   9   10
(NOT IMPORTANT)   (VERY IMPORTANT)

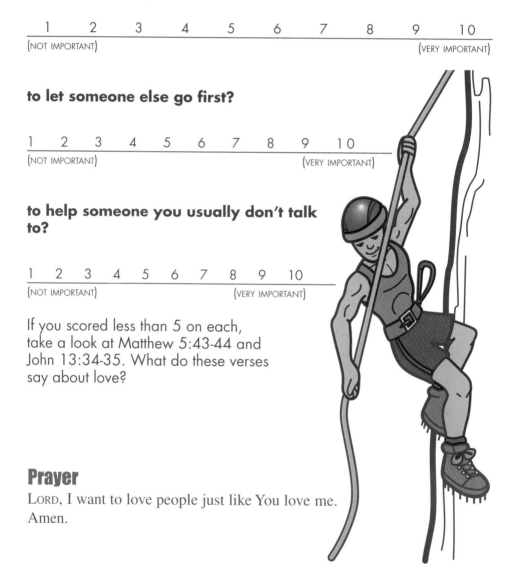

to let someone else go first?

1 2 3 4 5 6 7 8 9 10
(NOT IMPORTANT)   (VERY IMPORTANT)

to help someone you usually don't talk to?

1 2 3 4 5 6 7 8 9 10
(NOT IMPORTANT)   (VERY IMPORTANT)

If you scored less than 5 on each, take a look at Matthew 5:43-44 and John 13:34-35. What do these verses say about love?

Prayer

LORD, I want to love people just like You love me. Amen.

God Wants You to Be Compassionate

Be kind and compassionate to one another.
– Ephesians 4:32

Help for an Enemy

Paolo Martinez knew he didn't want to help Dennis. No way! Dennis was a bully. A complete and total menace just like bullies are in cartoons. Hadn't Dennis tried to pick a fight with him? Hadn't Dennis made fun of the way he pitched during gym class?

Now Dennis needed help. Paolo almost couldn't believe it. Dennis needed help in math. He was nearly crying when he asked Paolo for help.

"If I don't pass this math test, I'll get a bad grade," Dennis had said.

Paolo stared at him. Dennis had never seemed to care before.

Paolo was good at math. Everyone knew it. *I shouldn't help him,* Paolo thought. *I should just let him fail.* But then he thought about what God might want him to do. "Love your enemies. Show compassion." He knew compassion was a long word that means "imagine yourself in the other person's shoes." Paolo sighed. He couldn't help feeling sorry for Dennis. Dennis tried to act tough and mean, but he had trouble learning sometimes.

Well, Paolo decided, *I will help him.*

Your Turn

1. When has someone shown compassion to you?
2. How will you show compassion this week?

_____

_____

_____

Prayer

Jesus, show me someone to care for this week. Amen.

God Wants You to Be Compassionate

Be kind and compassionate to one another.
– Ephesians 4:32

Joy Even When You're Sad

Jack looked out his bedroom window. The backyard looked so empty now. He could hardly believe Buster was gone. One minute the little pug-chow mix was there looking at him with his sad eyes. The next minute the vet was telling Jack and his family that Buster hadn't survived the operation.

Buster had been so much fun. Thinking about him made Jack feel warm inside.

He soon felt a hand on his shoulder. His mother stood behind him.

"I know you're sad, honey," she said.

"Yeah, but I couldn't help remembering how silly Buster is…was." Jack's smile faded.

"Jack, this is part of how life is. We all have to face losses like this. That's why…"

"I know, Mom. God is with us." That's something his mother always said. It was funny though. That thought didn't annoy him this time. This time Jack was glad to know God was with him.

Your Turn

1. What does "joy" mean to you?
2. Describe a time you felt joyful amid sadness?
3. Which lasts longer—joy or happiness? Why?

_____

_____

_____

Prayer

Lord Jesus, You bring me joy. Thank You. Amen.

God Wants You to Be Compassionate

Be kind and compassionate to one another.
– Ephesians 4:32

Read All About It!

"What are you grinning at?" Jay asked.

Monica turned when she heard her friend approach her desk. They both had early detention. "I just became…"

"Hush!" Mr. Keller said.

Monica wrote on her notebook and flashed what she wrote to Jay. "I just became a Christian."

Jay wrote a big "Y" and a question mark on his arm.

Monica wrote fast. "Because I finally believe. I know Jesus won't leave me like my dad does. Dad is always traveling around. I just think it's so cool that Jesus…"

Monica suddenly realized Mr. Keller was standing at her desk. He had his hand out. She reluctantly handed over her notebook.

"Read chapter 17," Mr. Keller snapped over his shoulder.

Monica glanced at Jay and then opened her textbook.

Minutes later, Mr. Keller returned her notebook. Monica was surprised to see writing next to hers: "I think Jesus is pretty cool too." She looked up, and Mr. Keller smiled.

Your Turn

1. What does Monica's relationship with Jesus mean to her?
2. How does knowing Jesus bring you joy?
3. If you don't know Jesus, ask Him into your heart today.

_____

_____

Prayer

Jesus, I believe You are the Son of God. You died for my sins and rose again. Please live in my heart. Be my LORD and Savior forever. Amen.

God Wants You to Be Compassionate

Be kind and compassionate to one another.
– Ephesians 4:32

Stick with It

Alex turned off the lawn mower. He threw down his cap and folded his arms. The large backyard seemed to stretch on forever. Alex's back already hurt from pushing the mower.

"Taking a break already?" his father asked.

Glancing at his dad, Alex thought, *He looks nice and cool underneath the umbrella on the patio with a glass of lemonade on the table beside him.* "Dad, this is taking forever." Alex wiped the sweat off his forehead.

His dad said, "You begged me to let you earn some extra money. Cutting the lawn is a good way to do that. That's why I let you start this summer lawn-care business."

"But this yard will take all year to mow!"

"You've only been working ten minutes. Gotta stick with a job even when it's hard. Somebody else who hires you won't be as easy on you as I am." He grinned and raised his lemonade glass.

Alex rolled his eyes. His father was always on him about being committed to whatever he did. *So that's what this is all about,* he grumbled silently. With a sigh he turned back to mowing.

Your Turn

1. What do you think it takes to stay committed to something?
2. Why is commitment important?
3. What helps you to stick with a hard job?

_____

_____

Prayer

LORD, commitment takes hard work. Show me how to stay committed to You and to whatever I do. Amen.

God Wants You to Be Compassionate

Be kind and compassionate to one another.
– Ephesians 4:32

Stan's Choice

Stan went to be with his friends at the covered bridge, where most of the kids around the apartment complex hung out.

"She acts like she's a holy roller," Babette was saying.

Stan's blood seemed to freeze. "Who are you talking about?"

"Jennifer," Steve, who lived in Stan's building, replied.

Jennifer went to Stan's church. In fact, Babette did too.

"Why do you say she's a holy roller? And is that bad?" Stan asked.

"She's always talking about God. I mean, enough is enough, right?"

"Yeah," Steve agreed. "I go to church, but it's not my whole life."

At first Stan wasn't going to say anything, but he sensed God wouldn't be pleased. "I...I...I believe in God like Jennifer does," he admitted. He instantly felt embarrassed as Steve and Babette stared at him.

"Well...that's...cool," Babette finally said.

Your Turn

1. How did Stan show his commitment to God?
2. What might try to keep you from staying committed to Jesus?

_____

_____

_____

_____

Prayer

LORD, help me stay committed to You. Amen.

God Wants You to Be Compassionate

The Gospel According to You

What would you tell a friend about Jesus? The recorder is on. Use the speech balloon to share your message.

Prayer

LORD, give me the words and the opportunity to tell my friends about You. Amen.

God Wants You to Be Compassionate

Out of This World

Needed: game board; 1 die; 1 or 2 objects for game pieces

Ready to play a great game by yourself or with a friend? You don't travel in light years. You roll a die and move that number. All you need to know are multiples of four. If you land on a number that can't be divided evenly by four, you must say the word "space" before the other person moves or you go back to Earth. If you move around the board and make it back to Earth first, you win!

Prayer

LORD, help me stay committed to You even when it's hard. Amen.

God Wants You to Persevere

Pursue righteousness and a godly life, along with faith, love, perseverance, and gentleness.
– 1 Timothy 6:11 NLT

Throwing a Curve

"I'll never understand this!" Mort tossed down his glove.

"There's nothing to throwing a curve ball," Yasmine said.

"Go away!" Mort hated to admit that his nine-year-old sister was better at pitching than he was. He was athletic, but Yasmine was a natural when it came to throwing a baseball. He decided to quit and go back into the house. He was glad to see that his uncle was still there.

"Keep at it, Mort," Uncle James encouraged after Mort explained his problem. "That's the only way you'll get better."

"Yes, I know, but it's hard."

"How badly do you want to throw a curve ball?" Uncle James asked.

"Really bad!" Mort said.

"If you want something badly enough, you'll keep at it. That's what perseverance is all about. It means keep trying until you're successful."

Your Turn

1. What tasks require you to persevere?
2. What tempts you to quit? How do you keep going?

_____

_____

_____

_____

Prayer

Jesus, help me persevere at the tasks, activities, and skills You want me to. Amen.

God Wants You to Persevere

*Pursue righteousness and a godly life, along with
faith, love, perseverance, and gentleness.*
– 1 Timothy 6:11 NLT

Most Persistent

"The award for 'Most Persistent' goes to Lynnleigh Saunders! And the crowd goes wild!" Lynnleigh bowed, her hairbrush microphone held high.

"What is your problem?" her twin brother, Lyle, asked.

"Why are you barging into my room?" Lynnleigh asked.

"Why are you talking to your hairbrush?"

"Because I did it!" Lynnleigh said. Remember how I talked to Laura, the new girl in the neighborhood, about God two months ago? She acted like she didn't want to hear about Jesus."

"Yes. She made fun of you 'cause you asked her to come to church."

"Well, I kept being friendly. Today, she said she'd come to church this Sunday. Isn't that great?"

She and Lyle exchanged high-fives.

"You know," Lyle said, "sometimes you're not as crazy as I say you are."

Your Turn

1. Have you failed at doing something? What made you try again?
2. How many times are you willing to try to do right?

1 time   3 times   more than 5 times   as many times as it takes

_____

_____

_____

Prayer

Lord, please encourage me to persevere. Amen.

God Wants You to Persevere

Pursue righteousness and a godly life, along with faith, love, perseverance, and gentleness.
– 1 Timothy 6:11 NLT

Show Respect

Wyatt snorted with laughter from the back pew. A few heads turned in his direction, but he was having too much fun with his friends to really care.

After the church service was over, Wyatt's older brother, David, came looking for him. "I heard you've been clowning around in church," he said.

"Who said that?" Wyatt asked.

"Doesn't matter. You need to cool it when you're in church, little bro."

"I can't talk to my friends? You used to sit back there all the time and talk."

"Until I found out I wasn't showing respect for God by disturbing the people who were trying to worship Him."

As they went to the car, Wyatt felt a little ashamed, but he didn't want to admit it. He didn't think he was not respecting God by his actions. In fact, he hadn't even thought about God. *David's changed,* he decided. Ever since he went to college three months earlier, David had been different. *For one thing, he talks about God more.* Wyatt glanced at his brother. David was still the coolest person Wyatt knew. Maybe there was something to what his big brother had said.

Your Turn

1. "Reverence" means respect. Why is that important in worship?
2. How do you show reverence for God?

_____

_____

_____

Prayer

LORD, You are awesome. Amen.

God Wants You to Persevere

Pursue righteousness and a godly life, along with faith, love, perseverance, and gentleness.
— 1 Timothy 6:11 NLT

Where Angels Fear to Tread

"Why do you always have to do that?" Gwen asked as she poked her head into her brother's room.

"Do what?" Scott asked, looking puzzled.

"Misusing God's name like that just because your friends do." Gwen folded her arms. "My friends and I heard you at the mall today. Every time your friends are around, you do that."

Scott waved her away. "You're just mad because you and your friends aren't cool."

"At least I know one thing you don't: Disrespect for God's name isn't cool. And that makes you uncool." Gwen went to her room.

Scott threw a pillow after her, which landed harmlessly on the floor. *What does she know?* he thought. He hadn't meant anything by what he'd said at the mall. *God doesn't care about stuff like that. Or does He?* Suddenly, he wasn't so sure.

Your Turn

1. Do you think God cares about the way His name is used?
   Read Exodus 20:7. Did your answer change?
2. What will you do when a friend says something bad about God or uses God's name in a bad way?

_____

_____

_____

_____

Prayer

God, I want to respect You always. Please show me how. Amen.

God Wants You to Persevere

*Pursue righteousness and a godly life, along with
faith, love, perseverance, and gentleness.*
— 1 Timothy 6:11 NLT

Complete Trust

I've trotted 10 miles. I've sweated 5 gallons. These thoughts bounced around in Kyle's brain as he went up and down the sidewalk. Kyle's hair was sweaty, his shirt was sticking to his back, and his arms felt like lead weights. Teaching a five-year-old to bike ride wasn't easy.

"Hold on tight, Kyle," Evan yelled. "I'm going to fall!"

"No way!" encouraged Kyle. "Sit straight so you won't wobble."

Evan's short legs pumped up and down while Kyle's long legs ran alongside his brother's bike. He steadied the bike by holding the handlebars and the back of the seat. When the bike was going in a straight line, Kyle slowly let go of the handlebars.

When Evan saw only his hands on the handlebars, he panicked. "No, Kyle!" he yelled. "Hold on! I'm gonna fall!"

"You're doing great," Kyle said. "Trust me, I won't let you fall."

Kyle and Evan's mom had been watching. She brought out lemonade, and they all sat under a tree to cool off.

"Hey, Mom, I can almost ride. Kyle helped me, and he won't let me fall. Did you see me go?" asked Evan.

"You're doing super, Evan. And, Kyle, thanks a lot for helping him. He trusts you completely," said their mom.

Your Turn

1. Who do you trust and why?
2. What do you trust God to do for you?

_____

_____

Prayer

Dear God, thank You for always keeping Your promises. Help me to trust You in every situation. Amen.

God Wants You to Persevere

Go the Distance

A runner who isn't committed to finishing a race will seldom make it to the end. You get to decide whether you'll go the distance in your relationship with Jesus. The apostle Paul's pledge was, "Forgetting what is behind and straining toward what is ahead, I press on toward the goal to win the prize for which God has called me heavenward in Christ Jesus" (Philippians 3:13-14).

Write your own pledge on the trophy.

PAUL'S PLEDGE

FORGETTING WHAT IS BEHIND AND STRAINING TOWARD WHAT IS AHEAD, I PRESS ON TOWARD THE GOAL TO WIN THE PRIZE FOR WHICH GOD HAS CALLED ME HEAVENWARD IN CHRIST JESUS.

PHILIPPIANS 3:13-14

YOUR PLEDGE

Prayer

Dear LORD, I am committed to You. Help me run the race of life in a way that pleases You. Amen.

God Wants You to Persevere

Reverence Acrostic

To remind yourself that reverence for God is right, fill in the acrostic. Use words that begin with each letter to explain how you feel about God.

Prayer

LORD, help me listen to You and respect You. Amen.

Be Loyal to God

Love is patient, love is kind.
– 1 Corinthians 13:4

Erin's Dilemma

Rasheem's Sunday-school class was in the middle of their favorite game, called "Suppose."

"Suppose your best friend didn't believe in God and expected you to do something wrong. Would you go along with your friend?" Mr. Green asked.

"I wouldn't," Rasheem said immediately.

"Me neither," his cousin Erin said. But she didn't sound very convincing.

"You would too!" Rasheem hissed. "Remember what Laura asked you to do?"

Mr. Green overheard. "What was it?"

Erin shot Rasheem a look. She didn't want to discuss her life in front of the whole fifth- and sixth-grade class.

Since she hesitated, Rasheem jumped in. "Her friend wanted her to play a computer game my aunt didn't want Erin to play."

"I didn't want to play it either!" Erin said. "It's got occult stuff in it. Laura said she didn't see anything wrong with playing it. She said it was just a game and more interesting than going to church."

Some of the other kids talked all at once about what they'd do.

Mr. Green called for quiet. "God wants us to be loyal to Him. If you have to choose between loyalty to God and loyalty to a friend, which would you choose?"

Your Turn

1. Would you choose being loyal to Jesus over being loyal to a friend? Why?
2. How do you show your loyalty to God?

Prayer

Lord, I want to be a loyal friend to You always. I need Your help. Amen.

Be Loyal to God

Love is patient, love is kind.
– 1 Corinthians 13:4

A Cheerful Giver

"Clarence?"

Clarence looked up as his stepmother entered his room.

Mrs. Weaver sighed. "I know you think I force you to give money to our church every week. I wanted you to see how important it is to give. God has given us so much, and…" Mrs. Weaver stopped. "Anyway, your father and I have talked it over. The Bible says to be a *cheerful* giver, and we've decided that being cheerful is important, so…"

"I don't have to put money in the church basket if I don't want to?" Clarence cut in, looking hopeful.

"Starting next month, when you turn thirteen, you can make your own decision." Mrs. Weaver didn't look happy.

Clarence felt like jumping for joy. No more giving his money away! His father gave him an allowance every week. His stepmother was always on him to give some of it to the church. *No more giving!* Suddenly, he didn't feel all that great. "Thanks," he decided. "I think…maybe I'll still give."

Your Turn

1. Why do you think God "loves a cheerful giver"?
2. Are you a cheerful giver? How do your actions show this?

_____

_____

_____

_____

Prayer

Help me, LORD, to be a cheerful giver. Amen.

Be Loyal to God

Love is patient, love is kind.
– 1 Corinthians 13:4

The Gift

"Oh, I'm so embarrassed! I can't believe I don't have another dollar."

Ben felt sorry as he heard the woman ahead of him in line. He glanced at his mother, who looked annoyed. People in line were grumbling. Ben reached into his pocket. "Here," he said, as he gave the woman a dollar.

"I can't take…" the woman began.

"That's okay. Please let me help," Ben said.

The woman asked for his name and address to return the dollar.

Ben didn't think he'd get paid back. He was happy he could help.

"That was a very kind thing to do," his mother said.

Ben was pleased at her praise. He knew he'd done something God wanted him to do.

A few days later, a package came for him. Inside was a five-dollar bill, a video game, and a note: "Thank you for your generosity. Because of you, I made it to an important meeting."

"Wow," said Ben. "The lady paid me back—and more!"

Your Turn

1. Have you given a gift and received one in return? How did you feel?
2. Should people give without expecting something back?

_____

_____

_____

_____

Prayer

LORD, I want to give—not to receive, but to please You. Amen.

Be Loyal to God

Love is patient, love is kind.
– 1 Corinthians 13:4

Learning Patience

Casey was waiting in the car for his brother. Eric was driving him to the hobby shop downtown. Casey leaned over and blasted the horn.

"Knock it off!" Eric said as he got into the car. "What's the big rush?"

"Well, they have this really cool model of a 1957 Corvette on sale. I want to hurry and get one before they're all sold out," Casey answered.

"That is a neat model," Eric agreed. "But it has hundreds of pieces. Are you sure you're ready for that?"

Later, when Casey opened the box, he understood. It looked like zillions of pieces. And the directions were 10 pages long! He started sorting pieces and gluing them together. After two hours, he'd hardly made a dent. *This is taking too long,* Casey thought.

"How's the model coming?" Eric asked later, as he came into the room.

"Not so good," mumbled Casey. "I worked for hours and hardly anything is done. And it doesn't look right."

Eric asked, "Did you follow the directions step-by-step?"

"Well, most of them. I skipped some," Casey admitted.

"You have to carefully follow every direction," said Eric. "When you skip directions, you end up with a mess."

"It takes so long to do all that sanding, fitting, and gluing," Casey said.

"To build models, you need to be very patient. When it's finally finished, you can really be proud of it," said Eric.

This will be a masterpiece even if it takes me all winter, thought Casey as he carefully unglued a piece that was in the wrong place.

Your Turn

1. What makes you impatient?
2. What can happen when you're impatient?

Prayer

God, thanks for being patient with me. Help me learn to be patient. Amen.

Be Loyal to God

Love is patient, love is kind.
– 1 Corinthians 13:4

Blast Off!

Twelve-year-old Jeff jumped out of bed, hopped into his clothes, and rushed into the kitchen. He gulped down some juice and ate a bowl of cereal before bolting out to the garage. Andrew was home from college for the weekend. They were going to put the finishing touches on a remote-controlled rocket they'd built. When Jeff opened the garage door, he was annoyed to find their younger brother, Pete, with Andrew.

"Hey!" Andrew called. "Let's get this finished and onto the launchpad."

"Hooray!" yelled Pete as he shoved a stool into place for Jeff. Everything they needed was spread out on the workbench.

Jeff tightened two screws.

V-e-r-r-y slowly Pete turned the third screw.

"Hurry up!" said Jeff. Impatient, he started on the decals.

Soon Pete held a decal and was trying to decide where to stick it.

Jeff reached for the decal. "Let me do it! You're slower than a turtle!"

"I quit," Pete said and wiped at his eyes.

"Time out," Andrew said. "Jeff, we have all day to finish this rocket. Remember, you are five years older than Pete. He can't do things as quickly as you can. Be patient."

Andrew was right. Jeff gave Pete a friendly poke. "Hey, little bro. I'm sorry. Take as long as you want."

Your Turn

1. What makes you impatient?
2. What are some ways you help yourself be more patient?

_____

_____

Prayer

Father, help me be more patient with people. Amen.

Be Loyal to God

Loyalty Riddle

Time to solve another riddle! There are a number of clues you have to solve before you can figure out the answer. (Hint: Part of the answer is the name of a woman in the Bible.)

1. This disciple of Jesus walked on water.

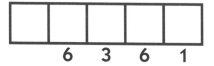

    6   3   6   1

2. Mary's loyal husband.

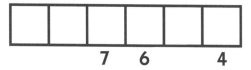

      7   6   4

3. Abraham was loyal to this nephew.

  5   3

4. The loyal apostle who wrote most of the New Testament.

  5   2

5. How would you describe a friend who isn't loyal?

  1   2   3   4   5   6   7   7   8

Prayer

LORD, I want to be a loyal friend to You and to my friends. Thank You for helping me. Amen.

Be Loyal to God

Patience, Patience

How much patience would you have in these situations? Check the patience level that fits. It may take patience to do this activity!

	Lots	Some	Little	None
Waiting for your turn in a game.				
Waiting for something you really want.				
Waiting in the dentist's or doctor's office.				
Waiting for your parents to decide if you can go somewhere with your friends.				
Waiting for your little brother or sister.				
Waiting for a big math test.				
Waiting for a special trip or holiday.				
Waiting for my own phone.				
Waiting for dinner.				
Waiting to mow the lawn.				
Waiting to find out if you made the team.				

Prayer

God, help me be more patient in all situations. Amen.

True Goodness Comes from God

Blessed are those who gain wisdom, those who gain understanding.
– Proverbs 3:13

True Goodness

"May I get this one, Mom?" Eric Nielson held up a CD.

Mom looked at the playlist on Eric's mp3 player. She said, "Isn't it funny that people can sing about evil and hate but nobody wants to sing about what is good?

Eric frowned. Whenever he heard the word "good," he thought of his cousin Michael. Michael always tried to be good, even though he was a big sneak. Everyone in the family talked about how great Michael was.

"I know that look. What's up?" Eric's mom asked.

"Michael."

Mrs. Nielson smiled. "I know you think everybody but you is fooled by Michael's behavior, but that's not true. Michael tries to look good, but he doesn't really want to be good. He's putting on an act. True goodness comes from God. It's His kindness and love shining in your heart."

Your Turn

1. Do you know someone like Michael? How do you respond to him?
2. Why is it important to have true goodness? Read Galatians 5:22-23 to find out.

_____

_____

_____

_____

Prayer

LORD, let the fruit of Your goodness grow and ripen in my life. Amen.

True Goodness Comes from God

Blessed are those who gain wisdom, those who gain understanding.
– Proverbs 3:13

Try, Try, Again?

"Dad, I'm so sick of trying to be good all the time!" Max Fielding flopped on a chair in his father's office.

"You mean you want to tease your sister." Mr. Fielding said.

"I can't help it, Dad."

"I heard that!" his sister yelled from the family room.

"You believe Jesus died for your sins, right?" his dad asked.

Max was thrown for a minute. What did that have to do with being free to tease his sister? "Yes…"

"Jesus lives inside you. His goodness resides in you, His goodness will help you treat others fairly. You have to let Him work through you by letting go of what you want and asking HIM what to do."

Your Turn

1. Have you felt frustrated by missing the goodness mark?
2. Since you can't be good all the time on your own, does that mean you don't have to try? Why or why not?

_____

_____

_____

_____

Prayer

LORD, with Your help, I can be kind and please You. Amen.

True Goodness Comes from God

Blessed are those who gain wisdom, those who gain understanding.
— **Proverbs 3:13**

A Wise Move

"How do you know what to do?" Devin asked his friend Jeff. The boys were at Jeff's house playing computer games.

"I already told you to hit the escape key to get out of that maze." Jeff pointed to the computer screen.

"I'm not talking about this." Devin paused the game. "How do you know…y'know, what's the right thing to do?"

Jeff knew that Devin wasn't a Christian, and that Devin was curious about God and about church. He usually asked Jeff lots of questions.

"My dad says you can ask God to help you know what to do. Knowing to ask God for help is the beginning of wisdom." Jeff grinned. "Just like you knew to ask for my help 'cause I'm so much better than you at this game. That was smart."

"Yeah, right. Then how come I'm beating your score?"

Jeff tried to wrestle the controller away from Devin.

Your Turn

1. When you're not sure what to do, where do you go for advice?
2. What's the difference between being smart and having wisdom?
3. What do you need wisdom for today?

_____

_____

_____

Prayer

LORD, I'm asking You for wisdom to live Your way. Amen.

True Goodness Comes from God

Blessed are those who gain wisdom, those who gain understanding.
– Proverbs 3:13

On the Road to Wisdom

"Your great-grandfather must be, like, two million years old," Richard whispered.

"Well, he is old," Kim whispered back. "I'm not sure how old he really is. Mom says he's pretty smart. He used to teach tae kwon do."

"Cool."

"I haven't lost my hearing," Kim's great-grandfather said, followed by a chuckle. "I'm 83. Want to know a secret—something I learned when I was a boy in Korea a long time ago?"

Richard and Kim looked at each other. "Sure," Jae said.

"God's Word will help you be wise."

Richard looked disappointed. He'd hoped Kim's great-grandfather knew something about being a ninja or a warrior.

"That's good advice, young man," Kim's great-grandfather said. "Even if you don't think so right now."

Richard looked embarrassed.

Kim grinned. "I told you he was smart!"

Your Turn

1. How does Jae's great-grandfather's advice help you?
2. If a friend needed advice, what would you tell him about God's Word?

_____

_____

_____

Prayer

Lord Jesus, thank You for Your Word. Amen.

True Goodness Comes from God

Blessed are those who gain wisdom, those who gain understanding.
– Proverbs 3:13

The Gift

Chris reluctantly unwrapped the gift from his great-aunt. She always gave him dumb things like sweaters and hats she'd knitted. *Why can't she ever buy me something?* he wondered.

"Did you tell your great-aunt thank you?" His mother frowned at him.

"Thanks," Chris mumbled. He didn't feel thankful at all.

"My pleasure," his great-aunt said as she beamed.

"Chris, we need to talk about your attitude," his mother said when they drove away from the retirement center where his great-aunt lived.

"Mom, why should I pretend I like these things?" Chris poked at the sweater in the box on his lap.

"I'm not asking you to pretend, Chris. I just want you to realize that your great-aunt didn't have to give you anything." His mother sighed. "I'm almost tempted to return this envelope." She handed him a worn-looking envelope. "Your great-aunt gave me this for you as well."

Inside was a twenty-dollar bill. "All right!" Chris said.

His mother sighed again. "Chris, we need to talk about being thankful."

Your Turn

1. Was Chris thankful for his great-aunt's first gift? Why or why not?
2. What are you most thankful for?

_____

_____

_____

Prayer

LORD, I want to have a thankful attitude all the time. Help me. Amen.

True Goodness Comes from God

Your Psalm of Thanks

Look up and read Psalm 66 in your Bible. This is a song of thanks to God. Praising God is a way of thanking Him. What would you like to thank God for? Use the space to write a thank-You to God. You can use pictures or words.

God,

Prayer

Heavenly Father, thank You for loving me and sending Your Son to die for me so that I might live with You for eternity. Amen.

True Goodness Comes from God

Problems, Problems

Your job is to help the kid use advice from the Word to solve the problems of sadness and loneliness. Which verses will you choose? Look up the Scriptures, and then write your advice based on the Scriptures.

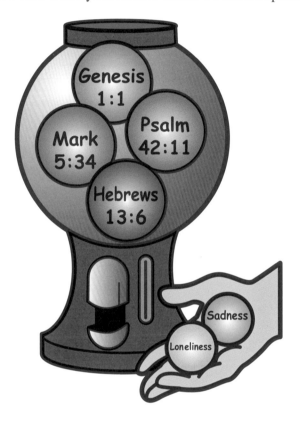

_____

_____

_____

_____

Prayer

Dear LORD, when I am lonely or sad, I know I can trust You to see me through the difficult times. Thank You. Amen.

Your Words Matter

Thanks be to God for his indescribable gift!
– 2 Corinthians 9:15

Canoe Trip

"Did you enjoy the trip?"

Kyle nodded at his stepfather's question. "This has been the best canoe trip ever!" He leaned back in his sleeping bag. He felt tired, but it was a good sort of tired. They had almost capsized on the river dozens of times, and Kyle had enjoyed the exciting ride.

He hadn't been thrilled when his mother remarried. He knew his stepfather had tried to win him over. At first, Kyle hadn't wanted to be bothered. But the love his stepfather had for his mother and for God had slowly worked on Kyle's heart too. His stepfather had brought him on this camping canoe trip to spend time together.

Just before he dropped off to sleep, Kyle said, "Thanks for bringing me, Dad." The "Dad" part had slipped out. Kyle had said he would never call his stepfather that precious name. But it felt right to say it now.

There was a long pause before his stepfather spoke. "You are welcome, son. Thank you."

"For what?"

"For agreeing to be my son."

Your Turn

1. How did Kyle show his thanks for the trip?
2. Think of a time when you were thankful. How did you express it?
3. Why is it important to say thank you?

_____

_____

_____

Prayer

LORD, help me remember to show my thanks. Amen.

Your Words Matter

Thanks be to God for his indescribable gift!
– 2 Corinthians 9:15

Tell the Whole Truth

Bernard did some fast thinking. How could he convince his grandmother the whole thing wasn't his fault? Quinn had made him mad—mad enough to cause the two of them to get into a shoving match. That had resulted in detention, which was why he was late getting home.

I'll just tell her that I had some schoolwork to do after school, he decided. That's sort of true. Bernard couldn't look his grandmother in the eye as he explained why he was late.

"Bernard, I've been your grandmother all your life and I know when you're about to lie to me or at least not tell me the whole truth. Are you telling me the whole story right now?"

Bernard squirmed. "Umm..." He finally told her everything.

Grandmother nodded shook her head. "Bernard, I know that telling the truth can sometimes be scary, but lying is wrong. You can lie to everyone, even to yourself, but not to God. The good news is that God and I love you no matter what you do, so you don't need to be afraid to tell the truth anymore. Now, that doesn't mean you won't have consequences for your actions today, but..."

Before Grandmother could finish, Bernard gave her a great big hug. He was relieved and thankful to know that God and grandmother would never stop loving him not matter what.

Your Turn

1. Why didn't Bernard want to tell the truth?
2. When are you tempted to lie?

Prayer

Lord, thank you for loving me even when You know I'm not being completely truthful. Amen.

Your Words Matter

Thanks be to God for his indescribable gift!
– 2 Corinthians 9:15

Speak the Truth in Love

"There!" Moira held up the project she'd just finished in pottery class. "What do you think?"

"What is it?" her brother Steve asked.

"It's a vase! What do you think?"

The words "hideous," "ugly," and "you've gotta be kidding" came to his mind. Steve couldn't help remembering how Moira had teased him about a drawing he'd once made. He looked at Moira. Her face revealed hope and joy. He knew she had worked hard on that vase, even though, to him, it looked as if an elephant had sat on it.

Steve had a second thought, "What would Jesus say to Moira?

"I know you worked hard on it," he said, knowing that was the truth. "Mom will really appreciate it." That was also true. Their mother liked anything they gave her.

"You think so? Thanks, Steve!" Moira left the room still looking happy.

Your Turn

1. Why do you think Steve didn't tell Moira exactly what he thought?
2. Was Steve's reply a good one?
3. How can you give an honest, gentle reply when the truth might sting?

_____

_____

_____

_____

Prayer

LORD, please help me to be honest and gentle at the same time. Amen.

Your Words Matter

Thanks be to God for his indescribable gift!
– **2 Corinthians 9:15**

Unforgiven

Stuart Leonard stared at his younger brother. He knew Linus wasn't sorry. Linus always took Stuart's stuff without asking. This time, Stuart had caught him red-handed.

"Are you gonna forgive me?" Linus asked.

I'm sick of forgiving him, Stuart thought. Aloud he said, "You're not really sorry, so no I'm not." Linus looked ready to cry, but Stuart didn't care. Linus didn't deserve to be forgiven.

Later, Mrs. Leonard called him into the living room. "Did you take one of your dad's tools without asking?" she asked.

Stuart knew that he had. "Oh…yes…yes, I did."

Mrs. Leonard folded her arms. "I've talked to you about this before."

"I'm sorry, Mom."

Mrs. Leonard shook her head. "Do you think you should be forgiven if you're not going to forgive your brother for doing a similar thing?"

Stuart stared at her. *She must've heard me talking to Linus.* "At least I'm sorry. Linus never is."

"That still doesn't give you the right to hold a grudge, does it?"

"I get the message," he said.

Your Turn

1. Did Stuart have the right to not forgive his brother? Why or why not?
2. Has someone ever not forgiven you? How did you feel?
3. Is there something a person could do that shouldn't be forgiven?
   Explain.

_____

_____

Prayer

Lord, thank You for the forgiveness You always offer. Amen.

Your Words Matter

Thanks be to God for his indescribable gift!
– 2 Corinthians 9:15

Forgiveness for a Friend

"What's wrong?" Megan asked when she saw her brother Joseph.

"Nothing." Joseph threw his backpack on the kitchen table, almost knocking over a vase.

"Something's wrong. Is it about that lie Nathan told about you?" Megan asked. She said even her fourth-grade class knew that Nathan had lied to avoid getting in trouble for something he had done.

The principal found out the truth, and called Nathan in to his office.

Joseph nodded. "Nathan told me he was sorry, but I don't know if I want to forgive him for what he did."

"Jesus said we're supposed to forgive people. If you can't on your own, He'll help you."

Joseph stared at her. He hadn't expected such good advice from her.

Megan grinned. "That's what Dad just told me a few minutes ago when I told him I didn't want to forgive you for making fun of my dress the other day."

Your Turn

1. Why do you think Joseph had a hard time forgiving Nathan?
2. When have you found it difficult to forgive? What did you do?

_____

_____

_____

_____

Prayer

LORD, thank You for the grace You give me so I can forgive others. Amen.

Your Words Matter

Gratitude Attitude

It's easy to spot the kid who has an attitude of gratitude. But some attitudes aren't so easy to see. They are attitudes of the heart. Check out the people listed and what they were given. Who had attitudes of gratitude?

Put a check mark under Column B. Who had attitudes of ingratitude? Put a check mark in Column A. Check the Scripture underneath each person to make sure you have the correct answers.

Gift	Column A	Column B
1. Hannah a son (1 Samuel 1:27–2:2)		
2. Adam Eve (Genesis 2:23)		
3. Israelites freedom from slavery (Exodus 16:2-3)		
4. Jewish leaders Jesus (bread of life) (John 6:41-42)		
5. People in Iconium The Gospel message (Acts 14:3, 5)		

Think of a gift you recently received. Under which column would you fall? Why?

Prayer

LORD, help me have an attitude of gratitude. Amen.

Your Words Matter

What's Wrong?

Can you find the eight wrong things in this scene? There is one wrong thing you can change to make this a picture of forgiveness. What is it?

Prayer

LORD, I want to forgive people like You forgive me. Amen.

Take Responsibility Seriously

Be on your guard; stand firm in the faith; be courageous; be strong.
– 1 Corinthians 16:13

Being Responsible

Gordon sighed when he looked out his bedroom window and saw his father talking to Mrs. Nakamura. Mrs. Nakamura had asked Gordon's father to give her bushes a trim. Gordon had begged his father to let him do it so he could earn some money.

Gordon didn't see what the big deal was. So he'd shown up a little late to her house. So he'd trimmed one bush until it looked like a lopsided egg. He'd said he'd come back and even it up after a game of street hockey with his friends.

His father came into Gordon's room. "I told you trimming bushes is a big responsibility."

"What's the big deal, Dad? I told her I'd finish later."

"The big deal, son, is that you were doing a job for someone else. Being responsible means showing up on time, doing a good job, and completing the job. Being late wasn't a good start, so Mrs. Nakamura started off upset and it went downhill when you left early."

Your Turn

1. How much responsibility did Gordon show? Circle your choice.

1	2	3	4	5	6	7	8	9	10
(Not much)									(A lot)

2. How do you handle responsibility? What can you improve on?

_____

_____

_____

Prayer

Lord Jesus, help me honor You by being responsible. Amen.

Take Responsibility Seriously

Be on your guard; stand firm in the faith; be courageous; be strong.
– 1 Corinthians 16:13

Who Is Responsible?

Gordon knew that his parents didn't think he was very responsible. But after the talking-to he had received from his father after slacking off on some bush trimming, he wanted to prove that he could be responsible. That included being able to stay at home by himself.

His parents exchanged a doubtful look.

"I'm almost thirteen!" Gordon declared. "I know not to let anybody come over or to let the house burn down." He looked slightly embarrassed. "I won't let what happened last time happen again."

The last time his parents had gone on a date, as they called it, Gordon had accidentally left the phone off the hook and was partially responsible for nearly setting fire to the kitchen table. But hadn't he proven himself more responsible this past week? He had done all of his chores, finished his homework without being forced to, and even returned some overdue library books.

"Okay, we're willing to trust you," Mr. Archer said. "We think you might be ready."

"Might be?" Gordon asked.

Mrs. Archer smiled. "We'll give it a trial run."

Your Turn

1. How did Gordon prove he was ready for more responsibility?
2. What big responsibilities do you think you're ready for? Why?

_____

_____

_____

Prayer

Lord, help me grow more responsible so I can honor You. Amen.

Take Responsibility Seriously

Be on your guard; stand firm in the faith; be courageous; be strong.
– 1 Corinthians 16:13

The Courage to Do What Is Right

"Did you see what happened?"

Keith wished he could suddenly fake amnesia to get out of answering the assistant principal's question. He had seen what had happened. His friend Terry had set off a firecracker in the restroom. The noise frightened someone into setting off the fire alarm.

Keith hadn't wanted to say anything, especially after the principal threatened to make everyone stay after school until someone confessed. Keith didn't want to get Terry in trouble, but he also didn't want Mr. Chavez to think he had something to do with it. *Terry has gotten all of us in trouble,* he thought. Suddenly he thought about prayer. His Sunday-school teacher had challenged the class to keep close to God during the week through prayer. LORD, *I'm afraid. Help me do what is right,* Keith prayed silently.

After a pause, Keith sighed and told what he'd seen. He was relieved that Mr. Chavez believed him. But what was even more of a relief was when Terry came in to confess what he'd done.

Thanks, God! Keith thought.

Your Turn

1. What did Keith need courage to do?
2. When have you needed courage to do the right thing?
3. When do you need courage the most?

_____

_____

_____

Prayer

Dear God, help me do what is right in Your eyes. Amen.

Take Responsibility Seriously

Be on your guard; stand firm in the faith; be courageous; be strong.
– 1 Corinthians 16:13

God Will Give You Courage

Fear? Chet wanted to laugh. *Fear is for big babies,* he told himself. But he was afraid. He hadn't really thought about it until his mother had said those dreaded words: "I'm taking you to the dentist."

Chet had begged and tried excuses as a way out. He'd even thrown a tantrum, which just made his mother mad.

You're going, and that's that!" she declared. "Everyone goes for regular checkups."

Chet sulked all the way to the dentist.

And that's when his mother had asked, "Are you afraid?"

Chet tried to bluff his way out, but he finally nodded.

"I thought so," his mother said. "Remember, you can ask God for courage when you're afraid. But the first thing you have to do is admit that you are afraid."

God, I'm afraid. Help me. Chet felt better just praying those words.

Your Turn

1. What was Chet afraid of?
2. What are you afraid of?
3. How do you deal with your fear? Is there a better way?

_____

_____

_____

_____

Prayer

LORD, when I'm afraid, I'm glad I can come to You for comfort and strength. Amen.

Take Responsibility Seriously

Be on your guard; stand firm in the faith; be courageous; be strong.
– 1 Corinthians 16:13

It's Not Fair!

"You sure look like a black thundercloud ready to spit lightning," Grandma Rogers said to Connor. "What has you all riled up?"

Connor flopped onto the couch. "It's just not fair! I practiced pitching for weeks, but Brad Hanson got picked. And he didn't practice."

Grandma listened as Connor complained. Then she spoke up. "I once knew a woman who had a husband and three kids. The woman was very happy. The children grew up and moved away. Then suddenly her husband died. And she started having physical problems and had trouble walking. She became very angry."

Grandma stopped to take a sip of tea. "People tried to help her, but all she did was whine that it just wasn't fair she had all these problems. A friend finally told her, 'Life is not fair. But even though the world doesn't always treat us fairly, God is always fair. Why not think about all the good things in your life that God has given you?'

Grandma smiled. "The woman kept thinking about what her friend had said. Gradually she smiled more than she frowned. She became more positive and complained less."

"How did the woman turn out?" asked Connor.

Grandma laughed and said, "That woman was me, Connor. What do you think?"

"I think you turned out great," Connor said. "Sorry I was such a grump."

"No offense taken," Grandma replied.

Your Turn

1. How can we know God is fair? How can we know He is just?
2. Look up "fairness" and "justice" in a dictionary. Are they different?

Prayer

Almighty God, I'm happy that You are always fair. Help me treat others fairly. Amen.

Take Responsibility Seriously

Ready, Willing, and Able

People who want to find jobs or get better jobs usually write a resumé. A resumé lists their work experiences. Are you ready for more responsibility? How can your past experience be used to show you are ready, willing, and able? Use the space below to list the responsibility you think you are ready for. Then take an inventory of your life and write down the experiences you've had that will show you are ready for the new responsibility. List everything you think will help. For example, you might include a project you were involved in or chores you have done successfully without complaining. Next list the "stoppers." These are items that might keep you from fulfilling your responsibilities, such as putting things off, being too busy, wanting to play baseball. How can you keep the stoppers from stopping you?

■ **Responsibility You Want**

_____

_____

_____

■ **Past Experiences**

_____

_____

_____

■ **Stoppers**

_____

_____

_____

Prayer

Father God, I want to take on more responsibility so I will grow up strong. Please help me be ready, willing, and able. Amen.

Take Responsibility Seriously

The Right Stuff

Having "the right stuff" means having the courage and determination to do what you need to do. God gave these people the right stuff to do what He wanted done. During one period in Israel's history, God gave judges the courage to lead the Israelites against their enemies. Most of the time the Israelites were outnumbered, but God made them victorious. Look up the Scriptures, and then match each person with the "nickname" that describes his or her task?

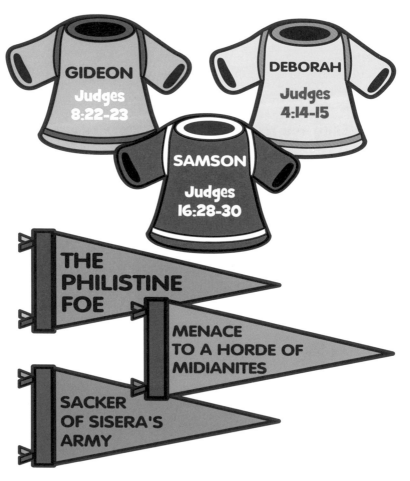

GIDEON
Judges 8:22-23

DEBORAH
Judges 4:14-15

SAMSON
Judges 16:28-30

THE PHILISTINE FOE

MENACE TO A HORDE OF MIDIANITES

SACKER OF SISERA'S ARMY

Prayer

God, I want the right stuff, and I know that You are the only One who can help me get it. That's why I want to stay close to You always. Amen.

Faith Is Believing Without Seeing

God has said, "Never will I leave you; never will I forsake you."
– Hebrews 13:5

Faith Test

Garrett tested the ice with one foot. He wasn't quite sure the pond was completely frozen over.

"Think it's okay?" his friend Mitchell asked.

Garrett shrugged and then suddenly grinned. "My dad once said faith is like this." He waved at the ice as they both began to skate. "Faith is like stepping out on the ice without really knowing whether it will hold you."

They began to slap a puck back and forth to each other using hockey sticks.

"I thought you had to see God to believe in Him," Mitchell said after a while. "Now, I know that's not true."

Neither spoke for a while, except to congratulate each other on good shots. Finally Mitchell said, "Sometimes you can have faith in the wrong things, though."

"Like what?"

"Like my dad said he had faith that I would be a boy, so he picked the name Mitchell. But I wasn't, and now I'm stuck with it. It's a good thing I like it!"

Your Turn

1. How would you describe faith?
2. In whom or what do you have faith?

_____

_____

_____

Prayer

Jesus, I trust You as my Savior and have faith in You. Amen.

Faith Is Believing Without Seeing

God has said, "Never will I leave you; never will I forsake you."
– Hebrews 13:5

A Prayer of Faith

Arnie felt foolish. He wasn't even sure half the time that God existed, let alone that He listened when a boy prayed. Now it was his turn to lead the closing prayer in Sunday school. The teacher always said no one had to pray aloud.

Arnie started to say "pass," but in a split-second the word "faith" came to mind. That was what they'd discussed in class: Having faith that God will hear you, even though you don't have any proof that He does. *I'm supposed to believe when I pray!* he thought.

"Arnie?" the teacher asked again.

"I'm ready! God, help us believe that You hear us when we pray. Amen."

Before Arnie could escape after class, the teacher called him. "Arnie, I know praying out loud is a struggle for you."

Arnie nodded. "It's starting to get easier. I choose to believe that God hears me."

His teacher smiled. "That's fantastic!"

Your Turn

1. Why do you think God wants you to know He hears you?
2. What helps you to believe that God hears you pray?

_____

_____

_____

Prayer

Lord, help me overcome my unbelief and have faith in You. Amen.

Faith Is Believing Without Seeing

God has said, "Never will I leave you; never will I forsake you."
– Hebrews 13:5

God Loves Everyone

The boys watched as Jed hit the baseball into Mr. Zane's backyard.

"Guess the game is over because we have no more balls," said Jim. "Unless someone wants to go and ask Old Zany to get our balls for us."

"No way!" said Jed. "I heard he yells at kids that come to the door."

"Maybe we should call him Prickly Porcupine because he's so grouchy," Jim hooted. "Matt, go get the ball. I hope you survive!"

Matt nervously rang Mr. Zane's doorbell. The door opened, and an old man looked out. "We hit a baseball into your backyard. May I please get it?"

Mr. Zane waved a gnarled hand at the backyard. Matt found the ball and two others they'd lost. As he came back around the house, Mr. Zane was sitting on the front porch. He said, "You kids are pretty good ball players. When you hit it over my fence, you leave before I can get to the ball and toss it back. I don't move very fast these days. I used to be called Speedy Sam when I played minor league ball. Boy, could I run those bases!" He invited Matt to "sit a spell."

Matt forgot all about the name Prickly Porcupine. He was having a great time listening to Mr. Zane's baseball stories. When it was time to go, Matt said, "Why don't you come over and watch us tomorrow?"

"I'd be honored!" Mr. Zane smiled.

Your Turn

1. How do you feel about old or sick people?
2. What are ways you can show love to old or sick people?

Prayer

God, thank You for loving everyone equally. Help me do the same. Amen.

Faith Is Believing Without Seeing

God has said, "Never will I leave you; never will I forsake you."
– Hebrews 13:5

Choosing Sides

When Andrew entered the classroom, he noticed the new boy from Poland, Boris, sitting in the back. He was being totally ignored. The fifth-graders were talking and laughing, using lots of slang expressions. *This must be confusing to someone learning English.*

Andrew walked to Boris' desk. "Hi, I'm Andrew. I sure had trouble with today's math assignment. What did you think?"

After getting over the shock of someone talking to him, Boris said, "I like math. In my Polish school we had even harder work. I can help you."

At lunchtime, Andrew saw Boris sitting alone and headed toward him. "Hey, 'Drew, where are you going? We saved you a seat," called Doug.

"Why are you sitting with him? He can't talk to you," Carl said.

Andrew stopped by the crowded table. "I'm eating with Boris today. We probably wouldn't sound so great if we had to speak Polish. Boris is a math genius."

After lunch, Ms. Conroy, the lunchroom monitor, came up to Andrew. "It was great how you stuck up for Boris. He needs help making friends."

Your Turn

1. List the names of people who are new in your school or church. What is a way you can help each one?

_____

_____

_____

Prayer

God, help me reach out and help people. Amen.

Faith Is Believing Without Seeing

God has said, "Never will I leave you; never will I forsake you."
– Hebrews 13:5

The Sign

Mark and his friends Juan and Toby liked to practice baseball on Saturdays. They all agreed that they would finish their chores and home-work before lunch so they could squeeze in as much playing time as possible before dinner. This particular Saturday, Mark and his family invited their new pastor and his family to dinner, so it was important that Mark was home on time.

As planned, the boys finished their chores and homework and met at the park right after lunch and started playing. They had such a good time that they lost track of time. Suddenly, Toby yelled out to Mark from the pitcher's mound, "Hey Mark, don't you have to be home soon?"

"Yikes, I gotta go!" exclaimed Mark as he looked at his watch.

Juan said, "You go Mark. We'll get the balls and equipment."

"Thanks guys! I'll text you later," said Mark as he hopped on his bike and sped home. He was going so fast that didn't see the sharp rock in the middle of the bike path. Before he knew it, he felt the tire pop under him.

"Oh no! I'll never get home on time. Oh God, please help me," Mark whispered.

Suddenly a familiar red van pulled to the curb next to him. It was the new pastor and his family. "Hi Mark, we're headed for your house for dinner. Could we give you a lift?

Your Turn

1. How did God provide for Mark and his friends?
2. What are some ways God shows His care for you?

Prayer

LORD, thank You for watching out for me. Amen.

Faith Is Believing Without Seeing

Unlovely People

Jesus often associated with people other people looked down on. Jesus truly loves everyone, even those some people might consider unlovely. To find out who some of the "unlovely" people were in Jesus' day, cross out every G, H, J, Q, U, V, W, Y, Z. Next write the letters left on the lines to read the message.

G Z S I U V N Y Y N E J R Q S

T Z W A J U X V Z M H E Y G N

W D Z V E H G A F L U A M Z E

G H L J Q U E V P E Y Z R S H

Z U B H W L Z Z J I Q J N D V

Q P O Y Z O U R S W I J C Z K

G G I H N J Q S U A V N E W Z

_____

_____

_____

_____

Prayer

Lord, when I think about how You love everyone equally, I know I can do better than I have been doing. Please help me show Your love to everyone I meet. Amen.

Faith Is Believing Without Seeing

What Do You Think?

God cares about your concerns and your world. Read each sentence starter and finish it with your own thoughts. When you are done, ask God to help you make a difference in your world.

If you could change...

YOUR NEIGHBORHOOD, what would it be like? Why?

_____

_____

YOUR SCHOOL, what would it be like? Why?

_____

_____

THE WORLD, what would you be like? Why?

_____

_____

YOURSELF, what would you be like? Why?

_____

_____

Prayer

Father, help me do my part each day to make this a better world. Amen.

Talking and Walking with God

The prayer of a righteous man is powerful and effective. . .
– James 5:16

Heart-to-Heart

Each kid in the sixth-grade Bible study was given a word to explain to the others at the next class. Kevin's word was "prayer."

I know how to pray, Kevin thought.

His Uncle Jack called. "Will you help me build my deck?"

Kevin and Uncle Jack sawed and hammered away. When they took a break, Uncle Jack asked, "Hey, Kev, what's new?"

Kevin said, "Not much. You know, same old thing—school, home, friends. Wait. There is something new in my Bible study. But my part is pretty much the same old thing, I guess." Kevin explained the project. "I've been praying forever. What more can I learn?"

Uncle Jack told Kevin to look around the half-finished deck. Then he asked, "What's the most important part?"

"Plans and measuring things exactly," Kevin decided.

"Those are important," his uncle agreed. "But the most important part of this deck is the nails. Without them, nothing would stay in place. Prayer is sort of like nails. It holds your faith together through heart-to-heart talks with God."

Back at work, Kevin said, "As I bang nails, I'll be praying. These may be the noisiest prayers ever!"

Your Turn

1. How do you feel about prayer? When do you pray?
2. Why is praying important in a Christian's life?

_____

_____

Prayer

God, I'm glad I can talk to You anytime about anything. Amen.

Talking and Walking with God

The prayer of a righteous man is powerful and effective. . .
– James 5:16

News Flash!

Brian was sprawled on the floor watching basketball. The program was interrupted and a news announcer said, "Strong earthquakes have shaken the Pacific islands. Thousands of people are homeless; hundreds are feared dead." Pictures of destruction flashed across the screen. People were walking around in a daze amid the rubble of homes and neighborhoods. Children were crying, and hurt people were waiting for help.

"Man, I really don't like this," Brian said to his dad.

Mr. Clark said, "The game will be back."

Brian interrupted, "I don't care about the game. Seeing the news made me scared and sad. Maybe if I never watched TV it would be better."

"Well, I don't think you'll do that," his father answered. "Not watching tragedies and bad news on TV won't improve anything. As long as there is sin in the world, all kinds of terrible things will keep right on happening. But there is something we can do about it right now."

"What's that?" Brian asked.

"We can pray for the people in trouble. God promises to hear our prayers and help those in need. Let's pray for the earthquake victims right now."

Your Turn

1. How do you feel when you hear or read distressing news?
2. How can you help people you don't know?

_____

_____

_____

Prayer

Merciful Father, please help people who are having trouble. Amen.

Talking and Walking with God

The prayer of a righteous man is powerful and effective. . .
– James 5:16

When God Speaks

Dale had his Bible open, but he didn't hear a word. Not one sound from God. "I thought God spoke through His Word?" he complained.

"He does," his dad said.

"I've been reading this Bible for ten whole minutes. I haven't heard God say one word."

His father chuckled. "He does help you understand what He wants you to do. Sometimes it helps to be quiet and listen. What are you reading?"

"The story of the lost son. I'm at the part where the mean older brother didn't want his brother to have a party."

"Kind of like the time when you didn't want us to take your brother out to celebrate his finally getting a 'C' in math on his report card instead of his usual 'D.' "

"That wasn't fair, Dad. I get 'A's' all the time, and you only took me out once."

"I think God is speaking to you now, Dale. Are you listening."

Your Turn

1. What do you think God is telling Dale?
2. How has God directed your footsteps through His Word?
3. What will you do this week to find out more through God's Word?

_____

_____

_____

_____

Prayer

LORD, thank You for Your Word. Amen.

Talking and Walking with God

The prayer of a righteous man is powerful and effective. . .
– James 5:16

Road Map

"Habakkuk!" Carey slammed his Bible shut. "It figures Joanie knew where it was. I can barely pronounce that book, let alone spell it."

"I never heard of it," his friend George said. "You're sure it's in the Bible?"

"Having trouble?" their small-group leader asked.

"Why do we have these Scripture drills? Joanie wins all the time." He made a face at Joanie, who sat at the next table smirking.

"That's because she's memorized the books of the Bible. Scripture drills are a fun way to help you learn the books."

"Sure, but who is going to read Habakkuk? Nobody can find it!" Carey declared. Some of the kids laughed.

"The Bible is like a road map, Carey. Every book contains part of God's plan. This is how He directs our steps each day. Habakkuk's like a little side street on a map. You may not think it's important, but someday you might need to go there."

Your Turn

1. How is the Bible like a road map?
2. How has knowing the Bible helped you recently?

_____

_____

_____

_____

Prayer

LORD, when I doubt, help me hear Your advice in Your Word. Amen.

Talking and Walking with God

The prayer of a righteous man is powerful and effective. . .
– James 5:16

Obedience Is Not a Request

"Are you listening to me?"

Claude never liked it when his mother said that. "Yes," he said. He glanced at her as she stood in the doorway to his room.

"Good," she said. "I suggest you have all of your chores done by the time I get back from the store…or else."

Claude nodded. He knew that tone. His mother wasn't really *suggesting* that he do it. She expected him to do it. He knew what "or else" meant too. If he didn't obey, he would be grounded for one thing. And no TV or video games for another. He also knew she only said "or else" the second time she asked him to do something.

His glance fell on the devotional his mother had bought him. Today's topic was "Why obey God?" *Everybody wants me to obey,* he thought. Claude sighed. "Why can't I order someone around?" he said out loud. Then another word caught his eye: "love."

He knew his mother loved him, even though she expected him to do things like chores. *Maybe God is like that too,* he thought.

Your Turn

1. What do you think "keeping God's commands" means?
2. What do you find hard and what do you find easy about obeying God?

_____

_____

_____

Prayer

Lord, help me obey Your commands. Amen.

Talking and Walking with God

Praying for Others

God promises to hear your prayers and to help you when you are in need. If you read about someone in the newspaper or hear about someone on TV who needs God's help, you can pray for him or her. You can pray for anyone, even people you don't know. God knows everyone in the entire world. He wants us to pray for each other and for anyone who has trouble. Fill in the blanks of the prayer. You can use it when you pray for others.

Dear God,

Sometimes I feel sad or scared or angry when I hear

or read about all the terrible things that happen in

the world. Today I want to pray for

_____

_____

because this has happened to them

_____.

Please help them and be with them.

Thank You, God, for Your love for all people.

In Jesus' name. Amen.

Talking and Walking with God

His Way to Obey

If Bible people kept reminder notes on their refrigerators (they didn't because they didn't have refrigerators back then!), which of the building projects would these notes represent? Write the building names next to the notes. Then write the name of the person who would obey God by following the note.

1. The temple
2. The ark
3. The tabernacle

A. Noah
B. Solomon
C. Moses/Aaron

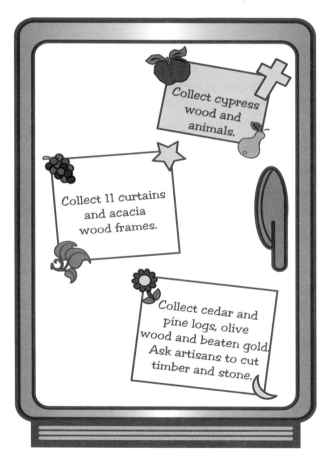

Prayer

Heavenly Father, I want to be used by You to help people and obey You. Amen.

Obey God Always

[Jesus said,] "If you love me, keep my commands."
– John 14:15

That's Telling Him!

"You go to church *every* Sunday?" Steve was shocked.

Faith nodded. She didn't want to talk to Steve. She had wandered into the family room where Steve was waiting for her brother.

"No wonder they call you Faith." Steve laughed at his own joke.

"Doofus" was on the tip of Faith's tongue, but she bit it back. "There's nothing wrong with going to church every Sunday, Steve. Lots of people do it."

"We only go twice a year—Christmas and Easter."

She stared at him. "Don't you believe in God and doing what He says?"

Steve got up and took off with her brother.

"Can you believe Clark's friends?" Faith asked her older sister, Karen.

"Faith, you said something about doing what God says, but you sure don't act like you believe it sometimes," said Karen. "You were snotty to Steve."

Faith sighed. "He is a total goofball."

"Yes, but what about 'judge not'? That's one of God's commands."

Faith hated to admit that her sister was right.

Your Turn

1. Is obedience to God something you want to do? Why or why not?
2. How well do you obey God? How can you improve?

_____

_____

_____

Prayer

Lord, help me trust You enough to willingly obey You. Amen.

Obey God Always

> *[Jesus said,] "If you love me, keep my commands."*
> **– John 14:15**

The Joy Factor

Ken usually liked Sundays. The whole family went to church. They stopped at a restaurant for lunch on the way home. Sunday afternoons were quiet—good for reading and relaxing. But this wasn't a good Sunday. Ken had been embarrassed in Sunday school when he'd tripped. Then his voice squeaked when he sang during church. To top off the morning, he'd spilled gravy on his pants at the restaurant. He slouched in a living room chair, reading the Sunday comics and feeling sorry for himself.

His little sister Katie marched around and sang "Alleluia" over and over in her loudest four-year-old voice.

"Enough already!" Ken said. "There's nothing to 'alleluia' about!" Katie ran to find their mom.

Oh, great, thought Ken. *Now I'll get chewed out too.*

Ken's mom came into the room and

handed him a small mirror. Ken looked at himself—a grumpy-looking kid with a big frown.

"His mother said, "I think your joy factor is about zero right now. Want to talk about it?"

Ken told his mom about his miserable morning.

"I think you need to think about 'alleluia' " said Mrs. Bartlett. "Alleluia is sort of like saying 'hooray' to God. God loves you even on hard days. He does lots of wonderful things for you. He deserves thanks and praise even when you feel like the clumsiest, sloppiest, most squeaky kid ever."

Ken thought about the good parts of the day—and smiled!

Your Turn

1. How do you praise God?
2. List three ways you can praise God. Then list three reasons to praise Him!

Prayer

Alleluia, alleluia, alleluia. I praise You, Lord. You are great! Amen.

Obey God Always

[Jesus said,] "If you love me, keep my commands."
– John 14:15

Worship God Every Day

"This sure is one huge blooper," Zach muttered. "They definitely need some better editors for this book."

His mom looked up from the newspaper. "Were you talking to me?" she asked.

"No," Zach answered. "I was talking to myself. But maybe you can help me figure out something."

"I'll do my best," Mom said as she laid down the paper.

"I'm doing a page in this book for Bible Club," Zach explained. "The whole lesson is about worship and the different parts of a church service. But this question asks, 'How do you worship God every day?' I think they meant to say 'on Sunday.' We don't go to church every day, so that question is impossible to answer." Zach gave a big sigh and closed the book.

"Zach, there's nothing wrong with the book," his mother explained. "You don't have to be in church to worship God. You worship Him every time you pray or sing songs of praise. It's even worshipping God when you obey Him and do what pleases Him. We have church services so everyone can worship God together, but we can also worship Him all alone."

Your Turn

1. How do you worship God in church?
2. How do you worship God when you're not in church?

_____

_____

_____

Prayer

Dear God, help me worship You in church and in my everyday life. Amen.

Obey God Always

[Jesus said,] "If you love me, keep my commands."
– **John 14:15**

Do You Mean It?

"Do you really mean it when you say you're sorry?" The junior high group leader's question stuck in Tom's mind. He'd just told his uncle he was sorry after being caught in a lie. He had lied about why he'd been late coming home from school. Being sent to the principal's office was not something he wanted to tell his uncle.

"Tom, that's the second time you've lied to me this week," his uncle had reminded him. "You know that lying is wrong."

Tom had promised that he wouldn't lie again. Now he wondered if he would be able to keep that promise.

"If you know you have a problem, you can ask God to help you turn away from wrong," the youth leader said. "First, you need to admit you can't do it on your own."

During prayer time, Tom did just that. Afterward, he felt better. He caught up with his uncle after church.

"I'm sorry I was late this week…and for lying and everything." Tom couldn't look him in the eye.

"You already told me you were sorry."

"Yes, but this time I really mean it."

Your Turn

1. What helped change Tom's mind about lying?
2. What are things you can do to help yourself not to repeat doing wrong?

_____

_____

_____

Prayer

Jesus, help me turn away from wrongdoing. Amen.

Obey God Always

[Jesus said,] "If you love me, keep my commands."
– John 14:15

Everyone Has Sinned

"Hey, Dad, look at that bumper sticker." Kenneth Simmons pointed to the car ahead.

"'I'm my own Savior,' " his father read. "I've seen clever bumper stickers that were just as wrong." He shot Kenneth a glance. "What would you put on a bumper sticker?"

Kenneth shrugged. He couldn't drive, so he didn't much care. Now if he had his own car… "I like video games?" he suggested.

Mr. Simmons smiled. "I meant about God."

Kenneth shrugged again. "What would you put, Dad?"

"A person who needs a Savior can't be his own Savior."

"Aren't we all just basically good?" Kenneth asked.

"Where did you hear that?"

Kenneth shrugged a third time. "Somebody said that at school. She said she heard it on some show on TV."

"Kenneth, according to God's Word, we have all sinned. It could be as simple as a lie or a harmful thought about someone. We were born in sin. Are you sure you haven't been wondering about this?"

Kenneth looked at his father and gave a sheepish grin.

Your Turn

1. Why can't you save yourself?
2. What would you write about repentance on a bumper sticker?

_____

_____

_____

Prayer

God, thank You for the forgiveness You give when I repent. Amen.

111

Obey God Always

Title?

"Alleluia" is sort of like cheering for God. Use each letter in the acrostic to name some of the things God gives you. Praise and thank Him for each one. For example, next to "A" you might write "All my family and friends."

A_____

L_____

L_____

E_____

L_____

U_____

I_____

A_____

Prayer

Dear LORD, You are worthy of praise. Alleluia! Amen.

Obey God Always

Your Bumper Sticker

Write a bumper sticker about God and then decorate it.

Prayer

Dear LORD, help me remember what it looks like to obey You. Amen.

Jesus Lives in You

In [Christ] we live and move and have our being...
– Acts 17:28

Meet My Friend

"I wish I could meet him," Denny said, waving a sports magazine at his friend Tyler.

"Who?" Tyler barely glanced up from the game in his hands. He already knew who. Denny only talked about one person—his favorite baseball player. "What would you do if you could?" he asked, finally looking up.

Denny shrugged. "Get to know him, I guess. Hang with him."

Tyler put the game on pause. "I've got someone you can meet. All you have to do is come to church with my family and me on Sunday."

Denny's eyes glazed over. "What? Not again."

"Really, this friend is way cool. All my friends at church think so, once they've gotten to know Him better."

"Does he play baseball?"

Tyler laughed.

Denny grinned. "I already know the punch line. God, right?"

Tyler went back to the game. "Want to come? Church is fun—because God's cooler than anyone you've ever met!

When you get to know Him, you'll want to stick with Him forever!"

Your Turn

1. Who is the person you would most like to meet? Why?
2. How have you gotten to know Jesus?

_____

_____

_____

Prayer

LORD, I want to know You better. Amen.

Jesus Lives in You

In [Christ] we live and move and have our being…
– Acts 17:28

The Answer

Jesse Collins silently followed the rest of the family to the van. He could hardly believe that Uncle Gary was dead. Jesse had prayed and prayed, asking God to make his uncle better. Now Uncle Gary was gone.

Jesse's father put a hand on his shoulder. "You're awfully quiet, buddy."

"I'll never pray again," Jesse said.

Mr. Collins paused to think. "Never is a long time."

"I asked God to make Uncle Gary better, and He didn't."

"You guys go on ahead," his father said to the others. He led Jesse to a stone bench. "Jesse, right now you're pretty mad at God, huh?"

Jesse nodded. God had let Uncle Gary die. His uncle was his favorite person in the world after his mom and dad.

"Remember how you told me that Jesus was your Savior and that you wanted to know more about Him?" Mr. Collins asked. "Well, one of the things is the fact that He's in control of our lives. That's what we agree to when we ask Him to be our Lord and Savior. We also trust that whatever He does is best for us. Right?"

Jesse shrugged.

"But now my brother is healed and in the best place ever! God does what is best," said Jesse's father.

Your Turn

1. What answer did Jesse receive to his prayer: yes, no, or maybe?
2. When are you most tempted to let go of God? What do you do?

_____

_____

Prayer

Lord, help me trust that You are in control of my life even when it's hard. Amen.

Jesus Lives in You

In [Christ] we live and move and have our being...
– Acts 17:28

Handling Things Peacefully

"Keep your junk off my side of the room." Richard threw a bowling shoe at his twin brother's bed.

"I said I was sorry!" Ray yelled.

"Can't we all just get along?" their mother said as she appeared in the doorway. "What's with you two?"

"He keeps breaking my stuff!" Richard showed her the cracked screen.

"You're fighting over that?" Mrs. Kean shook her head. "What did I tell you about handling things peacefully? It's important to get along. I don't want to hear you two always fighting."

"If he would just ask before taking my stuff," Richard complained.

Mrs. Kean threw Ray a look. "Ray, I told you about that."

"I just looked at it for a second, Mom. Okay! I'm sorry."

Mrs. Kean turned to Richard. "And Rich, what are three ways you can help yourself stop getting so mad over things?"

Richard had to think about that.

Your Turn

1. What kept Ray and Richard from getting along?
2. What can you do to live in harmony?

_____

_____

_____

_____

Prayer

LORD, help me live in harmony with others. Amen.

Jesus Lives in You

In [Christ] we live and move and have our being...
– Acts 17:28

Competition

"Okay, time!" Jim, the youth leader, blew his whistle. "You guys, the whole idea of Game Night is to have fun. You aren't having fun, except maybe Brian."

Brian had come up with idea to team the boys against the girls. But soon arguments had broken out.

"The girls are just mad because we're beating them four games to two," Brian declared.

"You cheat!" Vanessa replied. The other girls agreed.

Jim waved his hand for quiet. "The whole idea is to have fun, but getting along with each other is important. That's what God wants. Now, what do you think He'd want you to do?"

"He'd want Brian to stop cheating!" Vanessa yelled.

"He'd also want everyone to think about what he or she…" Jim looked hard at Vanessa, "could do to get along with others."

"Okay. I'll stop saying Brian's a cheater," Vanessa suggested.

"I'll stop cheating!" Brian said, and everyone laughed.

Your Turn

1. What needs to happen for everyone to get along?
2. What can you do to live peacefully with others?

_____

_____

_____

_____

Prayer

LORD, help me do what it takes to get along with people. Amen.

Jesus Lives in You

In [Christ] we live and move and have our being...
– Acts 17:28

A Life Shared

"Hey, Raul! Where are you going?"

Raul Guiterrez dreaded the sound of that voice. *Not today,* he thought. Just as he was on his way to youth church, he had to run into Cesar Hujar. Cesar was one of the toughest kids in the apartment complex. Raul didn't want Cesar to call him names just because he was going to church.

"Didn't you hear me, man?" Cesar asked when he caught up.

"Yeah." Raul sounded defensive. He didn't know what to say. His mother had once suggested that he invite Cesar to church. *Yeah, right,* he'd thought then. A new thought came to his mind now: *Pray.*

What do I say, God? he prayed silently. Suddenly he knew. All he had to do was be himself. He didn't have to be ashamed of going to church.

"I'm going to Parkside," Raul said. Parkside was the church in the neighborhood.

"You go there?" Cesar looked surprised. "Wow, maybe I'll go there sometime."

Raul thought he would die of shock and relief. "How 'bout today with me?" he asked.

Your Turn

1. What is the hardest thing about telling others about Jesus?
2. How can you help yourself do that?

_____

_____

_____

_____

Prayer

Dear God, let my life show that I trust You. Amen.

Jesus Lives in You

Fruit Basket Upset

When you stick with Jesus, you bear fruit. Does that mean you turn into a pear tree? No! But you do get the terrific attributes mentioned in Galatians 5:22-23. Unscramble the words to find out what you gain.

Ovle _____

Oyj _____

ecape _____

catenipe _____

dinksens _____

nodseogs _____

thaiffensuls _____

neteslengs _____

lefs-tooncrl _____

Fruit doesn't come up overnight! Which of these will you need to help you wait for God to work in your life?

_____

_____

_____

Prayer

LORD, please help me stick with You so that I will bear the fruit of Your Holy Spirit. Amen.

Jesus Lives in You

Ancient Hieroglyphics?

The text on the wall below is not newly discovered Egyptian hieroglyphics. Cross out the X's, Y's, and N's to discover items you can give to encourage peaceful relations.

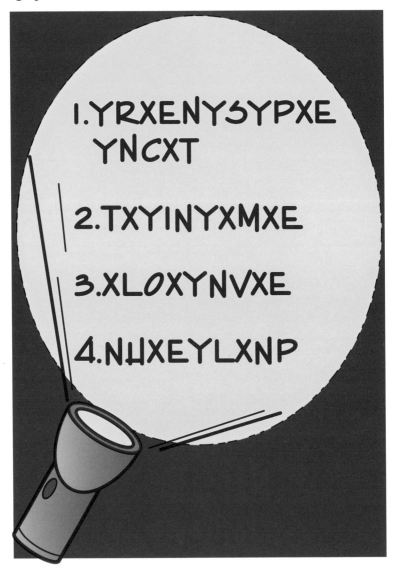

Prayer

LORD, help me live peacefully with my family and friends. Amen.

Life Lessons

*Let your light shine before others, that they may see
your good deeds and glorify your Father in heaven.*
– **Matthew 5:16**

The T-Shirt

"Mom, I can't wear this." Ethan Miniver held up the T-shirt his mother had just given him.

"What's wrong with a WWJD T-shirt?" his mother asked. "I think it's cute. It'll make your friends wonder what 'WWJD' stands for."

Ethan's eyes had taken on a glazed look when his mother said the word "cute." Now they blazed with indignation. "See, that's what I mean. They'll be asking me what it means."

"Is that a bad thing?" Mrs. Miniver looked puzzled.

"They'll be thinking I'm a weirdo or something."

His mother paused and then held up the T-shirt. "What would Jesus do?" she asked.

"Mommmmm!" Ethan whined.

"What would He do, Ethan? In this situation, what would He want? Would He want you to be ashamed of Him when you're with your friends? Would He want…well, you tell me."

Ethan shrugged. "I'm not ashamed of Him."

"I don't care about whether or not you wear this T-shirt," said his mom. "What matters is how important Jesus is to you. That is a question only you can answer. What do you think?"

Your Turn

1. What is a way you can tell if Jesus is important to someone?
2. How do you show Jesus is important to you?

_____

_____

Prayer

Lord, I want Your light to shine through me so people will want to know You. Amen.

Life Lessons

Let your light shine before others, that they may see your good deeds and glorify your Father in heaven.
– Matthew 5:16

All God's Creatures

"Most of the time, I'm glad I live on a farm," Cody said to his dad as they repaired a hole in the fence. "But these goats are a big pain. They're always getting out and running all over the place. Mom really gets mad when they chomp on her garden. Maybe we could sell them."

Mr. Daniels laughed as he gave the fence wire a final twist. "The goats are just being goats," he said. "They like to jump and have fun like you do. We make money selling their milk, so I think we'll keep them."

Cody and his dad sat on the fence watching the goats. Cody had to admit they really were funny. "I think they're the clowns of the farm."

Then they talked about the other farm animals—friendly dogs, squealing pigs, large cows, strong bulls, squawky chickens, cuddly kittens, frolicking lambs, and magnificent riding horses.

Cody was thinking about the tame farm animals and the wild animals that shared the farm. "I think it's great God made all the animals different," he said. "It's so much fun to watch them and learn about them."

Mr. Daniels agreed. "God gave us all these animals and hundreds more—just think of all the insects! But God doesn't just want us to look at the animals or use them. He wants us to take care of them too."

Your Turn

1. Why did God create animals?
2. How can you care for animals?

_____

_____

_____

Prayer

God, thanks for making all the wonderful animals. Amen.

Life Lessons

Let your light shine before others, that they may see your good deeds and glorify your Father in heaven.
– Matthew 5:16

Millions of Plants

Mr. and Mrs. Bartlett sat on their back porch and smiled as they watched the junior high youth group weed, mow, and trim their backyard.

Todd and Jamal were weeding a large flower bed. Todd tugged and pulled at a stubborn weed. "These roots must be buried in concrete!" he said as he braced his feet and gave a mighty yank. As the weed gave way, Todd lost his balance and sprawled in the dirt.

Jamal cracked up. "Hey, man, you are one messy dude," he teased. "Sitting in a pile of dirt, sweat running down your nose, and muddy streaks all over your face."

Just then Mr. Carlson called, "Take a break and cool off, everyone."

The kids rushed to the porch to enjoy the lemonade and cookies Mr. and Mrs. Bartlett served. "This is just a little thank-you for all your hard work," Mrs. Bartlett said.

"The yard looks good, but I hate plants!" Todd announced.

"The world wouldn't survive very long without them," Mr. Carlson said. "They provide food for people and animals, clean the air, make oxygen, hold soil in place, and keep us cool. They also give us products like lumber, medicine, and paper. And God made them all."

Todd sighed. "I wish the weeds would grow somewhere else!"

Your Turn

1. Have you ever taken care of plants? What did you do?
2. Why do you need to protect plants?

_____

_____

_____

Prayer

LORD, thank You for creating so many plants. Amen.

Life Lessons

Let your light shine before others, that they may see your good deeds and glorify your Father in heaven.
– Matthew 5:16

Camping Trip

"Smell that fresh air." Mrs. Clark paused to take a deep breath.

"Uh-huh," Reggie mumbled as he played his computer game. "Yeah!" he yelled. "I got 15,000 points!"

Mrs. Clark shook her head. "Reg, the whole idea of this mother-son camping trip is to look at what God created. Please put the game away."

"Okay, okay. Just one second." Reggie was soon interested in what was happening on the tiny screen before him. Suddenly, the game was taken out of his hands. "Mooooommm, I was almost a war warrior! I only needed one more point."

"Look." Mrs. Clark waved at the scenery before them. The horizon seemed a million miles away beyond a crystal lake near their campsite.

"It is sort of neat," Reggie admitted. "Hey, look over there!" He watched as a kingfisher suddenly made a dive into the water, coming up with a fish. "Cool."

His mother put her arm around him as she grabbed him in a quick hug. "God made you, too—a very cool part of His creation, in my opinion!" she said.

Your Turn

1. What do you appreciate about God's creation?
2. What are some things you notice about God's creation right now, where you are?

_____

_____

_____

Prayer

Lord, everything in Your creation points to how amazing You are. Amen.

Life Lessons

Let your light shine before others, that they may see your good deeds and glorify your Father in heaven.
– Matthew 5:16

Stars and Black Holes

Kyle Richards was fascinated in science class. The teacher had talked about black holes and stars brighter than the sun. Kyle had a lot of information to tell his dad.

"Did you know that the sun is a small star compared to some others?" Kyle announced that night.

"Interesting," his father said.

"The sun is 865,373.7 miles in diameter. To think that God made that!"

Mr. Richards chuckled. "Well, God's a pretty big God. The sun's size is nothing compared to Him."

"Did you know that the gravity of a black hole pulls stuff into it? Light and stuff," Kyle added. "Isn't that cool?"

"What's cool is that God is stronger than a black hole."

Kyle grinned. "I guess God would HAVE to be bigger and stronger than anything He made!"

Your Turn

1. What are some of the biggest things in creation?
2. What is the biggest animal or land form you've seen?
3. What are some reasons you can trust God?

_____

_____

_____

_____

Prayer

LORD, when I look around, I see Your hand everywhere. Amen.

Life Lessons

Bible Plants

The Bible mentions many plants by name. Look up the Scripture verses in a New International Version Bible (NIV) and decode the words to find some of the plants mentioned.

A	B	C	D	E	F	G	H	I	J	K	L	M
7	12	20	1	8	3	15	15	10	6	23	14	9	22

A	B	C	D	E	F	G	H	I	J	K	L	M
7	12	20	1	8	3	15	10	6	23	14	9	22

N	O	P	Q	R	S	T	U	V	W	X	Y	Z
17	4	19	24	18	13	21	2	5	11	26	16	25

_____ (Psalm 17:8)
7, 19, 19, 9, 8

_____ (1 Kings 5:6)
20, 8, 1, 7, 18, 13

_____ (John 12:24)
11, 10, 8, 7, 21

_____ (2 Samuel 6:19)
1, 7, 21, 8, 13

_____, _____ (Numbers 13:23)
19, 4, 22, 8, 15, 18, 7, 17, 7, 21, 8, 13   3, 6, 15, 13

_____ (John 6:9)
12, 7, 18, 9, 8, 16

_____ (Deuteronomy 24:21)
15, 18, 7, 19, 8, 13

_____ (Song of Songs 2:1)
18, 4, 13, 8

_____ (Revelation 11:4)
4, 9, 6, 5, 8

_____, _____, _____ (Numbers 11:5)
20, 2, 20, 2, 22, 12, 8, 18,13   22, 8, 9, 4, 17, 13   4, 17, 6, 4, 17, 13

Prayer

Heavenly Father, thank You for Your creation! Amen.

_____ (Luke 13:19)
22, 2, 13, 21, 7, 18, 1

Life Lessons

Learn All about It

What do you want to learn about God's creation? How will you go about discovering more? You could…

…check out a magazine like National Geographic or National Geographic World.

…check a book out of the library on animals or plants.

…check out creation around you by taking a walk.

…check out a film or TV show on the wonders of nature.

When you find some interesting facts,
don't forget to give God some praise!

Prayer

LORD, when I learn new things about Your creation, I am reminded of what a great God You are. Amen.

Taking Care of God's Creation

The LORD God placed the man in the Garden of Eden
as its gardener, to tend and care for it.
– Genesis 2:15 TLB

Someone to Care

Jennifer Brenner dropped the magazine on her brother's face as he lay on the couch watching TV. "You need to read this. This boy rescues sea turtles."

"So?" Connor asked.

"Mom, Connor has been harming animals!" she announced.

Connor waved her away. "Just because I threw one pebble at a goose."

Jennifer sighed heavily. "You know you shouldn't hurt a harmless animal."

"Harmless? It hissed at me. I thought it was going to bite me!"

"You looked like you were going to hurt her baby. She was protecting it—like we're supposed to protect what God made."

Connor said, "So, what do you want me to do? Say I'm sorry to the goose?"

"You should say you're sorry to God."

Your Turn

1. Do you agree with Jennifer? Why or why not?
2. What responsibility do you have regarding God's animals?

_____

_____

_____

_____

Prayer

LORD Jesus, thank You for trusting me to take care of Your creation. Amen.

Taking Care of God's Creation

*The LORD God placed the man in the Garden of Eden
as its gardener, to tend and care for it.*
– Genesis 2:15 TLB

Caretakers of the Planet

Connor tossed the can toward the park's overflowing garbage can. Instead of going in, it bounced off the rim and onto the ground.

"Aren't you going to recycle that?" his sister Jennifer asked.

Connor rolled his eyes. "Here we go again! I'm sick of recycling."

Jennifer put her hands on her hips. "Don't you care about the planet?"

"One little can isn't going to hurt the planet."

"It will if everybody thinks like you do."

"Who are you? Mother Nature?"

Jennifer gave him an exasperated look. "Well, if you won't, I will."

"Oh, fine," said Connor. He picked up the can and took it to the nearby recycling bin. "There. I saved the planet!"

Your Turn

1. What have you done to care for God's creation this week?
2. Do you think caring for the environment is everyone's responsibility?
3. Why do you think God wants people to care for His creation?

_____

_____

_____

_____

Prayer

God, help me be a considerate caretaker of Your creation. Amen.

Taking Care of God's Creation

*The LORD God placed the man in the Garden of Eden
as its gardener, to tend and care for it.*
– Genesis 2:15 TLB

Talent Talk

"You need a sand wedge for that," Marshall Albright suggested. Marshall and his brother were on the last hole of a nine-hole golf course.

"If I make the next two shots, I'll beat you by two strokes," Lawrence said. "You sure you want me to use a sand wedge?" Lawrence knew his younger brother's advice was good. Marshall was pretty good at golf. Lawrence only beat him occasionally. He chose the sand wedge, and the ball sailed crisply out of the sand and onto the green. One putt later, it was in the hole.

Marshall gave his brother a high-five as they went to the clubhouse.

"Who won?" Dad asked.

"I did!" Lawrence said proudly. He got his younger brother in a head-lock. "But I couldn't have done it without Marsh."

Marshall wriggled out of the headlock, pleased at his brother's words.

"I'm glad you're cooperating," their father said.

"I know I'm good," Marshall said. "That's why I can help those less fortunate." He grinned slyly at his brother.

Your Turn

1. What talents or abilities has God given you?
2. How will you use those talents to cooperate with others?

_____

_____

_____

_____

Prayer

LORD, help me use my talents to help others and praise You. Amen.

Taking Care of God's Creation

*The LORD God placed the man in the Garden of Eden
as its gardener, to tend and care for it.*
– Genesis 2:15 TLB

Helping Out of Love

"For the last time, no!" Dennis shooed his younger brother away.

"But it'll only take you a second to show me how to fold the paper to make a puppet." Terrence looked at Dennis with pleading eyes.

"I've got to finish sweeping out the garage. Unless…I'll make you a deal. You do the sweeping, and I'll make your puppet."

"Okay!" Terrence accepted the broom Dennis offered.

"Dennis!" their father called.

"Oh boy." Dennis reluctantly went out into the yard.

"Don't make your brother do your chores," Mr. Allen said.

"I wasn't making him. He wants me to help him, so I figured he could help me. That's cooperation," Dennis said. "Isn't that what you told me?"

"I know what 'cooperation' means. It also means helping someone out of love, not out of what you can get that person to do for you. That's what I've been trying to get you to see."

Your Turn

1. What's a way Dennis can follow his dad's advice?
2. How can you use your abilities to help others out of love?
3. How is helping others out of love different than "giving to get"?

_____

_____

_____

_____

Prayer

LORD, show me how to cooperate in ways that show Your love. Amen.

Taking Care of God's Creation

*The LORD God placed the man in the Garden of Eden
as its gardener, to tend and care for it.*
– Genesis 2:15 TLB

House for Sale

David looked at the "For Sale" sign in the front yard. He felt happy and sad about moving. He would miss the neighborhood and the climbing tree, but he was also looking forward to having his own room.

"Okay, troops!" Mr. Johnson said. "Everyone choose your weapon." He pointed to the mower, wheelbarrow, trimmers, a big mound of top soil, and several flats of colorful flowers.

David looked around at the long grass, the overgrown bushes, and the weedy flower beds. "Oh, yuck, this yard is a mess. It will take forever to make it look great," he said with a groan.

His sister, Erica, just rolled her eyes and gave a big sigh.

"If we work together, we can do it. You kids can start by weeding the flower beds. Start in the front and work your way around the house." Mr. Johnson started the lawnmower.

After a weekend of hard work and some complaining, the yard was ready to snag the attention of buyers. David rubbed the calluses on his hands. "I hope the people at our new house are getting that yard in tiptop shape. I don't want to do this again for a while."

Your Turn

1. How did David's cooperation help his family?
2. What are reasons you cooperate in your family?

_____

_____

_____

Prayer

LORD, help me cooperate with my family even when it's hard. Amen.

Taking Care of God's Creation

WCAGC

Congratulations! You've been drafted into the WCAGC! Those letters stand for "We Care About God's Creation." Members of this group do more than talk about God's creation. They take an active part in caring for it. As a member, you get to write the rules of membership. Answer the questions, and then design a WCAGC logo. Explain how your logo tells people about the importance of caring for God's creation.

■ How do you want to care for God's creation?

■ How will you recruit others to this cause?

■ How will the logo encourage people to get involved?

Prayer

God, I know You want Your people to care for the earth You created. Please help me be aware of the needs around me so I can help take care of them. Amen.

Taking Care of God's Creation

Working Together

Cooperation means working together to get something done. Use the code to figure out some people and groups who need to cooperate.

CODE

A	B	C	D	E	F	G	H	I	J	K	L	M
26	25	24	23	22	21	20	19	18	17	16	15	14

N	O	P	Q	R	S	T	U	V	W	X	Y	Z
13	12	11	10	9	8	7	6	5	4	3	2	1

— — — — —   — — — — —
8 11 12 9 7   7 22 26 14 8

— — — — — —   — — — — — — —
24 19 6 9 24 19   14 22 14 25 22 9 8

— — — — — — — — —
22 14 11 15 12 2 22 22 8

— — — —   — — — — — — — —
21 18 9 22   21 18 20 19 7 22 9 8

— — — —
26 9 14 2

— — — — — — — — —
12 9 24 19 22 8 7 9 26

— — — — — —
21 26 14 18 15 2

— — — — — — — —
8 7 6 23 22 13 7 8

Prayer

Dear God, help me be cooperative with my family and friends. Amen.

God Likes Cooperation

How good and pleasant it is when God's people live together in unity!
– Psalm 133:1

Unfinished Business

It was a beautiful fall day on Saturday. *Perfect football weather,* thought Bob as he hurried through his breakfast. Bob tucked his football under his arm and headed to the garage to get his bike.

Bob's father was in the garage looking around.

"Bob, your job was to clean the garage. You've got to do this now."

"Oh, Dad. It's such a great day. I'm meeting the guys at the park to play some football. It will take all day to get this garage into shape," Bob said. "I promise I'll do it tomorrow."

Mr. Tucker shook his head. "No way. You put it off all week. This is unfinished business with a deadline of today."

Bob sighed and kicked the garbage can. He started to work.

His dad said, "In a family, each person needs to do his or her part. That's called cooperation. Why don't you stop wasting energy complaining? You'll finish faster and maybe get some football in."

Bob moved faster as he thought of playing late-afternoon football.

Your Turn

1. What are some reasons everyone in a family needs to cooperate?
2. What jobs do you have in your family?

_____

_____

_____

_____

Prayer

Dear God, help my family work together in unity. Amen.

God Likes Cooperation

How good and pleasant it is when God's people live together in unity!
– Psalm 133:1

Help in Time of Need

"May I call you back? Someone's on the other line." Mark Gleason clicked the phone back to his friend Keith. "As I was saying…"

"Was that Karen again?" Keith interrupted.

"Yeah." Mark made a face. "Ever since the teacher put her in my math study group, she's been asking me for help. I wish she wouldn't bug me."

Keith laughed. "I think she likes you."

"Why couldn't it be Katy Shepherd? She's cute. I'd help her," Mark said.

"Mark, listen to yourself," his brother said. "You're not going to help the girl because you don't think she's cute?"

"I'm on the phone!" Mark yelled.

"So? As loud as you talk, I can't help but hear."

"Mom! Make Lance leave me alone!" Mark yelled.

"I agree with Lance," their mother replied.

"Keith, I'll call you later." Mark turned off the phone. "I'm going to my room!" He didn't want to admit he was wrong.

Your Turn

1. What are some ways you can be cooperative with kids at school?
2. Why cooperate with everyone, instead of just those you like?

_____

_____

_____

_____

Prayer

LORD, sometimes I don't want to cooperate. I'll do it for You. Amen.

God Likes Cooperation

How good and pleasant it is when God's people live together in unity!
– Psalm 133:1

Operation Cooperation

The mud puddle looked so inviting. And Mallory, the biggest know-it-all in the fifth grade, was close to it. Justin longed to stick out his foot as she hustled past him. Splat! She'd fall right in. Instead, he turned his attention to his serve.

"Mallory, you serve like this." Justin smacked the volleyball. It sailed across to Peter, who spiked it just as a teammate reached up to hit it.

"Oh, I see," Mallory said. "Thanks."

The gym teacher blew the whistle to call everyone back inside the school. Peter caught up to Justin as they headed in. "Why were you helping her?" Peter asked Justin. "I thought you couldn't stand her."

Justin replied, "She doesn't bother me as much as she used to."

Peter stared. "Who are you, and what have you done with my friend?"

Justin laughed. "I'm trying to…well…do what God wants for once."

"You've changed since you became a Christian. You said you would," Peter said. "There must be more to God than I thought."

Your Turn

1. Why did Justin help Mallory?
2. How does knowing Jesus help you cooperate with others?

_____

_____

_____

_____

Prayer

Dear God, show me ways to work well with others. Amen.

God Likes Cooperation

How good and pleasant it is when God's people live together in unity!
– Psalm 133:1

Doug's Turn

It was Doug's turn to pray at dinner. "Thank You, God, for giving us this food and all You do for us. Amen." A millisecond after the prayer, he said, "Please pass the pork chops."

"Are you really thankful to God?" his father asked.

"About the pork chops? Yes!" Doug loved pork-chop night.

His father threw him a measuring look and said, "About anything?"

Doug looked puzzled. "What do you mean, Dad?"

His father passed the pork chops. "I've been getting reports that you and your friends were making a lot of noise last week after youth church ended."

Doug quickly grabbed two chops. "We were just messing around in the gym. We didn't think anyone could hear us."

"I heard him too!" Benjie, the youngest, said.

"Nobody asked you!" Doug said.

"Well, you know the adult service sometimes runs a little long. If you disturb others, that cuts into their ability to worship God," Doug's dad said. "Considering others' needs is a great way to say thanks to God."

Your Turn

1. What could Doug have done to be considerate and cooperative?
2. How does cooperation help you show thanks to God?

_____

_____

_____

Prayer

LORD, I want to show my thanks to You by thinking of others and helping them in any way I can. Amen.

God Likes Cooperation

How good and pleasant it is when God's people live together in unity!
– Psalm 133:1

Volunteers, Anyone?

"We need volunteers to help in the nursery next Sunday," Mr. Philips said. Lloyd Mason half-listened. He wasn't about to volunteer.

"Why do we have to do this?" one girl asked.

"Another church is visiting ours," Mr. Philips said. "That means a lot of small children will be here. Taking care of their children will allow their parents to worship more."

"But that means we'll miss youth church," one boy brought up.

"It is a sacrifice," Mr. Philips replied. "That's why I'm asking for volunteers. How 'bout you, Lloyd?"

Lloyd snorted. "Hold some drooling babies? No way."

"Come on. I've been bragging to everyone about how cooperative and mature my class is. This is a way to worship God too."

"How does that work? We'll miss church," Lloyd said.

"God honors sacrifices made on behalf of someone else. Helping the kids so their parents can worship is an act of worship too."

"Well," Lloyd considered, "as long as I'm not the only one…"

Mr. Philips smiled. "Don't worry. I've just decided we all will volunteer. We need a lesson in cooperation."

Your Turn

1. What are some jobs at your church that require cooperation?
2. What are some things you can do to help others worship?

_____

_____

_____

Prayer

Lord, I want to cooperate with the people in my church. Amen.

God Likes Cooperation

Church Cooperation

When the Christian church first started, there was plenty of cooperation. You've been picked to report on church cooperation. Acts 2:41-47 is your beat. Your job as a reporter is to find out who, what, when, where, why, and how.

REPORT

O 1. Who cooperated?
(See verse 41)_____
_____
_____

O 2. How did they cooperate?
(See verses 42, 44, and 46) _____
_____
_____

3. What did they use to help each other?
(See verse 45)_____
_____
_____

4. When did they meet?
(See verse 46)_____
_____
_____

5. Why did they cooperate with each other?
(See verses 43 and 47) _____
O _____
_____

O Bonus Question: How do the people within
your church congregation cooperate with
O each other?_____
_____
_____

Prayer

Father God, help me cooperate with and show respect to the people in my church. Amen.

God Likes Cooperation

Living in Unity

Can you figure out the clues to find the answers? Write the answers on the blanks.

— — —   — — — . . .   — — — —   — — —
  1   5   4   12

— — — —   — — —   — — — — — — — —
   14   3   7

— — — — — —   — — — —   — — — —
      13   8   2

— — — — — .   — — — — — —   — — : —
     10   6   9 11

1. Fifth month of the year

2. Another word for "one" (rhymes with "peach")

3. Opposite of "out"

4. What you say when you're in trouble

5. Rhymes with "rod"

6. Sixth book in the New Testament

7. Opposite of "incomplete"

8. Add a "w" to the front of "it" and an "h" to the end

9. Number of disciples plus three

10. Rhymes with "mother"

11. 10-5

12. Opposite of "me"

13. Add "ony" to the end of a word that means "hurt"

14. Replace the "f" in "five" with an "L"

Prayer

Heavenly Father, please help me live in harmony with my family because I know that will please You. Amen.

Making Wise Decisions

[Jesus said,] "Anyone who listens to my teaching and follows it is wise."
– Matthew 7:24 NLT

A Wise Move

"Ooh!" Erick practically shoved his nose through the window as he stopped to check out the display. "They've got the new War Zone game!"

"You're not thinking about buying it. You owe me five bucks," Todd said.

"I'll pay you back later. Besides, didn't you just get paid?"

"What's that got to do with the fact that you owe me money?"

Erick looked pitiful. "I have to get by on my allowance."

"I don't feel sorry for you, bro. Pay up if you've got the money."

"I can hear you arguing," their mother said. "What is it now?"

"He won't give me the money he owes me," Todd announced. "He wants to buy a game instead."

"Mom, will you loan me five dollars to pay back Todd?" Erick asked. "I want to buy this game with my birthday money. You said I could."

"I didn't know you owed Todd. What's the wise thing to do?"

Erick grinned. "Beg Todd to wait a little longer?"

"Nice try," his mom said.

Your Turn

1. What was Erick's first responsibility?
2. Why is it important to pay people you owe?

_____

_____

_____

_____

Prayer

LORD, show me how to be wise about money. Amen.

Making Wise Decisions

[Jesus said,] "Anyone who listens to my teaching and follows it is wise."
– Matthew 7:24 NLT

Always Around

Desmond and his friend Alex pushed their way through the crowd of shoppers. They almost knocked over an elderly woman who was slowly making her way down the mall.

"Watch it!" the woman said.

"Old, crabby people!" Alex grumbled. His voice was loud enough to be heard by the elderly woman. The two boys continued walking.

"If they can't walk fast, why don't they stay at home?" Alex groused.

Desmond suddenly regretted not having said "excuse me" to the woman. Desmond argued with himself. Then he thought, *But God is.*

"Wait a sec," he told Alex. He ran back to the woman. "I'm sorry we accidentally pushed you."

The woman looked surprised. "It's all right."

Your Turn

1. How did Desmond show respect?
2. How do you show respect for those older than you?

_____

_____

_____

_____

_____

Prayer

LORD, show me how to be respectful to the adults in my life. Amen.

Making Wise Decisions

[Jesus said,] "Anyone who listens to my teaching and follows it is wise."
– Matthew 7:24 NLT

Respect + Respect = Respect

"I need you guys to be quiet while the announcements are read," Amy, one of the youth pastors, announced.

"What's with Amy? She looks tired," Jason said to Simon.

"I heard she's ready to quit," Simon replied. "Some of the kids have been mouthing off to her. You know, not showing her any respect."

The youth group had already lost one of the three youth pastors. Jason didn't want Amy to go. She seemed to really enjoy teaching the group, and she was fun to be around. Jason noticed some kids talking while Amy read the announcements.

Jason suddenly got up, put two fingers in his mouth, and whistled loudly. "Quiet, guys!" he hollered. "Didn't you hear Amy ask for quiet?"

"Thank you, Jason," Amy said.

After the meeting, Amy said, "That was a big help, Jason. I've been thinking about making changes. I've decided to choose some of you to be co-group leaders. I respect your judgment. I think you'd make a good group leader. What do you say?"

Jason grinned and nodded.

Your Turn

1. How did Jason earn respect?
2. How are you helped when you respect adults?

_____

_____

_____

Prayer

LORD, remind me to respect my parents, my teachers, and my church leaders. Amen.

Making Wise Decisions

[Jesus said,] "Anyone who listens to my teaching and follows it is wise."
– Matthew 7:24 NLT

The "In Crowd"

Cal and Henry heard Jim Hanson and his buddies before they saw them. The "in crowd" boys were hanging out in a corner of the gym, laughing and goofing around. They knew all the latest songs, had their own slang words, and always did things together.

Cal sighed. "Henry, wouldn't you like to be friends with Jim Hanson and the rest of his crowd?"

"I'm not sure," Henry replied.

Several days later, after gym class, one of the "in crowd" group, Mike, sauntered over to Cal. They talked as they walked to their next class. Then Mike said, "How about playing football with us after school today?"

Cal almost tripped over his feet, but he managed to say, "Sure."

They played every day for a week. The games were rough and tumble, but fun. Cal thought it was great to be part of this group.

"Will you do something special for us?" Mike asked on Friday.

Cal's stomach did a flip-flop. "Like what?"

"We're playing Wiley School tomorrow, and we want to beat them. You're our biggest guy. Tackle them super hard and punch them when no one is looking." Mike smacked his fist into his other hand.

Cal shook his head. "I won't do that. It's not playing fair."

"Jerk! I knew you didn't belong with us." Mike stomped off.

Cal felt relieved. *They really aren't so cool after all,* he thought.

Your Turn

1. What makes someone popular in your school?
2. Which of those things please God? Which don't?

_____

Prayer

Jesus, thank You for true friends who are honest. Amen.

Making Wise Decisions

[Jesus said,] "Anyone who listens to my teaching and follows it is wise."
– Matthew 7:24 NLT

Career Day

Career Day was in full swing in Aaron Barker's sixth-grade class.

"What are you doing now to prepare for the future?" one speaker asked the class.

One boy raised his hand. "I'm gonna be a rock musician," he said. "My dad just got me a new guitar."

"If that's what you want to do, what are you doing now to prepare for that career?" the speaker asked.

The boy shrugged his shoulders. "I dunno. My dad won't let me play the guitar much. He says it's too loud."

"I'm gonna play in the NBA," another boy said. "They make a lot of money."

Aaron listened while everyone shared their plans. He wasn't sure what he wanted to do.

"What's up?" his mom asked when he arrived home.

"I'm not sure what I want to do in the future," he said. "There's a lot to think about. Where should I go to college? What kind of job do I want?"

"It's good to think about that now so you have time prepare," his mother said. "But it's not something for you to worry about. Don't forget, you can always ask God for help."

Your Turn

1. What are your plans for the future?
2. What plans do you think God has for you?

_____

_____

Prayer

LORD, show me the plans You have for my life. Amen.

Making Wise Decisions

Respect Is Right

Have you ever heard your parents say, "Because I said so," when you asked why you had to do something? God wants obedience too. Respecting adults is one way to obey God. Respect doesn't mean you have to agree with them or do something wrong. In those cases, talk to your parents, or a teacher, or a youth leader at church.

How does the advice in each of these verses help you respect these individuals? How can you gain respect in the process? Use the letters next to the verses to make your choices.

1   **2**   **3**

1. Coach Franklin, who likes to tease kids who aren't very athletic
2. A parent who wants you to do chores you hate to do
3. A neighbor who wants you to do chores for her for little money

A. Honor your father and your mother (Exodus 20:12).
B. Obey your leaders and submit to their authority (Hebrews 13:17).
C. Rise in the presence of the aged, show respect for the elderly and revere your God. I am the LORD (Leviticus 19:32).
D. Show proper respect to everyone (1 Peter 2:17).
E. The worker deserves his wages (1 Timothy 5:18b).

1. I would use verse _____ because _____

2. I would use verse _____ because _____

3. I would use verse _____ because _____

Prayer

LORD, help me willingly respect all people. Amen.

Making Wise Decisions

How About You?

Are you ever like a chameleon—changing to fit in with whomever and whatever is around? Read the statements and mark the box that best describes you.

	Usually	Sometimes	Never
1. I use bad language because the kids I'm with talk that way.			
2. I laugh at things that aren't really funny because everyone else is laughing.			
3. I won't be friends with some kids because they aren't very popular.			
4. When someone starts to talk about church or God, I change the subject.			
5. I tell little lies to make myself seem more important.			
6. I go along with my friends when they want me to do something wrong.			

Prayer

Jesus, I want to be Your follower all the time, not just when it's convenient. Amen.

You Are Wonderful

– 1 John 3:16

Fitness Day

Corey waited for the whistle and then ran the 50-yard dash.

"Not bad," said his PE teacher, Mr. Grayson. He wrote Corey's time on a scorecard. "All right, everybody!" called Mr. Grayson. "Pair off and do sit-ups. See how many you can do in 60 seconds."

Corey held Manuel's feet firmly. When the whistle blew, Manuel did sit-ups as fast as he could. Then they traded places, and Corey took his turn. When he finished, they waited for Mr. Grayson to record their scores.

"Ha!" said Manuel. "I did three more sit-ups than you."

"Yeah, but I did two more chin-ups," Corey said. "This is fun."

Manuel said, "I like fitness testing day, except for the rope climb. Ugh! I burned my hands coming down."

"Just look at all this stuff we're doing," Corey said. "Isn't it amazing?"

"What do you mean?" Manuel asked.

"Think about everything your body can do," Corey said. "You jump, run, throw, swim, and climb."

"Yeah," said Manuel with a grin. "When God made me, He made the best. That means you must be second best."

Your Turn

1. If part of your body didn't work well, would you still be wonderful? Why or why not?

_____

_____

_____

Prayer

God, I love all the stuff my body can do. Thank You. Amen.

You Are Wonderful

This is how we know what love is: Jesus Christ laid down his life for us.
– 1 John 3:16

Love Can't Be Earned

Troy's dad was driving him to soccer practice. The radio played music from a Christian music station. Between songs, an announcer talked about God's love.

Troy said, "Does God love me because I'm good at soccer?"

Mr. Parker said, "God would love you if you were lousy at soccer."

"Does God love me because I got an 'A' in Spanish?"

"No. God would love you if you flunked every subject," Mr. Parker said. "Of course, you wouldn't get any allowance for a year."

"Does God love me because I always do my chores and you never have to ask me twice?"

Mr. Parker raised his eyebrows and looked at Troy.

"Okay, sometimes you have to ask me more than once." Troy laughed.

"God loves you whether you do your chores or not," Mr. Parker said. God loves you because you are you and God is God. God is pleased when you do good things, but that's not why He loves you. And doing bad things may disappoint Him, but it won't stop Him from loving you. God's love is a forever *gift*. God loves you because He wants to."

"Wow!" Troy said.

Your Turn

1. When you think about God's love, how do you feel about Him?

_____

_____

_____

Prayer

God, thanks for all the love. That's the best gift of all! Amen.

You Are Wonderful

This is how we know what love is: Jesus Christ laid down his life for us.
– 1 John 3:16

The Biggest Thing

On the drive home after the soccer game, Troy said, "I've been thinking about God loving me. I'm wondering how I can know for sure."

Mr. Parker thought for a moment. "Let me ask you a question first. How do you know your mom and I love you?"

"Because of all the stuff you do for me," Troy said. "You give me a home and food to eat. You buy clothes for me. When I'm sick, you take care of me. You drive me all over the place."

"So doing those things for you is one way of proving our love for you," Mr. Parker said. "What about God? What has He done for you?"

Now it was Troy's turn to think. "God made a beautiful world for me to live in. He gave me a strong, healthy body. He gave me a great family."

"So that proves God loves you," Mr. Parker asked. "But there's even more. God also sent Jesus to show His love."

They drove in silence for a few minutes.

"I can hardly imagine so much love," Mr. Parker said. "God loved us so much that He sent His Son to die for us."

Your Turn

1. How do you think God felt about sending Jesus to the world for you?

_____

_____

_____

Prayer

God, Your love is higher than the sky and deeper than the oceans. Wow! Amen.

You Are Wonderful

This is how we know what love is: Jesus Christ laid down his life for us.
— 1 John 3:16

The Ugly Cross

Hasin's family had moved from India, and this was his first time in a Christian church. He whispered, "Alan, over there on the wall...that's a cross, right?"

"Yes," Alan said. "Most churches display a cross somewhere."

"Don't be angry," Hasin said, "but isn't that a strange decoration? The Romans used crosses to kill people. A cross is a painful thing."

"We worship Jesus," Alan said. "Jesus died on a cross. The cross reminds us of that."

Hasin nodded. "Why do you remember such a sad story?"

Alan thought about that. "Jesus died on the cross because He loves us. He died to take away our sins. He died so we would understand how much God loves us. To us, the cross is beautiful because it reminds us of God's great love. It was sad when Jesus died, but He's not dead now. He rose from the dead, and now He's alive forever."

"Do you believe that?" Hasin asked.

"Yes," Alan said. "I believe Jesus died and rose from the dead for me."

"Then the story has a happy ending!" Hasin said.

Your Turn

1. Is there a cross in your church?
2. What do you think when you see a cross?

_____

_____

_____

_____

Prayer

Jesus, I don't get how much You love me, but I know You do. Amen.

You Are Wonderful

This is how we know what love is: Jesus Christ laid down his life for us.
– 1 John 3:16

Never, Ever

When Sunday school ended, the kids filed out of class, but Toby stayed. "Mr. Murdock," Toby said, "you told us Jesus lives in each Christian."

"That's right," Mr. Murdock said.

"But what if a person keeps making mistakes and doing the wrong things?" Toby asked.

The Sunday-school teacher smiled. "Toby, every Christian makes mistakes. Each morning I decide I'm going to live like Jesus, but by lunchtime I've already messed things up."

Toby had trouble imagining Mr. Murdock messing up. "What do you do about it?"

"When I go to bed, I think about my day," Mr. Murdock said. "I tell God I'm sorry for my sins and purpose to do better."

"That's all?" Toby asked.

"If Jesus lives in you, He knows your heart. He knows when you're really sorry and when you're trying to do right."

"And He won't move out of my life?" Toby asked.

"Jesus loves you, Toby. He will never leave you."

"Okay," Toby said. "Thanks, Mr. Murdock."

"Never, ever, Toby! Jesus will never, ever leave you."

Your Turn

1. What words do you use to ask God to forgive you?

_____

_____

_____

Prayer

God, Your love is bigger than my sins. Whew! Amen.

You Are Wonderful

If God Loves You, You Must Be Okay!

"Cinquain" is a kind of poem. It does not have to rhyme. The first line of a cinquain is the title, and the other four lines of the poem are about the title. Put your name on the first line and follow the directions to write a cinquain about you.

Line 1: Write your name.

Line 2: Write two words that describe you.

Line 3: Write three action words that apply to you.

Line 4: Write four feeling words about yourself.

Line 5: Rename the title by thinking of a different word for you.

Prayer

God, thank You for loving me no matter what. Amen.

You Are Wonderful

The Prodigal Chicken

Jesus told a parable to help us understand that God will forgive us when we make bad choices. (You can read about the prodigal son in Luke 15:11-24.)

Here is a messed-up version of that parable. It has eleven mistakes. Can you find them? Cross out the incorrect words and replace them with the correct words to see what Jesus taught about forgiveness.

••

There was a man who had two chickens. The fatter one said to his father, "Father, give me my share of the estate."

So he divided his property between them. Not long after that, the younger son got together all he had, set off for a distant circus, and there squandered his wealth in wild living.

After he had spent everything, there was a severe flood in that whole country, and he began to be in need. So he went and hired himself out to a window-washer of that country, who sent him to his pond to feed ducks.

He longed to fill his stomach with the sardines that the pigs were eating, but no one gave him anything.

So he got up and went to his cousin.

But while he was still a long way off, his father saw him and was filled with compassion for him; he ran to his son, threw his arms around him, and smacked him.

The son said to him, "Father, I have sinned against heaven and against you. I am no longer worthy to be called your pet dog."

But the father said to his servants, "Quick! Bring the best hat and put it on him. Put a tattoo on his finger and bells on his feet. Let's have a feast and celebrate. For this son of mine was dead and is alive again; he was lost and is found."

Prayer

Heavenly Father, I am so thankful that when I confess my sins to You, You forgive me. Please help me to do better next time. Amen.

God Knows Where You're Going

All the days ordained for me were written in your book before one of them came to be.

– Psalm 139:16

The Big Plan

"Do you ever wonder where you're going to end up?" Mike asked Rodney. They were watching a minor league baseball game. A new batter stepped up to the plate.

"I know where I'm going to end up," Rodney said. "After the game, I have to cut the grass. Then I'll shoot hoops until it gets dark."

"I don't mean today," Mike said. "Do you worry about where you'll go to college? What job you'll get? Whether you'll get married?"

The batter smacked the ball. Both boys jumped to their feet and cheered as the ball soared over the fence.

"No, I don't worry about how my life is going to end up," Rodney said. "I'll make plans, but I don't worry about it. You see, God's in charge. My pastor says God will make our lives turn out right if we have faith."

"Did God plan for you to paint your shirt with mustard?" Mike asked.

"No, that's just because I'm a slob," Rodney admitted. "I'm just saying God loves me, and He will make my life work out His way."

"Yeah," Mike admitted. "Maybe I think too much."

"I'm thinking I want another hot dog," Rodney said. "How about you?"

Your Turn

1. When is it easy to trust God to guide your life? When is it hard?

_____

_____

_____

Prayer

God, tomorrow is a mystery, but I know You'll be with me. Amen.

God Knows Where You're Going

*All the days ordained for me were written in your book
before one of them came to be.*
– Psalm 139:16

Best Friends

Quinn dropped his book bag, grabbed an apple from the kitchen, and hurried off to meet his best friend. After a short walk, Quinn reached the quiet spot where the creek formed a small pool under the trees. He settled on his favorite rock and said, "I love it here." Quinn and his friend sat in comfortable silence, listening to the gurgling water.

"What a great day in school," Quinn said. "My missing library book turned up. The librarian found it on the wrong shelf." He took a bite of his apple. "I got my English paper back, and I aced it! I got a 92. You know what? I kind of like poetry."

Quinn continued. "You'll never guess what we did in gym class." He grinned. "Well, maybe You already know. We played crab ball. That's my game, even though it gives me blisters on my palms." Quinn flicked pebbles into the pool. He smelled the sweet spearmint and enjoyed his friend's company. At last, Quinn stood up and brushed his pants clean. "I know You're with me all the time, but I like meeting here to tell You about my day."

Your Turn

1. Why do you think Jesus enjoys hearing about your day?

_____

_____

_____

Prayer

Jesus, help me remember I can talk to you anytime and anyplace. Amen.

God Knows Where You're Going

All the days ordained for me were written in your book before one of them came to be.
– Psalm 139:16

Tough Times

"Why so sad today?" Mrs. Stark asked as she gave Greg some toast.

Greg spread jam on it. "I heard Dad and you talking. Are we going to run out of money?"

Mrs. Stark sat down at the table and picked up her coffee cup. "We don't have much left in the bank. Your father's been laid off from work for months now. I'm not getting many hours at the drugstore. I might have to look for more work."

"I heard Dad say we might have to move out of this house," Greg said.

"Maybe," Mrs. Stark said. "We would save some money if we moved to an apartment. Or we might move in with Grandpa for a while."

"I'm scared," Greg said. "What if we can't buy groceries?"

Mrs. Stark reached out, gently lifted her son's face, and looked into his eyes. "You don't have to be scared. Your father and I have been in hard times before, and God has always taken care of us. He will do it again. God's big enough to handle today and our tomorrows."

Your Turn

1. What are some things you need? What are some things you want?
   What are ways you have seen God take care of you?

_____

_____

_____

Prayer

God, You've been taking care of me. I trust You. Amen.

God Knows Where You're Going

All the days ordained for me were written in your book
before one of them came to be.
– Psalm 139:16

24/7

Mickey saw a young robin cheeping frantically in the bushes near the porch. Mickey moved closer. *Maybe it needs help.* He reached for the little bird, but it cheeped and hopped into the yard. Mickey stepped forward.

Suddenly a shrill call came from a nearby tree. Mickey looked up. A fully grown robin squawked and swooped down, landing between Mickey and the baby bird. Mickey decided she was probably the mother. He took another step forward. The mother bird fluttered her wings and squawked. Mickey heard another call behind him. A second adult robin sat on the edge of the roof glaring. *The father?*

"Okay," Mickey said, laughing. He backed away from the young bird.

Mickey returned to the porch. The father flew back to the roof to keep watch. The mother cocked her head, plucked a worm from the soil, and dropped the worm into the mouth of the baby, who gobbled it eagerly.

Mickey decided the baby bird was going to be okay. Even though he hadn't seen the parents at first, they were nearby watching over their child. *Just like God,* Mickey thought. *Even when I forget God is nearby, He is still keeping a close eye on me because I'm His child.*

Your Turn

1. What helps you know God remembers you? What Bible promises about this can you remember?

_____

Prayer

Thanks, God, for watching over me 24/7. You never let me down. Amen.

God Knows Where You're Going

All the days ordained for me were written in your book
before one of them came to be.
– Psalm 139:16

The Lost Game

"I'm not going to pray anymore," Terry said as he and his twin brother, Perry, walked home after the game. "It's just a waste of time."

"How do you figure that?" Perry asked.

"I prayed for our team to win this game so we could go to district, but we lost," Terry said. "Either God wasn't listening or God doesn't care."

Perry shook his head. "I know we're twins, but I must have gotten most of the brains. Do you know how goofy you are?"

"I don't care what you say," Terry told him. "I prayed and God didn't give me what I wanted. I say prayer doesn't work."

"God isn't going to give you everything you ask for," Perry said. "What if you prayed for somebody's house to burn down? Would God do that?"

"But I just wanted our team to win," Terry said. "That's a good thing."

"It is also praying for the other team to lose!" said Perry. "Besides, God is not a vending machine. He is our loving Father. He loves us too much to give us everything we think we want. That would be bad for us."

"I still say God should have answered my prayer," Terry insisted.

"God did answer you," Perry said. "'No' is an answer. Try praying for God to do His will, whatever HE wants. He'll answer that one with a 'yes'!"

Your Turn

1. Make a list of times God answered your prayer. How do you know
   He answered?

_____

Prayer

God, I ask You for lots of stuff, but You give me the things that will be best for me and honor You. Thanks for watching over me. Amen.

God Knows Where You're Going

Meandering Moses

It took Moses forty years to lead God's people through the wilderness to the Promised Land. Sometimes they wandered around, and other times they ran into trouble. Moses always trusted that God would get them to their new home. He did his best along the way, and he trusted God to fulfill His promises. On the winding trail, draw pictures about a few of the things that happened while the Israelites wandered through the desert.

Prayer

Dear Lord, like Moses, I don't know what's going to happen tomorrow, but I know that You will always be with me wherever I go. Amen.

God Knows Where You're Going

Under God's Protection

We talk about the eyes and ears and hands of God, although we know God is Spirit. It's easier for us to think about God if we imagine Him as we are, with a physical body. Sometimes the Bible describes God with body parts we don't have. Did you know that? Decipher this passage and find out more. You'll also be reminded how faithfully God watches over you. Move each letter back one place in the alphabet. For example, B becomes A, and K becomes J.

IF   XJMM   DPWFS   ZPV   XJUI   IJT

_____ _____ _____ _____ _____ _____

GFBUIFST   BOE   VOEFS   IJT   XJOHT

_____, _____ _____ _____ _____

ZPV   XJMM   GJOE   SFGVHF.

_____ _____ _____ _____   ~ Psalm 91:4

Prayer

Heavenly Father, thank You for watching over me. Amen.

Jesus Lives in You

[Jesus said,] "I am in my Father, and you are in me, and I am in you."
– John 14:20

Cleaning House for Jesus

Mr. Murdock said to his Sunday-school class, "If Jesus were moving into your house, what would you do to get ready?"

"We'd clean out the guest room," Toby said.

"Good," said Mr. Murdock, writing on the chalkboard. "What else?"

"Weed the garden," one girl said.

"Finish painting the porch."

"Wash all the windows."

Toby thought of some movies and books his family would throw out. They weren't so bad unless Jesus was visiting.

The kids kept sharing until the board was full.

"That's a long list," Mr. Murdock said. "I guess you'd really want your house to look its best if Jesus is going to live there. Now I have another question. What would you do to get ready if Jesus was going to live inside you?"

Nobody said anything.

Mr. Murdock went on. "What thoughts would you clean out? What habits would you change?"

No more lying, Toby thought. *A lot more Bible reading. Less time watching horror movies.*

"Guess what?" Mr. Murdock said. "If you're a Christian, Jesus already lives in you! Jesus makes His home in your life."

Toby thought of Jesus living in him. It was a good feeling knowing Jesus loved him. Toby decided it was time for some spring cleaning.

Your Turn

1. What changes do you need to make so Jesus will feel more at home in you?

_____

Prayer

Jesus, thanks for living in me and loving me. Amen.

Jesus Lives in You

[Jesus said,] "I am in my Father, and you are in me, and I am in you."
– John 14:20

God's Gift

"You smoke?" Grant asked in surprise as Steve took a pack of cigarettes from his pocket. Steve was new in school, and Grant hadn't known him long.

"It's no big deal," Steve said. "Do you want one?"

"No way," Grant said. "Smoking trashes your health."

"It's my body," Steve said with a shrug.

"Not exactly," Grant replied. "You like to draw, right? Say you spent days on a beautiful ink drawing and you gave it to me as a present. How would you feel if I scribbled on it or left it out in the rain?"

"I'd be hurt, I guess," Steve said. "So what?"

"Your body is a gift from God," Grant said. "God made it just for you. How do you think He feels when you mess up His gift?"

"I never thought of that," Steve said, looking at the unlit cigarette.

"Think of the great stuff you might do with your life. What a shame to mess everything up by not taking care of your health."

"Well," Steve said, "maybe it wouldn't be hard to stop."

"Now you're talking!" Grant slapped Steve on the back.

Your Turn

1. What are ways you can tell God's Spirit is living in you?
   How does that make you feel?

_____

_____

_____

Prayer

Thank You for this incredible body, LORD. Amen…and wow!

Jesus Lives in You

[Jesus said,] "I am in my Father, and you are in me, and I am in you."
– John 14:20

No Fooling

Mr. Jordan said, "Please put away all your books and notes."

Peter nervously fingered the cheat sheet inside his sleeve. He'd never cheated before, but he couldn't figure out this biology stuff.

The teacher looked at the class. "You will be taking two tests today. One in biology and one in integrity. Will you be biologists when you grow up? Probably not. But your choices today shape your character. What kind of person do you want to be? Trustworthy? Honest? Successful?"

As he handed out the tests, Mr. Jordan said, "You might be able to cheat without getting caught. Maybe I'll never know, but you will."

Peter slipped the cheat sheet into his book bag. *I'm not a cheater,* he decided. *That's not who I want to be. Even if I get a bad grade, it's what I earned. God will know too.*

Your Turn

1. Have you done the right thing when no one was watching?
2. Have you done the wrong thing without getting caught?
   Are you sorry?

_____

_____

_____

_____

_____

Prayer

Lord, I want to make You proud of me. Help me do the right things. Amen.

Jesus Lives in You

[Jesus said,] "I am in my Father, and you are in me, and I am in you."
– John 14:20

The Pool Date

Hamadi danced around the living room playing air guitar. He was totally excited. In a radio contest, his friend Brady had won tickets to the Kicking Parrots concert on Saturday. Brady had invited him to go!

Hamadi's father called, "Please turn that music down!"

As Hamadi did, he heard his little brother on the phone.

"Yeah, Hamadi is taking me to the pool Saturday. I can hardly wait!"

Oh, man, Hamadi thought. *I forgot all about taking Musa swimming. We'll just have to make it a different day. Hopefully he won't mind.*

"He's already called it off twice," Musa continued. "But he promised we'd go this Saturday for sure. We'll take sandwiches and snacks. Hamadi's the best!"

This is so unfair, Hamadi thought. *I didn't know I'd get a chance to see the Kicking Parrots! The pool will be there all summer; the Parrots won't.*

Musa was silent for a minute. "No, he won't forget. He promised."

Hamadi settled on the couch. This swimming trip was a big deal. If he broke his promise again, Musa might think he wasn't loved. That his big brother cared more about everything else.

Hamadi called Brady to tell him he couldn't go. Something more important had come up.

Your Turn

1. Have you made a promise you wanted to take back? What happened?
2. Do you think keeping your word is important? Why?

_____

_____

Prayer

LORD, You keep all Your promises. Help me be like You. Amen.

Jesus Lives in You

[Jesus said,] "I am in my Father, and you are in me, and I am in you."
– John 14:20

New Music

Billy Garrick's mother pounded on the door of his bedroom. "What in the world are you listening to?"

Billy pushed the pause button. "It's my favorite music group, Mom. You said I could buy it."

"Maybe I did," Mrs. Garrick said. "But I didn't know it had that kind of language."

"Sorry, Mom," Billy said. "I'll use my headphones."

"No, I don't want you listening to it," Mrs. Garrick said.

"But, Mom!" Billy protested. "Everybody listens to this group!"

"Billy," Mrs. Garrick said, "I know, but some of this music isn't good for you. Just like everything else, words are a gift from God. God wants us to use words to encourage people and to praise Him."

"I'm not using those words," Billy said.

Mrs. Garrick held up her hand. "When you bought the music, you gave your money to the people who made it. You were saying 'I approve of these dirty words. Keep it up!' "

Billy looked miserable. "I guess you're right," he said.

"I'll go with you to the store, and we'll get your money back. You can find music you like that also pleases God."

Your Turn

1. What are some ways you can use words to please God?
2. Do you have questionable music or games? ? What will you do?

_____

_____

Prayer

God, I want every part of me to serve You, including my mouth. Amen.

Jesus Lives in You

Taking Care of the Gift

God makes all kinds of bodies. Yours is special because He made it, and God doesn't make junk! When you take care of your body and protect your health, you give honor to your Maker. Look at the pictures. Draw an "X" through the ones that disrespect God's gift, and draw a heart around the ones that honor God.

Prayer

LORD, I know that You made me special. You created me in Your image. Please help me take good care of my body. Amen.

Jesus Lives in You

Rock Steady

God is a promise maker and a promise keeper! When He makes a promise, you can stand on it like it's solid rock. God never breaks a promise. Never! Can you match the person on the left with the promise God gave him or her? If you need help, look up the Scripture verses.

Abraham (Genesis 12:6-7)   "I will give you wisdom."

Sarah (Genesis 18:9-10)   "I will help you defeat the Midianites."

Moses (Exodus 3:7-8)   "I will make you as strong as an iron pillar."

Joshua (Joshua 1:5)   "I will bring my people out of Egypt."

Gideon (Judges 6:14-16)   "I will not leave you or forsake you."

Jeremiah (Jeremiah 1:17-19)   "I will give you a land of your own."

Solomon (1 Kings 3:10-12)   "I will give you a child."

Prayer

LORD, You are a promise keeper. I want to be just like You. Please help me keep my promises. Amen.

Do Your Best Always

Whatever you hand finds to do, do it with all your might.
–Ecclesiastes 9:10

The Grass or the Game?

"We're going to miss the game," Harris said.

Tyler paused in sweeping the grass clippings from the driveway and looked around the big yard. He mowed Mrs. Queen's grass on Thursdays, but rain had forced him to postpone the job until Saturday. "I'm not finished yet," he told his friend.

Harris pointed to his watch impatiently. "That's good enough."

Tyler said, "I still have to trim around the bushes, and there are places I ought to rake."

"It's just grass!" Harris protested. "What's the big deal if you take a few shortcuts? Mrs. Queen won't know if you skip the trimming."

"When Mrs. Queen hired me, I promised I'd do it right," Tyler insisted.

"But you're the best fielder on the team," Harris pleaded.

"Do you know what makes me a good fielder?" Tyler asked. "When I'm playing ball, I don't goof around. I give it my very best. When I do anything, I do it as well as I possibly can."

Harris shook his head and climbed on his bike. "Get to the park as soon as you can," he called as he rode off.

"I'll be there when I finish this job," Tyler yelled back.

Your Turn

1. When you do your best work, how do you think God feels about it? How do you feel about it?
2. List jobs at which you've done your best.

_____

_____

Prayer

LORD, help me do my best every time. Amen.

Do Your Best Always

Whatever you hand finds to do, do it with all your might.
–Ecclesiastes 9:10

The Free Throw

When Buddy walked to the free-throw line, the crowd cheered like crazy. He bounced the ball a few times and looked at the basket. Gradually, the noise died down. Buddy concentrated. The whole game was riding on him. Only two seconds were left on the clock. The score was tied, and Buddy had one foul shot.

Buddy glanced at his coach. The coach nodded. He seemed to be saying, "Go for it." The coach always told his team that they worked hard in practice so the games would come easy. Buddy spent hours practicing free throws—lobbing one ball after another over and over and over. The coach called that "perseverance."

Buddy rolled the word around in his mouth: "perseverance." It meant hanging in there. It meant practicing and practicing. It meant not quitting, not getting discouraged, not throwing in the towel. Perseverance meant making up his mind to become the best free-throw shooter on the team, and then working hard to make that come true.

I've definitely got perseverance. I've shot a thousand free throws to get ready for this shot. Nobody's perfect. If I miss, I'll just practice more. He raised the ball, rose on his toes, and lofted the ball toward the basket. It dropped cleanly through the net.

Your Turn

1. When is it hard to persevere?
2. What have you practiced over and over? Has your skill improved?

_____

_____

Prayer

God, some of the things I want in life aren't going to come easy. Give me the strength and perseverance to to do what pleases You. Amen.

Do Your Best Always

Whatever you hand finds to do, do it with all your might.
–Ecclesiastes 9:10

Getting Smart

Jay looked over his grades. Four "B's" and two "A's." Excellent! And it was all because of his planning book. He'd always worked hard in school, but his grades weren't very good because he was so disorganized. One weekend his world crashed. He was supposed to clean the garage. He'd made plans to go to the movies on Saturday. Then he remembered his science project was due Monday. He'd also promised to help the church youth group with a food drive.

Jay panicked. He cancelled going to the movie, and his friends got mad. He cleaned the garage, but he did a lousy job and lost his allowance. He explained to his youth-group leader why he couldn't help but felt guilty. He spent Sunday on his science project, but it stank.

That terrible weekend convinced Jay to get organized. He bought a planning book. He wrote down every assignment and its due date. He included events, plans with friends, chores, and family activities. It wasn't easy to make new habits, but soon Jay's grades improved. He learned to plan and use his time carefully.

Jay opened the book to today's date and wrote: Show grades to Mom and ask for favorite dessert!"

Your Turn

1. Do you ever get mixed up and behind?
2. What can you do to help yourself get organized?

_____

_____

_____

Prayer

God, help me be smart in how I use every day. Amen.

Do Your Best Always

Whatever you hand finds to do, do it with all your might.
–Ecclesiastes 9:10

More Than Inches

Rashid stood straight while his father measured him against the doorframe. On every birthday, Rashid's father made a new notch to show that year's growth.

"You're almost an inch taller than last year," Rashid's father said.

"That's all?" Rashid said. "I'm the shortest guy in my class."

"I'm not very tall, Rashid. Neither is my father."

"Great," Rashid mumbled. "I'll probably never grow up."

Rashid's father laid his hands on his son's shoulders and looked at him. "Rashid, there's more to growing than just getting taller."

"Like what?" Rashid asked.

"For your birthday last year I gave you a pair of in-line skates. Do you remember how you kept falling at first?"

"Yep. Now I outrace everybody and can do skating tricks."

"And last year," his father continued, "you barely passed math. But this year you've brought your grade up to a 'B.' "

"Hey, that's right," Rashid agreed.

His father smiled and squeezed Rashid's shoulders. "In all the important ways, Rashid, you've grown at least a foot this year!"

Your Turn

1. Name three ways you grew last year.
2. Now name three ways you hope to grow in the year ahead.

_____

_____

Prayer

God, You've packed me full of possibilities. I'm excited about what's next. Amen.

Do Your Best Always

Whatever you hand finds to do, do it with all your might.
–Ecclesiastes 9:10

Getting Stronger

Jason's father was a big man. Every time he swung the axe, the muscles moved and bulged in his arms and back. Wood chips flew from the old stump. He sat down for a break.

Jason brought him water and sat down. "Do you think I'll ever be as big as you?"

"Oh, sure," his father said. "Look how big your feet are. You're going to be a tall man. You'll pass me up one of these days."

"But will I be strong?" Jason persisted.

"Strong isn't the same as big," Jason's father said. "Strong is up to you. Some people think strong is about how much weight you can carry or how hard you swing a hammer, but that's nothing." He pulled a red bandanna from his pocket and wiped his face. "Listen, Jason. Strong is about being a man. And being a man means keeping promises, taking care of your family, walking away from fights when you can, respecting people—especially women—and honoring the LORD."

Jason's father smiled. "Son, I've seen you hold the door open for your mom. I've watched you stand by your friends and look out for your brother. You're on your way to becoming a strong man." He gave Jason a sweaty hug and stood up. "Are you ready to try out this ax?"

Your Turn

1. Was Jesus a strong man? Why or why not?
2. How are you working toward becoming strong?

_____

_____

Prayer

LORD, help me grow strong in love and faith. Amen.

Do Your Best Always

Hang in There

Sometimes it's hard to keep trying when everything and everyone seems to be working against you. God will help you keep your promises and do the things you need to do—if you depend on Him and His strength. Complete the following sentences as reminders to turn to God for help when things get tough.

I will trust God to help me hang in there when

My parents want me to...

_____

I am embarrassed by...

_____

I have trouble learning to...

_____

My friends don't understand why...

_____

My brother/sister is mean to me because...

_____

Prayer

LORD, remind me that when things get tough in my life, I can turn to You for help and encouragement. Amen.

Do Your Best Always

Growing Is More Than Getting Taller

There are lots of ways to grow. Sometimes your decisions and choices show that you are growing in ways that make God happy. In each pair of statements, one choice will help the person grow, the other will not. Circle the statements that will help the boys grow into the kind of person God wants them to be.

Dylan pretended to be sick so he could watch extra TV.

Matt helped his dad rake leaves.

Rod offered to help his little brother start his science experiment.

Keith cancelled a movie date with his little brother in order to play baseball with friends.

John explained to Scott how he had broken Scott's scooter and then offered to pay for the repairs.

Jeff broke Scott's scooter, but told Scott he didn't know how it got broken.

Tim went to the movies with friends and didn't get his math homework finished.

Kevin told his friends he couldn't go to the movies because he had to finish his homework.

Prayer

Heavenly Father, I want to grow into the type of person You want me to be. Amen.

God Wants to Help You

*[The LORD said,] "Call on me when you are in trouble,
and I will rescue you."*
– Psalm 50:15 NLT

The Growling Belly

As Barrett watched television, his stomach growled. When a commercial came on, Barrett went to the kitchen for something to eat. The coach wanted Barrett to lose a few pounds, but losing weight wasn't easy.

"Just lay off the sweets between meals," the coach had told him.

Barrett was trying, but he loved snacking. In the kitchen he found a chocolate pie. Mom had probably baked the pie for dessert tonight. But why wait? He could have a piece now and one for dessert.

As he got out a plate and reached for a knife, he heard his coach's words: "Just lay off the sweets between meals." Barrett hesitated. He didn't want to spend the season on the bench, and he knew his game would be better if he lost weight. He could smell the chocolate pie and his mouth watered. He wanted a piece right now! Could he live without it? Yes. Could he wait until after dinner? Yes.

Barrett pushed the pie away. He picked up an apple and returned to his television program.

Your Turn

1. Have you talked yourself into doing something bad for you?
   How'd it go?
2. Have you talked yourself into doing something good for you?
   How'd it go?

_____

_____

_____

Prayer

God, when I want to do things I shouldn't, help me do the right thing. Amen.

God Wants to Help You

*[The LORD said,] "Call on me when you are in trouble,
and I will rescue you."*

– Psalm 50:15 NLT

Holy Joe

Tim sat down next to Reed. "What a pile of books," Tim said. "You must have a lot of homework. Wait…is that a Bible? Are you a 'Holy Joe' or something?"

Reed liked going to church, but he didn't want to be teased about it. He could pretend he was using his Bible for an assignment in World Lit. But Reed didn't feel right lying or denying his faith. "Yes, I bring my Bible to school," Reed said. "Sometimes when I get my homework finished I have time to read my Bible in study hall. The Bible has great stories!" Reed said. "There are battles, and giants, and miracles." Reed swallowed. "My favorites are stories about Jesus."

"I don't know anything about Jesus," Tim said. "We don't have a Bible."

"I can show you some of the good stories," Reed offered.

Tim stood as the bus came to a stop. "Maybe. I get off here. See you later, Reed."

Tim didn't tease me, and I didn't lie. Perfect! thought Reed.

Your Turn

1. Does it bother you to talk about what you believe? Why or why not?
2. What are three ways you can share your faith?

_____

_____

_____

_____

Prayer

Jesus, I'm proud You are my Friend. Amen.

God Wants to Help You

[The LORD said,] "Call on me when you are in trouble, and I will rescue you."
– Psalm 50:15 NLT

Last-Place Louie

Wally loved kickball, and he loved winning. Today he was team captain. The captains chose teams carefully, picking the best players first.

Some of the kids waved their hands and pleaded, "Pick me! Pick me!" Louie stood off to one side, quietly scuffing the asphalt with one shoe. Louie was always the last to be chosen. He just wasn't any good at sports.

Wally felt a little sorry for Louie. Wally also felt sorry for himself. He counted how many players were left and realized Louie was going to end up on his team. Soon he was about to call Louie. Stuart came jogging from the school building. Wally's heart jumped! Stuart was great at every sport. With Stuart on his team, they'd win for sure. Then Wally saw the sad look on Louie's face. Somebody shouted, "Choose Stuart!" Somebody else yelled, "Yeah! We didn't get stuck with Last-Place Louie."

Wally wondered how it felt to always be chosen last. He decided that maybe winning wasn't the most important thing after all. To everyone's shock, Wally chose Louie. Wally's team got stomped, but he didn't feel bad. In fact, he felt good. He'd rather do what pleased God than what made his friends happy.

Your Turn

1. Do you know someone who is always chosen last?
2. What's a way you can include him or her?

_____

_____

_____

Prayer

Jesus, when I see people get left out, help me be kind. Amen

God Wants to Help You

[The LORD said,] "Call on me when you are in trouble,
and I will rescue you."
– Psalm 50:15 NLT

Bugged

"That Joseph drives me crazy," Neal said. Neal and Adam were shooting hoops. Neal paused and took a shot from the free-throw line. The ball hit the rim, bounced high, and fell through the net. "Joseph thinks he knows more than everybody else. No matter what you say, he tells you you're wrong. Doesn't that drive you nuts?"

Adam shrugged. "I don't let him get to me." He took a shot.

Neal jumped for the rebound and put the ball through the net again. "Doesn't anything bug you? I've never heard you complain about anybody."

Adam did a perfect lay-up and bounced the ball back to Neal.

"What's the point in getting all bent out of shape?" Adam asked. "God put all types of people on earth. I just try to get along with everybody."

Neal took a long hook shot and missed completely. He retrieved the ball and took another shot. "Some people are so annoying."

"You can always find something you don't like about a person," Adam said. "Try to make the best of any relationship. People can probably think of something they don't like about you too."

"Not me!" Neal grinned. "Everything about me is likeable."

"Yeah, you're the exception," Adam said, grinning back. "In fact, it really irritates me that you're so perfect."

Your Turn

1. What can you do to get along with people who annoy you?
2. What can you do to be a better friend?

_____

_____

Prayer

God, help me remember that everybody is worth knowing. Amen.

God Wants to Help You

*[The LORD said,] "Call on me when you are in trouble,
and I will rescue you."*

– Psalm 50:15 NLT

Bad Company

"I'm going out for a while," Rich said, heading out the door.

"If you're going to Wayne's house, we need to talk first," Rich's mother said.

She sat on the front steps, and Rich settled beside her.

"Have you noticed that Wayne keeps getting you into trouble?"

"That's not true," Rich said.

"No? Who put a cherry bomb in Mrs. Worthington's mailbox?"

"Wayne did that, not me," Rich said.

"You were there, and you had to help pay for the mailbox. Last week you were accused of cheating."

"I told you I didn't cheat."

"I believed you, but the teacher saw Wayne copying answers from your paper. You both had to see the principal, right?"

"Yes," Rich said quietly.

"Let's see," Mrs. Corrigan said. "There were the broken bottles in the school parking lot. The graffiti. The prank phone calls. The…"

"Okay! Wayne likes to fool around. But I'm not doing that stuff."

"Maybe not," Mrs. Corrigan said. "Wayne needs for your ways to rub off on him, not the other way around. If you can't help him change, find another friend."

Rich stood. "I think I'll go see if Jerry wants to hang out."

Your Turn

1. What qualities make a good friend?
2. Are you a good friend?

Prayer

God, help me find good friends who love and honor You. Amen.

God Wants to Help You

Passing the Test

Before Jesus started His ministry, He went away to pray alone about what following God meant to Him. While He was alone, He was tempted by the devil to disobey God. Read Matthew 4:1-11, and then match each of the temptations to the statement that best describes Jesus' reason for refusing the temptation.

1. Jesus was tempted to turn stones into bread.

2. Jesus was tempted to jump off a mountain and command angels to save Him.

3. Jesus was tempted to worship the devil and become ruler of the world.

A. Worshiping the one, true God is more important than power or money.

B. Obeying God is more important than showing off to impress other people.

C. Doing God's will is more important than physical comforts.

Prayer

LORD, I know there will be times when I'm tempted to do something I shouldn't. Please be with me during those times so I can stand strong. Amen.

God Wants to Help You

Different Is Good

Isn't it great that God made everyone different? The world would be a boring place if we all liked to do the same things, looked alike, and were interested in the same things. Sometimes the key to getting along with another person is finding out how you are alike and how you are different.

Put your name in one of the three large triangles. Write things about yourself in that triangle. Put the names of two of your friends in the other two triangles, and write things about them that are different from you. In the space in the middle where the triangles come together, make a list of some of the ways you and your friends are the same.

Prayer

God, it's easy for me to get along with friends and family who are like me, but sometimes I need Your help to get along with people who are different. Amen.

Working Together

Plans fail for lack of counsel, but with many advisers they succeed.
– Proverbs 15:22

The Lightning Bolt

Harper looked at his go-kart with disappointment. It was a downhill coaster, but the racer hadn't turned out the way he'd hoped. In his mind, the Lightning Bolt was going to be a beauty, but it turned out to be a rolling mess. As Harper frowned, his father came into the garage.

"How's it going?" Mr. Summers asked. "Are you ready for NASCAR yet?"

Harper shook his head. "The front wheels barely turn. One rear wheel wobbles. I tried to paint lightning on the side, but it looks like a lumpy banana."

"Didn't your friend Kenny build a go-kart?" Mr. Summers asked. "Why didn't you get him to help you with the wheels?"

"I don't know," Harper said. "I guess I wanted to do it by myself."

Mr. Summers said, "Sometimes it makes sense to ask for help. God gives us friends and family so we can help each other."

"I wish I'd thought of that before I messed up my go-kart," Harper said.

"Who says it's too late?" asked Mr. Summers. "Let's get busy. Say, Willy is taking art classes," Harper's father said. "I'll bet he could turn that banana into lightning."

Your Turn

1. How do you learn to do new things?
2. Are you good at asking for help? At offering help?

_____

_____

Prayer

God, I like to do things myself. Help me know when to ask for help. Amen.

Working Together

Plans fail for lack of counsel, but with many advisers they succeed.
– Proverbs 15:22

Better Late Than Never

"I'm not mad," Carl told Ted. "But I'm tired of waiting for you."

"That's just how I am," Ted said. "Running late is my superpower."

"You can joke about it if you want," Carl said, "but I'm serious. Every time we get together, I end up waiting at least fifteen minutes for you to get here. Last week you were a half-hour late!"

"I don't see the big deal," Ted said. He was starting to get angry.

"The big deal," Carl said calmly, "is that when you're late over and over, I feel like I don't matter. That my time isn't important. That you don't care if I'm twiddling my thumbs waiting for you."

"That's not true," Ted said. "You're my friend."

"That's why I'm telling you how I feel," Carl said. "We're friends."

"Are you saying we can't be friends if I keep being late?" Ted asked.

"Of course not," Carl said. "But good friends care about each other, and that includes being on time."

Ted's face relaxed into a grin. "From now on I'll try not to keep you waiting. I can't promise perfection."

"And I can't promise I won't leave without you next time," Carl said.

"Fair enough," Ted said.

Your Turn

1. Was it hard for Carl to tell Ted what was bothering him? Why?

2: Do you think Carl and Ted will become even better friends? Why?

_____

_____

Prayer

God, help me know when to speak up. Amen.

Working Together

Plans fail for lack of counsel, but with many advisers they succeed.
– Proverbs 15:22

Jumbo Popcorn

"This is going to be a great movie," Nick said as they waited in line for the tickets. "I love science fiction. Someday I want to be an astronaut."

"The special effects are supposed to be awesome," Evan said. "The aliens are all computer generated."

Nick bought his ticket first, and then waited for his friend. He noticed that Evan counted out the dollar bills carefully.

As they walked past the concession stand in the lobby, Evan said, "That popcorn sure smells good."

"Let's get some," Nick said.

Evan reached for his wallet but dropped his hand. "I'm not really hungry after all. You go ahead."

Evan's dad had been laid off from work for a few months, so money was probably tight, Nick realized. He hoped Evan's dad could get back to work soon. Evan seldom talked about his dad's being out of a job, but Nick could tell he was worried.

Nick studied the prices at the concession stand. He glanced at his friend. "You get a lot more for the money if you buy the jumbo popcorn. That's more than I can eat. Will you help me out?"

"Uh, sure," Evan said. "I guess so. Thanks."

"Good," Nick said. "It's no fun eating popcorn by myself."

Your Turn

1. Do you think sharing makes things more fun? Why or why not?

_____

_____

_____

Prayer

God, I don't have everything I want, but I have enough to share. Amen.

Working Together

Plans fail for lack of counsel, but with many advisers they succeed.
– Proverbs 15:22

Better Than a Ball Glove

"Dad, may I talk to you?" Roger Harper asked.

"Sure," his father said, lowering the Sunday paper. "What's up?"

"I've saved $25 to buy a new baseball glove," Roger said.

"Getting close," Mr. Harper said. "The new glove is $35, right?"

"You've been helping me, Dad," Roger said. "You've let me do extra jobs to make money. That's why I wanted to talk to you."

"Roger, are you going to ask to borrow the $10 you need?" Mr. Harper frowned. "I thought we agreed you'd wait until you had all the money."

"That's not it," Roger said. "I'm not sure I want to buy it."

Mr. Harper looked at his son in surprise. "I thought you had your heart set on that glove," he said.

"I did," Roger said. "But now I think I want to use the money for something else."

"Like what?" Mr. Harper asked.

"Remember in church they talked about that family whose house burned down?" Roger asked. "One of the guys in that family is in one of my classes. I've been thinking how awful it would be to lose everything. My old glove isn't so bad I was thinking I might give my savings to help him."

"All of it?" Mr. Harper asked.

"Yes, if it is okay with you."

"Roger," Mr. Harper said, "it is more than okay. I'm proud of you."

Your Turn

1. After Roger gave away his money, how do you think he felt?
2. Is there something you can give to help someone this week?

_____

_____

Prayer

Lord, teach me to be generous with others. Amen.

Working Together

Plans fail for lack of counsel, but with many advisers they succeed.
– Proverbs 15:22

Open Ears

"I brought the snacks for our study time," Gavin said. "My mom always says the brain needs good food to do good work."

"Great!" Josh said. "Let's see the goodies."

Gavin opened the bag and set two cans of root beer on the table.

Josh made a face.

"What's the matter?" Gavin asked. "You said to get root beer for you."

"I told you to get me anything but root beer. I can't stand that stuff."

"Sorry about that. But wait until you bite into this candy," Gavin said, holding out two Peanut Paradise bars.

Josh frowned and shook his head.

"Gavin, we've been friends almost two years. Are you telling me you don't know that I'm allergic to peanuts?"

"How am I supposed to know if you keep it a big secret?" Gavin snapped.

"I've only told you about a hundred times. You never listen…"

"Yes, I do!" Gavin interrupted.

"You talk instead of listen," Josh said. "Yesterday you asked what snacks I like. While I was telling you, you started talking about a movie."

Gavin's face turned red. His parents and teachers always complained that he never listened too. "Maybe you're right," Gavin admitted.

Your Turn

1. What makes a person a good listener?
2. What can you do to be a better listener?

_____

_____

Prayer

God, remind me to give my mouth a rest and my ears a work-out. Amen.

Working Together

Enough to Go Around

Sharing with others is one of the ways you can say "thank You" to God for all the things He gives you. Read the story and follow the directions to help the boys share their lunches.

Zach, Ian, Tyler, and Luis were going on an all-day bike trip. They were going to meet at the park at nine and head up a mountain path that Zach's dad had shown him. Everyone was supposed to bring his own water and sack lunch.

When the boys stopped for lunch, Zach realized he had forgotten his lunch. The other boys decided to share their lunches so Zach would have some food too.

Choose things from each of the three sack lunches the boys could share with Zach. Write or draw these items in Zach's empty lunch bag.

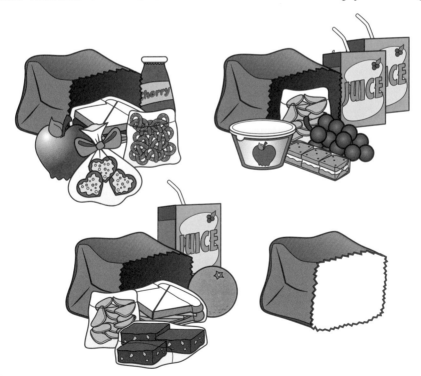

Prayer

Lord, I want to be more generous with what I have and share my things. Amen.

189

Working Together

What Did You Say?

Sometimes you might think you know what someone said, but you didn't really understand what he or she meant. Good communication involves saying what you mean and listening carefully so you really hear what the other person is saying. Look at the statements below and circle the explanation that best describes what the person really means to say. Your answers may not be the same as someone else's.

1. **"I've already seen that movie, but I'm not too tired for a game."**

   a. I'd like to go to the movie with you.
   b. I'd rather play basketball than go see that movie again.
   c. I'll go to the movie if you buy my ticket.

2. **" I guess Matt's not so bad."**

   a. I think we should invite Matt to our party.
   b. Matt's okay at school, but I don't want to hang out with him.
   c. Let's play a trick on Matt.

3. **"Why do I have to have my little brother tag along everywhere I go?"**

   a. Having a little brother is no fun.
   b. I wish I had sisters.
   c. I'll still do things with my brother, but sometimes I want to do things just with my friends.

4. **"I've got to have a remote-controlled car."**

   a. All my friends have remote-controlled cars and I feel left out when they play with them.
   b. You are bad parents for not getting me something I need.
   c. I can make a lot of money racing a remote-controlled car.

Prayer

LORD, please help me to really listen before I speak. I want to understand what people are saying to me. Amen.

Choose to Forgive

Love prospers when a fault is forgiven, but
dwelling on it separates close friends.
– Proverbs 17:9 NLT

The Invitation

Aaron opened the envelope and pulled out an invitation to Carter's surprise birthday party. *Yeah, like I'd go,* Aaron thought.

A month before, Aaron had a birthday party and invited Carter. Carter had promised he'd come. Aaron spent the whole evening watching for him, but he never showed up. The next day at church, Aaron asked Carter, "Where were you last night?"

"I was at the mall," Carter said. "Why?"

"You missed my party!" Aaron said. "I thought we were friends, but a real friend wouldn't have blown off my birthday."

Carter apologized and the next day brought a present to Aaron.

"I got plenty of presents," Aaron said. "I don't need more."

Carter apologized again, but Aaron wouldn't listen.

Aaron read the invitation again. It was a surprise party, so Carter's mom must have sent it. He tore it up and shoved it into his pocket. But maybe he was being silly. He missed Carter, and this party might be a way to patch things up. It still hurt that Carter had forgotten his party, but everyone makes mistakes. Aaron took the torn pieces out of his pocket and slid them together on the porch. Should he go?

Your Turn

1. Do you think Aaron should go to the party?
2. Think of a time when you were forgiven. How did you feel?

_____

_____

Prayer

God, You have forgiven me so many times. Help me forgive others. Amen.

Choose to Forgive

Love prospers when a fault is forgiven, but
dwelling on it separates close friends.
— **Proverbs 17:9 NLT**

Papers in the Wind

Owen and Vic were at the bus stop as Ellen trudged up the hill. As usual, she carried a huge stack of books.

"Here comes superbrain," Vic said.

"I bet she never gets less than 100 on her papers," Owen said.

"As many books as she carries around, she must have muscles like a lumberjack," Vic joked.

The school bus came around the corner, its gears grinding. Ellen heard the bus and started to trot up the hill. As she hurried, a book slid out of her grip. When she grabbed at it, all the other books fell onto the street. Some flopped open, and the wind scattered the papers tucked in the pages.

Watching the papers tumble through the streets, Vic laughed.

"Come on," Owen said. "We'd better give her a hand."

"Help superbrain?" Vic asked. "You've got to be kidding."

Owen ran down the hill and helped Ellen chase the papers.

"Thanks so much," Ellen said when the papers were back in her grip.

"No problem," Owen said as he picked up the books.

Owen sat by Vic on the bus. Vic asked, "Why did you do that?"

Owen shrugged. "I thought how I'd feel if that were me. I'd want somebody to help me, so that's what I did for her. It's the golden rule."

Your Turn

1. What is the golden rule?
2. What would your school be like if everyone followed that rule?

_____

_____

_____

Prayer

LORD, help me remember that other people have feelings too. Amen.

Choose to Forgive

*Love prospers when a fault is forgiven, but
dwelling on it separates close friends.*
– Proverbs 17:9 NLT

Taming the Tongue

"I didn't mean to hurt his feelings," Dylan said. "I was joking."

"Well, it wasn't a joke to Sam," said Dylan's father. "His parents called and told me Sam's been really upset. What happened?"

Dylan didn't want to look his father in the eye, so he stared down at his own shoes. "Sam got a bad grade on a homework assignment."

"And?" his father asked.

"I sort of told him he was dumber than a doorknob," Dylan admitted. "But I didn't mean it!"

His father said, "Next time, think before you speak. Once the words come out of your mouth, you can't take them back."

Dylan nodded. "I wish I'd never said it. Sam's feelings are hurt, his parents are mad at me, and I feel terrible. All because of a few dumb words."

"Words are powerful," said Mr. McCoy. "Your tongue is probably the most powerful muscle in your body."

"May I call Sam, Dad?" asked Dylan. "I want to say I'm sorry."

"Those are strong words too," Mr. McCoy said. "Make things right."

"I guess so," said Dylan. "It would have been a lot simpler if I'd just kept my mouth shut in the first place."

Your Turn

1. Make a list of good things you can do with your words.
2. Have you said something you're sorry for? Did you apologize?

_____

_____

Prayer

LORD, help me use my words to build up people. Amen.

Choose to Forgive

*Love prospers when a fault is forgiven, but
dwelling on it separates close friends.*
– Proverbs 17:9 NLT

Grumbling Makes Things Worse

Zach returned to the dugout shaking his head in disgust.

"Don't worry about it," Diego said. "Everybody strikes out sometimes."

"Wasn't my fault," Zach said. "That's the worst pitcher, and the umpire is worse. Can you believe he called that last pitch a strike?"

Diego sighed quietly. Nothing ever suited Zach.

"That bat I used is no good," Zach said. "I think it must be warped."

Diego had hit a double with it the last inning.

"Our batting order is a mess," Zach said.

Diego said nothing. He remembered a conversation with his *abuela*, his grandma. In a gentle voice, his grandma had said, "Grumbling only makes things worse, Diego. Smiling never hurt anyone. If the world is such a bad place, then do something to make it better."

"Even if I got a hit, I'd probably never make it around the bases," Zach said. "What a crummy field, and the baselines are crooked."

"When the game's over," Diego said, "we can get a lawnmower and cut down the weeds in the outfield. That would help."

"Are you joking?" Zach asked. "It's too hot for that. Let somebody else do it." Zach paused. Hey, what are you smiling at?"

Your Turn

1. How does frowning make you feel? What about smiling?
2. Do you grumble? What can you do instead of complaining?

_____

_____

Prayer

Lord, help me be happy about the good things and work to improve the bad things. Amen.

Choose to Forgive

Love prospers when a fault is forgiven, but
dwelling on it separates close friends.
– Proverbs 17:9 NLT

The Sleepover Secret

"You told what happened Friday night, didn't you, Jack?" Kirby asked. His face was red and he looked angry.

"I might have mentioned it to a couple of the guys."

"I can't believe this," Kirby said. "I can't believe you'd talk about it." On Friday, Jack had spent the night. After the boys had gone to bed, Kirby's father had come home shouting and slamming doors. In a miserable voice, Kirby had admitted his father was drunk again. "Don't tell anybody, okay?" Kirby had asked.

On Monday, Jack felt important talking about Kirby's dad. Jack had shared Kirby's secret with three people but asked them not to spread it around. They had told others, and soon the whole class knew. Now Kirby was angry, and Jack knew he'd made a mistake.

"I'm sorry," Jack said. "It's not your fault your dad gets drunk."

"No, but it's your fault everybody knows about it," Kirby said. He turned and walked away.

Your Turn

1. Do you think Kirby and Jack will still be friends?
2. Is it hard for you to keep quiet about things you know?

_____

_____

_____

_____

Prayer

God, help me be wise about what I share. Amen.

Choose to Forgive

The Golden Rule

Jesus told a parable about a person who didn't follow the Golden Rule. Read the parable in Matthew 18:23-34. How would the story Jesus told be different if the servant had followed the Golden Rule and treated others the way he wanted to be treated? Rewrite the ending of the parable to show the happier ending the story could have had.

One day a king called in all his officials to find out what they owed him. One official was brought in who owed the king 50 million silver coins, but he didn't any money to pay back the debt. The king ordered the official, his wife, and children to be sold into slavery to pay back the debt. The official begged the king for mercy and forgiveness and promised to pay back the money. The king felt sorry for the man and told him he could go free and didn't even have to pay back the money.

As the official was leaving, he met another man who owed him 100 silver coins. He grabbed the man and started choking him and demanded payment of the money owed. The man begged for mercy and forgiveness and promised to pay back the money he owed. The official…

_____

_____

_____

_____

Prayer

Dear LORD, I want to be quick to forgive others even when my feelings are hurt. Help them be quick to forgive me too. Amen.

Choose to Forgive

A Downer or a Doer?

Some people would rather complain than do something about a problem. You can be a person who chooses to take action rather than complain. Read the problem situations and create an action plan to change each situation.

■ Your parents don't want to raise your allowance, but you want more money.

Action Plan:_____

_____

■ You seldom get to watch TV on weeknights because you have too much homework.

Action Plan:_____

■ Your friends want you to go to a baseball game on Saturday, but your parents expect you to help clean out the garage on Saturday.

Action Plan:_____

■ You've lost your homework assignment for the weekend and your parents won't let you go out with your friends until your homework is finished.

Action Plan:_____

■ You want to swap trading cards with a particular friend, but other people always get to him before you.

Action Plan:_____

Prayer

LORD, when things don't turn out how I would like them to, please help me remember not to grumble. Show me possible solutions. Amen.

Be an Encourager

Encourage one another and build each other up.
– 1 Thessalonians 5:11

Good Words on a Bad Day

"What a lousy day!" Ned stomped into the bedroom he shared with his brother, threw his schoolbooks down, and fell on his bed.

Paul looked up from his homework. "What's up?"

"Nothing is up." Ned moaned. "Everything is down. I barely passed my history test—the one I thought I was going to ace. Baseball was horrible. I did nothing but swing at air. I had to make a speech in English class but forgot my notes. I worked hard on that speech, but I couldn't remember anything. I bumbled around for five minutes." Ned stared at the ceiling. "My history teacher thinks I didn't study, coach thinks I'm a loser, and my English class thinks I'm stupid. The whole world thinks I'm a dork."

"Not the whole world," Paul said. "I don't."

"Yeah, great!" Ned snorted.

"Hey, if you were stupid, you couldn't have helped me pass math last year," Paul said. "And I know you can bat because you taught me. You're just having a bad day. Everyone has those. You're still my favorite brother!"

"I'm your only brother," Ned said.

"See?" Paul said. "You really are my favorite."

Your Turn

1. What are five kind things you could say to someone who's having a bad day?
2. Who will you encourage this week?

_____

_____

Prayer

God, give me the words to make someone's day better. Amen.

198

Be an Encourager

Encourage one another and build each other up.
– 1 Thessalonians 5:11

The Bowling Buddy

Eric lifted the bowling ball, stumbled, and dropped the ball. It bounced and crashed into the gutter. He wished he could turn invisible. He slunk back to his friend Isaac, who had invited him. "I haven't gotten the hang of it yet." He looked at the floor.

Isaac slapped him on the back. "You're doing great for your first time out. If you hadn't slipped, you would have really nailed that one."

Eric looked at the score sheet and moaned.

"Don't worry about your score," Isaac said. "Just have fun."

"Everybody else is having fun laughing at me," Eric said.

"Nah!" Isaac said. "Nobody's paying any attention to you."

Isaac stepped onto the floor and picked up his ball. He knocked down seven pins, and then picked off the other three on his second try.

When he sat beside Eric, Isaac said, "You should have seen me the first time I ever came bowling. I only got five pins all night."

"I know the feeling," Eric said.

"Twice I dropped the ball—and it rolled back here to the seats. I thought I was going to die of embarrassment. And that wasn't the worst," Aaron said. "Once I bounced my ball into someone else's lane. Don't ask me how I managed that. That's how I got those five pins."

Now Eric was laughing.

On Eric's next turn he knocked over eight pins and Aaron cheered.

Your Turn

1. When have you let someone else choose? What happened?
2. Who needs encouragement today? What will you say to help?

_____

_____

Prayer

LORD, I want to be an encourager. Show me who I can build up. Amen.

Be an Encourager

Encourage one another and build each other up.
– 1 Thessalonians 5:11

Nine Ways to Make God Smile

Uncle Hal asked, "Remember the apple tree you helped plant?"

"Yep!" said Price. "That was hard work."

"The hard work paid off!" Uncle Hal led Price to the tree.

"Wow!" Price said when he saw the tree full of shiny, red fruit.

Uncle Hal plucked an apple and pitched it to Price before picking one for himself. He bit into it, and a grin spread across his face.

"Uncle Hal, you're really proud of this tree, aren't you?"

Price's uncle nodded happily. "You and I dug the hole and staked the tree in place. I watered it and sprayed it to keep the bugs away. Every summer I've looked for apples, and here they are!"

Price bit into his own juicy apple.

"A healthy tree bears fruit," said Uncle Hal. "This tree is doing what God meant for it to do. It's no different for people."

"People don't bear fruit," Price said.

"Christians do," Uncle Hal said. "God's Spirit loves us and helps us grow, and after a while fruit grows in our lives."

Price imagined himself planted in the ground with apples hanging from his fingers. He shared the vision with his uncle.

Uncle Hal laughed. "The fruit of God's Spirit isn't apples. It's qualities such as love, joy, and kindness."

Your Turn

1. Read Galatians 5:22-23. What is growing in your life?

_____

_____

Prayer

God, fill my life with Your Holy Spirit so I can grow fruit. Amen.

Be an Encourager

Encourage one another and build each other up.
– 1 Thessalonians 5:11

Burger Battle

"School's out," Mrs. Logan said. "Let's celebrate!"

"I want to go to Pancake Kitchen!" Maggie said.

"Yuck!" shouted Price. "Let's go to Burger Barn!"

"Pancake Kitchen has chocolate-chip waffles," Maggie said.

"Burger Barn has a playground," Price said. "And with the super-large cheesy fries, you get a free toy."

"I want chocolate-chip waffles with marshmallow syrup," Maggie said. "If I can't go to Burger Barn…"

"Stop it!" Mrs. Logan cut in. "You have five minutes to work this out in a loving way or we'll stay home."

Price wondered what love had to do with eating out. Then he remembered Sunday's Bible lesson: Love doesn't insist on getting its own way. "Last time we ate at Burger Barn, didn't we?"

"Yes," Maggie said. "And the time before that."

"Then I guess it's your turn to pick where we eat, Maggie," Price said.

Maggie hugged him and shouted, "We're going to Pancake Kitchen!"

Price felt good. Uncle Hal had told him that every time the fruit of the Spirit grows, God smiles. Price smiled too.

Your Turn

1. When was the last time you showed love?
2. How will you show love today?

_____

_____

Prayer

Lord, love isn't just something I say; love is something I do. Amen.

Be an Encourager

Encourage one another and build each other up.
– 1 Thessalonians 5:11

Pumpkin Pie and Joy

Price reached into the back of the cabinet and pulled out a can of pumpkin.

"Thank you, Price," Granny said. "My knees would hurt all day if I had to get down there." She handed him a can opener. "My fingers aren't in such great shape, either," she said with a chuckle.

Price opened the can. "How can you laugh when you're hurting?"

Granny spooned the pumpkin into a bowl. "Life has good and bad things," she said. "I learned long ago to focus on the good stuff."

"Like what?" Price asked.

"Like pumpkin pie and visits from my grandson," Granny said. "Flowers in the yard and good friends. Most off all Jesus." Granny added spices and brown sugar to the pumpkin. "Jesus is my best friend. If I get sad, I just think about everything He has done for me and how much He loves me." She poured the pumpkin mixture into two pans and slid them into the oven.

"Why did you make two pies, Granny?"

"One for us," she said, "and one for my neighbor. I like giving presents."

So does Jesus, Price thought. *He gave Granny the gift of joy. She probably has other fruit of the Spirit, but joy fills her life the way the smell of pumpkin pie fills her kitchen.*

Your Turn

1. What brings you joy?
2. How can you help someone feel joy this week?

_____

_____

Prayer

God, give me Your joy to share with others. Amen.

Be an Encourager

Barnabas, the Encourager

In the book of Acts, we meet a fellow named Joseph who was always encouraging other people. Joseph was so kind and helpful that nobody called him by his real name. Instead, he was nicknamed Barnabas. In the language of those days, "Barnabas" meant "encourager." In the following scenarios, think like Barnabas and write down how you'd help. Look up the Scriptures to see if you were correct.

1. Paul, a new Christian, came to Jerusalem to work with the church, but the other Christians were afraid of him and the church leaders avoided him. What do you think Barnabas did? (Acts 9:26-28)

_____

_____

2. In the city of Antioch, many people were becoming Christians. The church there needed help making those new Christians part of the family. What do you think Barnabas did? (Acts 11:19-26)

_____

_____

3. John Mark was a young Christian who had gotten halfway through a mission trip and quit. Now he wanted to join another mission trip, but Paul said he couldn't be trusted and refused to take him along. What do you think Barnabas did? (Acts 15:36-39)

_____

_____

Prayer

God, I want to be like Barnabas. He was an encourager. Show me ways I can encourage people. Amen.

Be an Encourager

God's Favorite Fruit

Paul writes to his Galatian friends about nine aspects of the fruit of the Holy Spirit. Here is a list of fruit with the words jumbled. Unscramble each word and write it on the tree. (If you need help, read Galatians 5:22-23.)

FNLOE-RSOLTC   VELO

LETNENESGS   SKENDINS

OJY   ACEPE

NIACTEEP   DONSESOG

STFNHFEIUSLA

Prayer

God, help me memorize the fruit of Your Spirit so I am reminded that You are at work in me. Amen.

Let Peace Fill Your Heart

Let the peace of Christ rule in your hearts.
– Colossians 3:15

The Storm Party

Ba-Ba-THOOOOM! The thunder roared so loudly that the house shook. A moment later the lights went out.

"Mommy!" squealed Maggie. "Why is it dark?"

"Don't be afraid," Mrs. Logan said. "The storm has blown down the power lines somewhere."

"I'll get a flashlight," Price said.

"I'm scared," Maggie whined.

"Don't worry. The four of us will be fine," Mrs. Logan said.

"Four?" asked Price.

"Sure," his mother said. "You, Maggie, Jesus, and me."

Thunder boomed again.

"Take Maggie downstairs," Mrs. Logan said. "I'll be down in a minute, and we'll have a storm party."

Maggie sat up straight on the couch. "That sounds like fun!"

As Price led Maggie downstairs, he said, "Maggie, we'll be okay. Jesus really is here. Ask Him to fill your heart with peace."

Their mom joined them. She set down a lit candle, and they sat around it. She handed both kids a skewer and opened a bag of marshmallows. "Have you ever roasted marshmallows over a candle?"

Your Turn

1. When your thoughts are filled with Jesus, how do you feel?
2. The next time you're scared, what can you do to find peace?

_____

_____

Prayer

Jesus, thanks for taking away my worries and giving me Your peace. Amen.

Let Peace Fill Your Heart

Let the peace of Christ rule in your hearts.
– Colossians 3:15

Knot Patient

Price's little sister, Maggie, came into his room carrying a shoe in her hand. The laces were tangled in knots.

"Will you show me again how to tie my shoes?" Maggie asked.

Price closed the history book and looked at Maggie. A dozen mean answers flashed through his head, such as, "I've already shown you 287 times." Instead, he reminded himself that patience is a fruit of the Holy Spirit. "Let's see if I can get the knots out first."

Price untangled the knots. "Put this on your foot, and try again."

Price put one foot next to Maggie's and untied his own shoe.

"We'll go slowly," he said. "I'll tie my shoe and you tie yours."

Price tied an overhand knot, and Maggie did the same. He gathered one lace in a loop and wrapped the other lace around it. Maggie did the same with her chubby fingers.

"Now push this part through and pull," Price said, leading the way.

Maggie squealed with delight. "It worked! I tied it!" She ran out.

Your Turn

1. When is it hard for you to be patient?
2. What helps you to be patient when you don't feel patient?

_____

_____

_____

_____

Prayer

God, You're always patient with me, so I want to be patient with others. Amen.

Let Peace Fill Your Heart

Let the peace of Christ rule in your hearts.
– Colossians 3:15

Wet and Late

"Mom, I'm home!" Price called.

"Don't take another step, young man!" his mother said. "You are soaked to the skin, and you're dripping water on my clean floor."

Mrs. Logan brought a towel. She watched as Price dried himself off.

Price's little sister, Maggie, joined them at the back door.

"You're wetter than a goldfish," Maggie said.

"And you're late for dinner," Mrs. Logan told him.

"I'm sorry, Mom," Price said. "I was on my way home when I saw Mrs. Curry in her front yard trying to get her lawnmower started. Her grass was almost up to my knees," so I mowed her lawn."

"Did you finish before the rain started?" Mrs. Logan asked.

"Barely." Price grinned. "I rode my bike home in the storm."

Mrs. Logan smiled at her son. "Price, I'm very proud of you."

As Price came from his room wearing dry clothes, he heard Maggie ask, "Why did Price cut that lady's grass?"

His mother answered, "Because Price is kind."

Kindness, Price remembered, *is a fruit of the Spirit.* He sat down at the table and his mother set dinner in front of him.

"Are you cold?" Mrs. Logan asked.

"No, I feel great," Price said. "Just great!"

Your Turn

1. Have you been kind to anyone this week? What did you do?

_____

_____

Prayer

God, help me notice people who need some kindness. Amen.

Let Peace Fill Your Heart

Let the peace of Christ rule in your hearts.
– Colossians 3:15

Treasure in a Trash Bag

Price leaped for the football, but it sailed overhead and bounced crookedly into thick bushes. Price pushed through the green branches and picked up the football. He noticed an open garbage bag, and a shiny coin caught his eye.

"Hey, Tomas!" he yelled. "Take a look at this."

"Wow! That's a gold coin," Tomas said.

Price peered into the trash bag. He saw a few old coins, but mostly empty coin wrappers and containers.

"This is somebody's coin collection," Price said. "Or what's left of it."

"What's it doing here?" Tomas asked.

"I think this stuff is stolen," Price said slowly. "Somebody stole all this, shoved it in the bag, and brought it here to sort through it."

"Why'd he leave the gold coin behind?"

"Maybe it was dark, and the person missed it," Price said.

"Man, you have all the luck," Tomas complained.

Price looked at his friend with surprise. "I'm not going to keep it. I'm going to call the police. There's not much left here, but maybe they can get it back to the person it belongs to."

A few days later the owner of the coin collection phoned Price. "I'm glad I got the coin back. It was a gift from my grandfather and means a lot to me. Thanks for doing such a good thing."

Your Turn

1. Do you ever ask, "What would Jesus do?"
2. When you get the wrong change, do you give back the extra?

Prayer

Jesus, I want to be like You. Show me some good things I can do. Amen.

Let Peace Fill Your Heart

Let the peace of Christ rule in your hearts.
– Colossians 3:15

The Boring Meeting

"I don't want to go to youth group tonight," Price said. "Our meetings are so boring, and we do the same things. We eat dinner—always hot dogs and chips. We have a Bible study. We play volleyball."

"I guess that could get boring," his mother agreed.

"A lot of the kids have stopped going," Price told her.

"That's a shame," she said. "But you've got new leaders, right? Didn't the Connors start a couple of weeks ago?"

"Yes. They're nice," Price said, "but the meetings are still boring."

"Maybe you can talk to them about doing new things," Mom suggested.

Price shrugged. "I don't know…"

"I'll bet the Connors are counting on faithful members to pull the youth group together. They are making a commitment to you kids. Are you willing to make a commitment to them?"

Price knew faithfulness was part of the fruit God grows in people. *Is this what faithfulness is? Keeping a commitment even when I want to quit?* "Okay," Price said. "Will you drive me to church?"

"Sure," Mrs. Logan said. "Tell the Connors I'll fix dinner for the youth group next week. And I promise no hot dogs!"

Your Turn

1. In what areas of your life is faithfulness important?

_____

_____

_____

Prayer

God, You never give up on me. Thank You for Your faithfulness. Amen.

Let Peace Fill Your Heart

Random Acts of Kindness

Sometimes you might miss chances to be kind just because you're not paying attention. In the spaces below, write the names of four people you expect to see this week. Beside each name write one kind thing you might do for that person. Now circle one kind deed you will commit to doing this week.

_____   _____

_____   _____

_____   _____

_____   _____

Prayer

Heavenly Father, help me be kind to everyone I see today, even if it's just giving a friendly smile. Amen.

Let Peace Fill Your Heart

For Goodness Sake

The Bible says Jesus went around doing good (Acts 10:38). Do you know the kinds of things Jesus did? A few are listed below. Draw each good deed the way you imagine it might have looked. (If you want to find out more, you can look up the stories in your Bible.)

Jesus fed a hungry crowd (Matthew 14:15-21).	Jesus raised a little girl from the dead (Matthew 9:18-26).
When the disciples were in a boat, Jesus stopped a storm that was scaring them (Matthew 8:23-26).	Jesus gave sight to blind people (John 9:1-7).

Prayer

Jesus, I want to be more like You. Please help me see ways I can do good things for others. Amen.

Being Gentle Is Good

Let your gentleness be evident to all.
– Philippians 4:5

The Splinter

Maggie extended one finger. A splinter was buried under her skin.

"We have to get that out," her brother, Price, said.

His sister jerked her hand back. "No!" she yelled.

"If it hurts too much, just tell me," Price said. "But first I'll show you my secret way of keeping splinters from hurting."

He went into the house and returned with a needle and an ice cube. "Hold this ice cube on the splinter," Price said. "The cold will keep your finger from hurting." After a few minutes, he took the ice cube and dropped it on the grass. He held his sister's finger firmly. "As soon as it hurts too much, you tell me," Price said. "Don't watch. Look at that dog across the street and tell me what he's doing."

"He's trying to sneak up on a squirrel," Maggie said. "Ouch!"

"I'm finished!" Price held out the splinter for Maggie to see.

"That's a big one! It only hurt a little at the end. You're very...very...I can't think of the word. You're very..."

"Gentle?" asked Price. "Mom says that God smiles when He sees gentleness."

"When God sees gentleness in us, He smiles."

"God must be smiling at you like I am," Maggie exclaimed.

Your Turn

1. Write the names of three people you know who are gentle with you.
2. When was the last time your gentleness showed?

_____

_____

Prayer

God, thanks for being gentle with me. Help me be gentle with others. Amen.

Being Gentle Is Good

Let your gentleness be evident to all.
– Philippians 4:5

Almost Batty

"The last time I was here, Uncle Hal," Price said, "you told me about the fruit of the Holy Spirit."

"When God's Spirit comes into our lives, good things start growing," Uncle Hal said. "Things like love, joy, and peace."

"And patience, kindness, goodness, and faithfulness," Price added with a grin.

"Somebody's been reading his Bible," Uncle Hal said and smiled.

Something flitted through the darkening sky.

"Was that a bird?" Price asked.

"No," Uncle Hal said. "The bats are coming out."

"Bats?" Price asked, his eyes big. "Do they bite?"

"They won't bother us. They're after moths and mosquitoes."

"They scare me a little bit," Price admitted.

"Then we'll go inside," Uncle Hal said.

Once they were in the house, Price felt better. "I almost ran for cover," he said.

"I'm glad you kept calm," Uncle Hal said. "Bats aren't dangerous, but running through the dark is. You might have stepped in a hole." He pretended to pluck something from his nephew's ear. "What's this?" he asked. "It looks like the fruit of self-control."

Your Turn

1. Do you sometimes do things you later wish you hadn't? Explain.
2. What other times do you use self-control?

_____

_____

Prayer

God, help me stay in control when I'm scared or upset. Amen.

Being Gentle Is Good

Let your gentleness be evident to all.
– Philippians 4:5

Cabbage and Coconut

"I can't believe I flunked that biology test," Foster said to his friend Hiroshi as they walked home from school. "What did you get?"

"It was a tough test," Hiroshi agreed. "I got a 'B.' "

"I don't get it," Foster moaned. "I ate cabbage for a week."

"Cabbage?"

"Yep. A woman on TV said cabbage improves memory. I switched to coconut shampoo because the smell makes brains work better. I even slept with my biology book under my pillow. A guy on the radio said information will seep into my head that way." He kicked a rock. "I did everything to get ready for that test."

"Did you study?" Hiroshi asked.

"Not exactly," Foster said. "I didn't think I needed to study."

"Foster, you've got to stop believing goofy stuff you see and hear," Hiroshi said. "Get a clue, buddy."

"I guess you're right," Foster said. "I'd better check things out from now on and be more careful about what I believe."

Your Turn

1. Are all ads true? Why or why not?
2. What can you do to check what you see and hear?

_____

_____

_____

_____

Prayer

God, remind me to ask questions so I'll know if someone isn't telling the truth. Amen.

Being Gentle Is Good

Let your gentleness be evident to all.
– Philippians 4:5

Getting Even

Ollie went over to Vince in the school cafeteria. "I know what you did," Ollie accused. "You squirted epoxy glue into my bicycle lock."

Everybody at Vince's table laughed.

"Yeah, it was really funny," Ollie said. "I had to walk all the way home. I delivered newspapers on foot, and after dinner my dad brought me back here to cut the lock off."

Vince leaned back in his chair.

"I've been thinking about how to pay you back," Ollie said. "I could do something mean, but you'd do something mean back."

"Sounds like fun," Vince said.

"Not really," Ollie said. "So I thought I'd try something different."

Ollie dropped a ticket onto Vince's tray. "There's a rock concert at my church Saturday. The band is pretty good. You like rock, don't you?"

"You know it," Vince said.

"Great! My dad and I will pick you up around seven. Okay?"

"Sure," Vince said. He looked at the ticket and then at Ollie. "About the lock, Ollie. I didn't mean to cause you so much trouble."

"Okay," Ollie said. "See you Saturday."

Your Turn

1. What might have happened if Ollie had tried to get revenge?
2. What would you have done in Ollie's situation?

_____

_____

_____

Prayer

God, it's not easy, but making peace is better than revenge. Amen.

Being Gentle Is Good

Let your gentleness be evident to all.
– Philippians 4:5

Turning the Tables

Danny grinned as they came out of the drugstore. He reached into his coat pocket and pulled out two chocolate bars. "How about a snack?"

"I didn't see you pay for them," Chris said.

"Five-finger discount," Danny said with a wink.

"You stole them?" Chris asked.

"Nah. They sort of fell into my pocket," Danny said. "Cool off." He unwrapped a candy bar. "Wait!" he yelled. "Where's my skateboard?" I left it right there. It's gone!" He ran up and down the sidewalk looking in every direction. "Some stinking thief stole my board! I can't believe it!"

"Cool off," Chris said. "Maybe it 'sort of fell into someone's pocket.' "

"It's my skateboard!" Danny yelled.

"I guess a five-finger discount isn't so cool," Chris said.

"This is different," Danny said.

"No, it's not," Chris said. "Whether it's a candy bar or a skateboard, whether you rip off a person or a store, stealing is still stealing."

Your Turn

1. Has anything of yours ever been stolen? If so, how did you feel?
2. What will you do if you're with a friend who steals something?

_____

_____

_____

_____

Prayer

God, I want to honor You by being honest always. Amen.

Being Gentle Is Good

Getting a Grip

Everyone needs help with self-control sometimes. Circle the areas where you would like to have more self-control in your life. Write some of your own ideas on the blanks.

GETTING ANGRY

SPENDING

GETTING
SCARED

SAYING DUMB
THINGS

TELLING LIES

EATING TOO
MUCH

The next time you find yourself doing something for which you'll be sorry, try out the **Four Secrets of Self-Control:**

- **Stop and think first!** Ask yourself if this is really what you want to do. How will it turn out? How will you feel about it tomorrow?

- **Plan ahead!** Before you get into hard situations, figure out ahead of time how you want to handle them. Make a plan and stick to it.

- **Ask God for help!** Say a quick prayer when you have trouble. Ask God to help you to decide and to do the right thing.

- **Don't give up!** It takes time to change the way you think and act. But you really can change if you keep trying and asking for God's help.

Being Gentle Is Good

Sticky Fingers

Stealing isn't funny, and it isn't right. God expects you to show respect for things that belong to other people. Follow the word wheel to find a message Paul sent to the church in Ephesus. Start with the circled letter on top of the wheel and read every others letter. Keep going around the circle until you return to the circled letter again.

Prayer

Heavenly Father, I know that stealing is wrong. If I'm tempted to take something that doesn't belong to me, please help me say no. Amen.

Following the Rules

Be obedient, always ready to do what is good.
– Titus 3:1 NLT

Pool Rules

Derek ignored the lifeguard's whistle as he ran beside the pool. After all, the lifeguard was his older brother, Keegan. With a cheery wave, Derek dove into the pool. When he came up, Keegan was waiting.

"What part of my whistle don't you understand?" Keegan asked him. "No running! No diving in this end!"

"You're not my boss, Mr. Big Man!"

"I am when you're in this pool," Keegan said.

Derek said, "You care more about the dumb rules than about me."

"I do care about you," Keegan said. "What if you slipped on the wet concrete or dove on top of somebody?"

"Big deal," Derek said.

"Last summer a kid dove in the shallow end and hit his head," Keegan said. "He'll be in a wheelchair for the rest of his life. Is that a big deal?"

"That's awful," Derek said in a small voice.

Keegan laid a hand on Derek's shoulder. "I want you to have fun but be safe."

Your Turn

1. If no one followed the rules, what would your life be like?
2. What rules do you need to work on following?

_____

_____

_____

_____

Prayer

Lord, help me follow Your rules so I will be safe and happy. Amen.

Following the Rules

Be obedient, always ready to do what is good.
– Titus 3:1 NLT

The Second Mistake

"I have some homework to do," Sam said as he stood.

"We need to talk to you first," his dad said.

Sam sat back down. His parents looked serious.

Mom laid a ticket stub on the table next to Sam's plate. "I found that in your pocket while I was doing laundry. It's a movie ticket stub for *Blood Party* last Friday."

Sam stared at the stub. He couldn't think of anything to say.

"Remember when I asked you on Saturday what movie you and your friends had gone to see?" Dad asked. "You lied to me, didn't you?"

"I'm sorry, Dad," Sam said. "The movie we wanted to see was sold out. I knew you wouldn't approve, but I went along with the crowd."

"What bothers us even more is that you lied about it," said Mom. "Why didn't you tell us what happened?"

"I thought you'd be mad," Sam said.

Dad said, "We wouldn't have been happy, true. But we would have understood."

"But you turned one mistake into two mistakes," Mom said.

"I'm really sorry," Sam said. "I should have told the truth."

Your Turn

1. Why is it important to tell your parents the truth?
2. Why is it important to tell God about your mistakes?

_____

_____

_____

Prayer

God, bad choices get worse when I try to cover them up. Amen.

Following the Rules

Be obedient, always ready to do what is good.
– Titus 3:1 NLT

In God's Strong Hand

Nathan walked into the hospital room and looked around. Grandpa was lying in a bed with blinking machines hanging on the wall overhead.

"Hey, Nate," Grandpa called. "Come here and give an old man a hug."

Nathan leaned over and hugged his grandfather. "Doing okay?"

"I feel fine," Grandpa said. "I'm having surgery tomorrow."

"I know," Nathan said. "Mom says it's dangerous. Are you scared?"

"No," Grandpa said, smiling. "I'm not scared even a little bit."

"I'm worried," Nathan said.

"Well, don't be," Grandpa said. "Jesus has been taking care of me my whole life, and He won't let me down now."

"So you'll be okay after the surgery?" Nathan asked.

Grandpa said, "I hope so. I'd like more summers to take you fishing. But all people die. If I die tomorrow, I've had a good life with a lot of blessings." Grandpa stuck out one hand, palm up. "God is holding me. Do you think He will accidentally drop me?"

"Never," Nathan said.

Your Turn

1. What makes you afraid?
2. What can you remember when you're afraid? What can you tell God?

_____

_____

_____

_____

Prayer

Jesus, when I'm afraid, remind me You are always in charge. Amen.

Following the Rules

Be obedient, always ready to do what is good.
– Titus 3:1 NLT

A House Made of Love

"Hi, Mom," Nathan said as his mother came into the house. "Where have you been?"

"I spent the afternoon at Grandpa's house," she said as she flopped wearily on the couch. "There are a lot of things to repair before we can sell the house."

Nathan's grandfather had died two days after surgery.

"I miss Grandpa," Nathan said.

"Me too," his mother said.

"Remember at Grandpa's funeral, the pastor said going to heaven is like moving into a beautiful new house? Do you think so?"

"Heaven is so wonderful that we don't have the words to describe it," Nathan's mother said. "But I guess it is a little like moving into a new house. Grandpa's old house has a leaky roof and rain gets into the basement. The furnace is old, and the house gets cold in the winter…"

"Now Grandpa's in a new house!" Nathan finished. He decided Grandpa must be very happy in heaven. A house made of love would be just right for him.

Your Turn

1. Do you believe in Jesus? Is He your LORD and Savior?
2. If you do, will heaven be your home someday?

_____

_____

_____

_____

Prayer

LORD, this world is wonderful, and You say heaven is better. Wow! Amen.

Following the Rules

Be obedient, always ready to do what is good.
– Titus 3:1 NLT

The Best Batter in the Neighborhood

Luis picked up a bat and swung it a few times. He shook his head, dropped the bat, and tried another.

"Come on! Come on!" yelled the pitcher. "Ya waitin' for Christmas?"

As Luis walked slowly toward home plate, he thought, *I had to be a big shot. Why did I tell them I'm a great batter?*

Earlier, when the captains were choosing players, Luis had yelled, "Hey! If you want some runs, pick me! I can knock the hide off that ball!" He was always saying that kind of stuff. He wanted to have friends, and he thought bragging would help people like him.

This is going to be awful, Luis thought as he planted his feet beside home plate. *I'm going to strike out. Why do I have to brag?* He missed the first pitch and fouled the second. On the third pitch, Luis slammed the ball, and it sailed into right field. The fielder fumbled the catch then overthrew second base. By the time the other team found the ball, Luis was home.

His captain gave Luis a high-five. "You really are a great batter!"

"I'm really not. I just got lucky."

The captain smiled. "Stick around after the game, and I'll give you some pointers if you'd like."

Your Turn

1. Why do you think Luis bragged a lot?
2. What makes you want to be friends with someone? What makes you a good friend?

_____

_____

Prayer

Lord, I want people to like me. Help me relax and be myself. Amen.

223

Following the Rules

Follow the Leaders

Jesus is the ultimate authority you should obey, but He gives you other leaders too. Your parents, teachers, and police, for example, help guide you in life and keep you safe. Jesus wants you to be obedient and respectful to them.

Fill in the blanks below to remember some of the leaders who watch over you each day. (The picture to the right shows something that person might use in his or her job.)

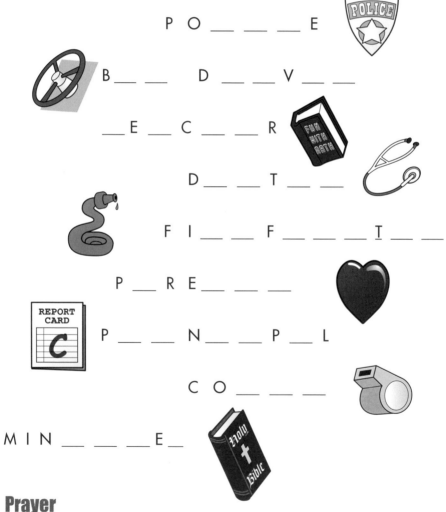

P O __ __ __ E

B __ __   D __ __ V __ __

__ E __ C __ __ R

D __ __ T __ __

F I __ __ F __ __ __ T __ __

P __ R E __ __ __

P __ __ N __ __ P __ L

C O __ __ __

M I N __ __ __ E __

Prayer

God, help me obey the leaders you have set in my life. Amen.

Following the Rules

The Best Place of All

Nobody is completely sure what heaven will be like, but you can trust God and know it will be a wonderful place. Nobody knows you better than God, so He knows just what you need to be happy forever. Even if you don't know everything about heaven, you can be pretty sure of some good things that will be there, and some bad things that definitely won't be there. Make an X through the things on this page that you believe will not be in heaven. Circle the things you believe will be there. When you are finished, draw a picture that shows how you feel about heaven.

death   love   hate

sickness

life   happiness   peace

fear

family   joy   health

pain

Jesus

beauty   music   laughter

Prayer

LORD, I don't know exactly what heaven will be like, but I believe it will be perfect because You are there! Amen.

Being Content

A heart at peace gives life to the body, but envy rots the bones.
– Proverbs 14:30

The Comic Book Collection

Rudy stared at his comic book collection. He had three boxes. Each book was sealed carefully in plastic to protect it. He used to bring friends to his room to show off his collection. He'd pull out special issues and tell how much each comic was worth. But not anymore. Not since he'd visited his cousin Garrett.

While on vacation, Rudy's family had spent the night with relatives. Rudy and Garrett were the same age and quickly became friends. Garrett invited his cousin to see his comic book collection.

What an incredible sight! Garrett had had gotten comics from his father, who collected when he was a boy. Some of Garrett's books were more than 40 years old. As Rudy carefully held *Spider Man #1* in his hands, Garrett had said, "Tell me about your collection." "It's not really a collection," Rudy had mumbled. "Just a few books I picked up."

Rudy had been back from vacation for over a month, but he couldn't stop thinking of the wonderful comics Garrett owned. Rudy's collection now seemed puny. He wished he'd never seen Garrett's collection.

Your Turn

1. Why is it so easy to envy what others have?
2. Are you content with what you have?

Prayer

God, help me be content with and appreciate what I have. Amen.

Being Content

A heart at peace gives life to the body, but envy rots the bones.
– Proverbs 14:30

The Vacant Lot

Ike's dad lifted the lawnmower out of the truck and set it on the sidewalk. The grass was high, and the vacant lot was scattered with fast-food cups and paper. Mr. Richards had hired Ike to mow the lot.

Ike's dad said, "Before you start the mower, walk the lot. Pick up the garbage and make sure there aren't hidden obstacles. You'll save time in the end."

As soon as his dad drove away, Ike started the mower. Picking up garbage was too slow. He pushed the mower through the tall grass. When he came to paper, he ran over it. He reached the end of the lot and turned to start back. He stopped abruptly. Paper had been cut into tiny bits and scattered everywhere. He groaned. *What a mess!*

He moved forward. There was a loud clunk and the mower died. He'd hit a brick buried in the tall grass. He threw it angrily onto the sidewalk. Ike pulled the cord on the mower, but it didn't start. He pulled and pulled until he was sweaty and out of breath.

Ike looked at the messy lot and the broken mower. *I should have listened to dad.*

Your Turn

1. When was the last time you didn't listen to advice? Were you sorry?
2. Why is it easy to insist on doing things your own way?

_____

_____

_____

Prayer

God, give me wisdom so I'll listen more. Maybe I'll learn something good. Amen.

Being Content

A heart at peace gives life to the body, but envy rots the bones.
– Proverbs 14:30

The Excuse

"I wish I hadn't watched TV last night," Ellis said to Norman as they entered their school. "I didn't get my science report done."

The boys stopped at their lockers and hung up their coats.

"I'll just have to come up with a good excuse," Ellis said. "Maybe I'll tell Mrs. Corrigan that our dog got hit by a car, and we had to take him to the vet last night. She'll probably give me more time, don't you think?"

"Maybe," Norman said. "She's a nice teacher."

"Yeah," Ellis agreed. "She's so nice she might call my parents to ask how the dog's doing." He hung his coat in the locker. "I know! I'll pretend that my computer crashed. Do you think that will fool her?"

"Ellis, why don't you just tell Mrs. Corrigan the truth?"

"I'll get in trouble," Ellis protested.

"You might get in more trouble for lying," Norman said. "Besides, won't you feel crummy telling a lie? That's a lousy way to treat Mrs. Corrigan."

When Ellis got to science class, he told Mrs. Corrigan that he didn't have his report. He asked if he could turn it in tomorrow.

"Do you have a good reason?" Mrs. Corrigan asked.

"No," Ellis said. "I just put it off too long."

Mrs. Corrigan nodded. "Bring it in tomorrow. I'll take off five points for being late, but if you do a good job you can still get an A."

Your Turn

1. Does lying solve problems or cause problems? Explain.

_____

_____

Prayer

God, everything You do and say is true. Help me be more like You. Amen.

Being Content

A heart at peace gives life to the body, but envy rots the bones.
– Proverbs 14:30

More Than Talk

My parents are mean, Enrique thought as he moved boxes. He wanted a dog, but his parents said he wasn't responsible. Enrique had promised, but his parents said he didn't work to make his plans happen. He'd promised to clean the garage, but it was still a mess. So, Enrique was out in the garage to prove his parents wrong.

Enrique peeked into a cardboard box and saw his in-line skates. In-line skating was harder than he'd expected. A dusty guitar leaned in the corner. Practicing made his fingers hurt. Next to the guitar was a dirty aquarium. When he'd realized how often he had to clean the aquarium, he gave the fish away.

Maybe he was better at talking than working. But he really wanted a dog. How could he prove he was ready? He studied the aquarium. It would take a lot of work to clean it and get it set up, but if he showed his parents he could take care of fish, they might let him have a dog. He picked it up and then stopped. *Maybe I'd better finish cleaning the garage first.*

Your Turn

1. Do you think Enrique will get a dog?
2. When have you had to work hard to make a plan work?

_____

_____

_____

_____

Prayer

God, help me remember to ask You to show me what plans to work on. Amen.

Being Content

A heart at peace gives life to the body, but envy rots the bones.
– Proverbs 14:30

Learning to Obey

"Heel," Judd said as Rex took off to chase a butterfly. "Rex, if you want a treat, you'd better get back here!"

When he heard the word "treat," Rex ran back to Judd.

"Heel!" Judd commanded.

Rex rose up on his hind legs and planted his front paws on Judd's chest. The dog licked Judd's face.

"I love you," Judd said, laughing, "but you're dumber than a rock."

Rex wagged his tail and bounded across the yard to sniff a molehill and explore. Eventually he trotted over and flopped down beside his master sitting on the grass.

Judd rubbed behind Rex's floppy ears. "I'm not just bossing you around. I'm trying to take care of you. If you'll obey me, we can take long walks. We can go to the lake so you can chase rabbits."

Rex looked at Judd.

"I'm not mad at you, Rex," Judd said. "I guess Jesus has the same problem trying to get me to obey. He's my LORD, and I don't always do what He tells me. When I obey Him, I get along fine. Jesus wants me to obey so I will be safe and happy."

Judd stood up. "Let's try it again, Rex."

Your Turn

1. Do you find it hard to obey?
2. How will talking to Jesus help you obey?

_____

_____

_____

Prayer

Jesus, Your help is what I need to live a safe and happy life. Amen.

Being Content

Wise Words for Wise People

The book of Proverbs is packed with pithy advise to help you live a great life. Some are funny, some are tough, some are hard to understand. Here are a few nuggets of wisdom.

Laziness: Lazy hands make for poverty, but diligent hands bring wealth. (Proverbs 10:4)

Kind Words: Gracious words are a honeycomb, sweet to the soul and healing to the bones. (Proverbs 16:24)

Stopping an Argument: A gentle answer turns away wrath, but a harsh word stirs up anger. (Proverbs 15:1)

Anger: For as churning cream produces butter, and as twisting the nose produces blood, so stirring up anger produces strife. (Proverbs 30:33)

Honesty: An honest answer is like a kiss on the lips. (Proverbs 24:26)

Neighbors: It is a sin to despise one's neighbor, but blessed is the one who is kind to the needy. (Proverbs 14:21)

Making Money: Dishonest money dwindles away, but he who gathers money little by little makes it grow. (Proverbs 13:11)

Here's one more proverb—and you get to decipher it.
Key: 1 stands for A, 2 stands for B, 11 stands for K, and so on.

1-16-16-12-25   25-15-21-18   8-5-1-18-20   20-15

_____

9-14-19-20-18-21-3-20-9-15-14   1-14-4   25-15-21-18

_____

5-1-18-19   20-15   23-15-18-4-19   15-6

_____

11-14-15-23-12-5-4-7-5.

_____

Prayer

LORD, help me understand Your wisdom in Your Word. Amen.

Being Content

What Would You Do?

In John 9 there is a story about Jesus meeting a blind man. Use your imagination to put yourself in the story. In your mind, picture each part of the story. Think about the questions and what you would have done if you were the blind man.

One day, Jesus and the disciples came upon a man who had been blind since birth. In his whole life he had never seen a bird or a star. Jesus wanted to help this man, so He spit on the ground, made some mud, and rubbed it on the man's eyes.

- Would you let Jesus rub spit and mud on your eyes?
- Would you wonder why He didn't heal you on the spot?
- Would you trust Him even if you didn't understand Him?

Jesus told the man to go to the Pool of Siloam and wash the mud from his eyes.

- Why would Jesus want you to walk to a specific pool to get your sight back?
- Would you have gone all the way to the pool?

The blind man got up and headed to the Pool of Siloam. He probably felt silly with mud caked on his eyes. Maybe the people in the crowd were laughing at him and making jokes as he walked along.

- Would you have changed your mind halfway to the pool?
- Would you have been so embarrassed that you rubbed the mud off your face and went back to begging?

When the man got to the pool, he splashed water on his face and washed away the mud. When he opened his eyes, he could see for the first time!

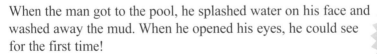

**How would you react if you were blind
and Jesus healed you?**

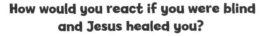

Prayer

Dear God, help me to trust You and do what You say, even when I don't understand. You want what's best for me. Amen.

Jesus—Your Lord and Savior

[Jesus said,] "I am the gate; whoever enters through me will be saved."
– John 10:9

The One and Only

"Remember that story on TV about firefighters who helped people get out of the burning building in New York?" Harley asked.

"Yep," Drew said. "Those firefighters were real heroes."

"Here's what I'm wondering," Harley said. "Were the firefighters saviors to those people?"

"I guess so," Drew said. "They did save them."

"Right," said Harley. "Firefighters save people all the time. So do cops, and doctors, and lifeguards. How is Jesus different from them?"

"That's easy," Drew told his friend. "Jesus is the only One who saves people for all time."

"What does that mean?"

"Let's say there's a guy named Joe," Drew said. "A doctor saves Joe after a heart attack. What happens to Joe?"

"I guess he goes on living."

"How long?" Drew asked.

"Let's say 50 more years."

"Then what?"

"Then Joe dies."

"Right," said Drew. "So the doctor saved Joe for a time—not for all time. Only Jesus can give Joe eternal life."

"I get it!" Harley said. "People can save each other for a while, but Jesus can save us so we'll live with Him forever."

Your Turn

1. Have you trusted Jesus to save you forever?
2. If you haven't, take time today to ask Him to be your Savior forever!

Prayer

Jesus, You're my biggest hero. I love You. Amen.

Jesus—Your Lord and Savior

[Jesus said,] "I am the gate; whoever enters through me will be saved."
— **John 10:9**

The Lost Lamb

"Did you hear that?" Uncle Clark asked. He turned off the engine.
Bruce listened through the open window of the truck. He loved visiting his uncle's sheep ranch. Somewhere a dog was barking.

"Over there in those rocks," Uncle Clark said, getting out of the truck.

Some of the boulders were as large as the truck. They were jumbled together, and thorny bushes grew between them. Uncle Clark and Bruce walked around the rocks quietly. A soft "baaa" came from somewhere in the brush.

"Sounds like a lamb," Uncle Clark said quietly. He got down on his hands and knees and squeezed between the boulders. In a few minutes he came out with a black-and-white lamb. He pulled thorns from its wool and checked it over. "No harm done."

"But what about you?" Bruce asked. He saw bloody scratches on his uncle's arms where the thorns had stabbed him.

"Goes with the job," Uncle Clark said. "I'm a shepherd, and I take care of my sheep. Now, let's get this lamb back to the flock." He got behind the wheel, and Bruce rode with the lamb on his lap.

The lamb was peaceful. Bruce scratched the wool between its ears. "You're a lucky guy to have such a good shepherd."

Your Turn

1. Jesus is your good Shepherd. What does that mean to you?
2. What are ways Jesus takes care of you?

_____

_____

Prayer

Jesus, thanks for keeping a close eye on me. I'm glad You never forget. Amen.

Jesus—Your Lord and Savior

[Jesus said,] "I am the gate; whoever enters through me will be saved."
– John 10:9

A Loaf of Love

John sniffed the air. He followed the warm, sweet scent into the kitchen. "It smells good when you make bread, Mom."

Mrs. Grey said, "When I was growing up, my mother taught me to make bread, and her mother taught her. Someday, I'll teach you."

"How long have people been making bread?" John asked.

"A long, long time," Mrs. Grey said. "I'm sure Jesus grew up eating His mother's homemade bread."

"I like bologna on my bread," John said. "Did Jesus eat sandwiches?"

Mrs. Grey laughed. "No, but bread was part of the meal. People would eat a little cheese or a piece of fish on the side, maybe a few figs and olives." She took a long, golden loaf of bread from the oven and shook it gently from the pan. "That's why Jesus said, 'I am the bread of life.' He is the most important thing in life. Nothing matters more than Him. He gives us true life."

Mrs. Grey cut two fat slices from the steaming loaf and laid them on a plate. "Do you want honey or jam?" she asked.

"Neither," said John. "Your bread is good enough all by itself."

Your Turn

1. Food gives you health and life. What does Jesus give you?

_____

_____

_____

_____

Prayer

God, thank You for food. Thank You even more for Jesus. Amen.

Jesus—Your Lord and Savior

[Jesus said,] "I am the gate; whoever enters through me will be saved."
– John 10:9

An Open and Shut Case

Jorge and his father lifted the front gate from the hinges and laid it carefully on the picnic table. Jorge's father brushed on white paint in long strokes. "When we finish," he said, "we'll let it dry for a couple of hours. We'll hang the gate before we go to bed."

Jorge said, "That's good. I feel safer when the gate is closed."

"Sure," his father agreed. "A gate has two jobs. One job is to protect us by keeping robbers outside. The other one is to let people in. You don't expect your friends to jump over the fence, do you?"

Jorge laughed. "Here, let me take a turn," he said. He spread white paint evenly over the wood. "Jesus called Himself a gate. I didn't understand that before, but I get it now. Jesus is like a closed gate keeping bad things from happening and an open gate letting God's love into my life."

"Yep!" agreed Mr. Ayala. He studied the gate. "Good job! I bet you don't know what painters do while they wait for paint to dry."

Jorge shook his head.

"We sit under a tree and drink lemonade."

Your Turn

1. What good things have come into your life because of Jesus?
2. What can you tell your friends about Jesus?

_____

_____

_____

_____

Prayer

Jesus, You are a strong gate to protect me. You are my gate to blessings. Amen.

Jesus—Your Lord and Savior

[Jesus said,] "I am the gate; whoever enters through me will be saved."
– **John 10:9**

The Darkest Dark

"When I turn out the lights, you might be frightened," said the park ranger.

Kyle's family was touring a cave in a national park. Hidden electrical lights made the cave beautiful and helped the tourists stay on the path. Now they were going to experience the cave without lights.

"Oooooooh," Kyle moaned to his little brother. "Try not to cry in the spooky, creepy dark."

When the ranger flipped the light switch, Kyle caught his breath. The darkness was so deep it swallowed everything. Kyle knew his family was only inches away, but he couldn't see anything! When the ranger spoke, Kyle couldn't tell where he was.

"Without the light," the ranger said, "we'd be lost in here until someone came to save us." The lights came back on. Bryan whispered to Kyle, "That really was a little scary."

"Yes," Kyle agreed. "It made me think of Jesus. The world was lost in the dark until Jesus came to light our way to God."

Your Turn

1. Have you been scared in the dark?
2. How does Jesus help you see light and dark in a new way?

_____

_____

_____

_____

Prayer

Jesus, thank You for giving us light so that we can know God through You. Amen.

Jesus—Your Lord and Savior

No Other Savior

Do you sometimes forget that Jesus is the only One who can truly save your soul? Here's a fun trick to remind your friends and you that Jesus is your light. You'll need a regular sheet of paper and a pair of scissors.

Here's a way to make a reminder for you and your friends.
You'll need a piece of paper and a pair of scissors for this paper trick.

1. Fold down the top left corner of your paper.

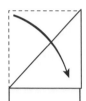

2. Then fold down the top right corner.

3. Fold the left side over the right side.

4. Cut the paper as shown and throw away the part on the right.

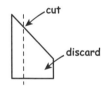

5. Open up the folded part and you will find a reminder of the Savior!

Prayer

Jesus, I am so thankful that God sent You to be the Savior of the world—including me. Amen.

Jesus—Your LORD and Savior

First Things First

There are many things you need in life. Look at the list below and decide what things are most important to you. Put a #1 beside the thing you need most in life, then a #2 beside the second most important thing. Work through the whole list. When you finish, ask someone else to give his or her own answers on the same list. Compare your answers. Did you agree on everything? Did you agree on what comes first?

Friends ____

Clothes ____

Home ____

Healthcare ____

Education ____

Jesus ____

Air ____

Food ____

Money ____

Water ____

Bicycle ____

Prayer

Jesus, with You as my LORD and Savior, I am content. Amen.

Getting to Know God

[Jesus said,] "I am the vine; you are the branches. If you remain in me and I in you, you will bear much fruit."

– John 15:5

Keeping Connected

Kevin Walker stood at the back door holding a long, broken branch.

His mother frowned at the leafy branch that held several clusters of tiny, green grapes. "What happened?"

"Ruff and I were chasing the ball around and we crashed into the grapes," Kevin said apologetically. "I guess this branch broke off."

"You didn't hurt yourself, did you?" Mrs. Parker asked.

"No, we're fine," Kevin said. "Can we do anything with this branch? Is there any way to keep it alive so the grapes can ripen?"

Mrs. Parker looked at her son thoughtfully. "Do you remember what Jesus said about grapevines?"

"Didn't He say He is the vine and we believers are His branches?"

"That's right," Mrs. Walker said. "As long as we stick to Christ, He'll fill us with His life. But if we break away, we'll shrivel up."

Kevin looked at the branch in his hand. Already, the leaves were drooping. "So what do I do with this branch?"

"Throw it on the fire pile," his mother said. "That branch has no life of its own. We'll get our grapes from the branches that hang on the living vines."

Your Turn

1. Did Kevin do the right thing by confessing he'd broken the branch?
2. Jesus said you will bear fruit if you stick to Him. What fruit?

_____

_____

_____

Prayer

Jesus, You're the vine and I am Your branch. Amen.

Getting to Know God

[Jesus said,] "I am the vine; you are the branches. If you remain in me and I in you, you will bear much fruit."

– John 15:5

The Long Shortcut

Barry and Lyle could hardly wait to get to the cool, country stream and the swimming hole their uncle had told them about. They were wearing old shorts so they could leap into the deep pool. Uncle Ollie said, "Stay on the path so you'll find it."

Barry mopped sweat from his face. "I'll bet there's a shorter way. The trail curves left up ahead. We can cut through the woods."

"I don't know," Lyle said. "Uncle Ollie said to follow the path."

"Come on!" Barry urged, pushing through the bushes. "How hard can it be? All we have to do is head downhill and listen for water."

Two hours later, Barry and Lyle still hadn't reached the swimming hole. Barry flopped down in some green vines and looked at the briar scratches on his legs. "I guess we're lost."

"And it's getting late," Lyle added. "We're going to have to go back the way we came and hope we can get back to the farm before dark."

"Back through those blackberry bushes?" Barry moaned. "If only we'd stayed on the path. I'm hot and tired and bleeding. Could this get any worse?"

"You'll find out," Lyle said. "You're sitting in poison ivy."

Your Turn

1. Have you ever gotten lost? How did you find your way back?
2. Think of a time you didn't follow Jesus. What happened?
   How did you feel?

_____

_____

_____

Prayer

Jesus, help me follow wherever You lead. Amen.

Getting to Know God

[Jesus said,] "I am the vine; you are the branches. If you remain in me and I in you, you will bear much fruit."
– John 15:5

Extra Groceries

Jamal looked up and down the aisles of the supermarket until he found his mother pushing her cart. He dropped a can of tuna into the cart.

"You don't like tuna," his mother said.

"No, I don't," Jamal admitted. "I'd still like to buy it. I'll pay you for it when we get home."

"You don't have to pay for groceries," Jamal's mother said. "Just tell me why you want to take home a can of tuna."

"I don't want to take it home," Jamal said. "I want to leave it here. We'll put it in the big box by the front door—the box where they collect food for people."

"You want to help hungry people?"

Jamal nodded. "I used to think hungry people lived in other countries," Jamal said. "But I found out there are people here who don't have enough to eat. The food collected by the supermarket helps people who live nearby. Jesus fed hungry people!"

"Yes, He did," Jamal's mother said. "Here's what we'll do. You can pay me for this can of tuna when we get home. Now you can get three more cans. I'll pay for those. We'll leave all four in the box for the hungry."

Your Turn

1. Can you think of any way you can feed hungry people?
2. What else can you do to help people?

_____

_____

Prayer

Jesus, show me how to share with people who don't have enough. Amen.

Getting to Know God

[Jesus said,] "I am the vine; you are the branches. If you remain in me and I in you, you will bear much fruit."
– John 15:5

Touching Lepers

"What's a leper?" Chris asked. "Isn't that an animal?"

"You're thinking of a leopard," his brother Adam told him. "A leper is someone who has leprosy. Leprosy is a skin disease."

"Like zits?" Chris asked.

"Leprosy is a zillion times worse," Adam explained. "Lepers get terrible sores. Sometimes their fingers and toes fall off. Their skin sort of rots."

"Gross," Chris said. "I just read a story about Jesus healing a leper."

"Back in Bible times, it was awful for lepers," Adam said. "People were afraid of catching the disease. A person with leprosy couldn't stay with his family. He had to live with other lepers outside of town."

"They must have been lonely and sad," Chris said.

"Yes," Adam agreed. "If they went into town, people might throw rocks at them to drive them off. Nobody was supposed to touch a leper."

"Jesus did," Chris said. "He touched the leper and made him well."

"Jesus loves people, even those nobody else wants to have around," Adam said. "Jesus helped the blind, the crippled, the deaf, and the mute."

"And lepers too," Chris said. "Don't forget the lepers."

Your Turn

1. When you get sick, what do you want most?
2. What can you ask Jesus when you are sick?

_____

_____

_____

Prayer

Jesus, thanks for being a friend to the sick and hurting. Amen.

Getting to Know God

[Jesus said,] "I am the vine; you are the branches. If you remain in me and I in you, you will bear much fruit."
– John 15:5

Make Room for the Kids

Dennis ran into the Sunday-school room. He opened his Bible and laid it on the table. "I found a great story! You gotta hear it!"

Mr. Kord, the teacher, smiled. "Tell us the story before you burst."

"Okay," Dennis said, rubbing his hands together. "Jesus is out one day teaching. There are whole families there—kids and everybody. They're all listening. And then I guess Jesus takes a break or something." Dennis looked at his Bible before he went on. "So some of the kids want to see Jesus. Their parents want them to meet Him and be blessed by him. But the disciples are hanging around acting like bodyguards. They're like, 'Hey, get those kids out of here!' "

Everybody laughed. They were enjoying the story.

"No, really," Dennis said. "The disciples are like, 'We're big stuff, and we can hang with the Master, but those kids are just a waste of time.' "

"Now here's the best part," Dennis said. "Jesus sees what's going on. You know, how the disciples are pushing the kids to the back of the line. Jesus says, 'Don't run those kids off! Bring them to me. Kids are exactly the kind of people God cares about!' "

Your Turn

1. How do you feel knowing you're important to Jesus?
2. Do you know kids Jesus would like to meet?

_____

_____

_____

Prayer

Jesus, You always have time for me. Thanks for loving kids! Amen.

Getting to Know God

Finding Your Way

Life has many twists and turns, but as long as you follow Jesus, you'll always be on the right path. Need some practice following Him? Try the maze below! You'll always make the right turn as long as you follow J-E-S-U-S.

Prayer

Jesus, I want to follow You all the days of my life. Your ways are perfect. Amen.

Getting to Know God

Adults Only?

You might think the stories in the Bible are all about grown-ups. No way!
There are plenty of kids who served God. How many of these kids do you
know? Match the kid on the left with what he or she did on the right. Look
up the Bible passages if you need help.

Boy with a sack lunch (John 6:1-11)	**Sang praises to Jesus**
David (1 Samuel 17:41-49)	**Helped feed 5,000 people**
Jesus (Luke 2:41-47)	**Guarded her little brother on the river**
Samuel (1 Samuel 3:2-9)	**Became king when seven years old**
Miriam (Exodus 2:1-4)	**Heard God's voice in the night**
Joash (2 Kings 11:21)	**Talked with the wise men in the temple**
Children of Jerusalem (Matthew 21:15)	**He killed a giant**

Prayer

Jesus, I'm so glad You love kids! Amen.

Jesus Is Lord of All

*[Jesus says,] "I am the Alpha and the Omega, the
First and the Last, the Beginning and the End."*
— **Revelation 22:13**

Jesus Has It All

As Jimmy and Duncan entered the mall, they noticed the sign over the entrance: "From A to Z—This Mall Has It All!"

"That's so bogus," Jimmy said. "There's stuff you can't get at this mall."

"No joke." Duncan laughed. "You mean they don't sell kangaroos here?"

"Well, they shouldn't say it if it's not true," Jimmy argued.

"Come on, Jimmy," Duncan said. "Nobody could really have everything."

"Jesus does!" Jimmy said. "He said, 'I am the alpha and the omega.' That means He's everything from A to Z."

"What does that mean?" Duncan asked.

"Jesus is LORD over the whole world. There's nothing He can't help us with. He will give us everything we need if we ask Him."

"Jesus will give me a kangaroo if I ask for one?" Duncan asked.

"Sure, Jesus could give you a kangaroo," Jimmy said. "Except you don't really need a kangaroo. Your family lives in an apartment. You don't have a pasture. If Jesus gave you a kangaroo, it would be bad for you and worse for the kangaroo."

"Never mind the kangaroo," Duncan said. "Let's paint a sign over the church door: From A to Z—Jesus Has It All!"

Your Turn

1. Does Jesus care about stuff that's not religious? Why or why not?

_____

_____

Prayer

Jesus, nothing's too big or too hard for You. Zilch! Zero! Amen.

Jesus Is Lord of All

[Jesus says,] "I am the Alpha and the Omega, the
First and the Last, the Beginning and the End."
– Revelation 22:13

A Message in the Sky

The campfire had burned to a heap of coals when Counselor Dean said, "Time for our Bible study. Who has their Bibles with them?"

Randy raised his hand, along with a couple of other boys.

"But it's too dark to read," Randy said. "Do you want me to throw some more wood on the fire?"

"No," said Dean. "Just look up and tell me what you see."

The boys tilted back their heads.

"All I see is the sky and a bunch of stars," Randy said.

Woody nodded. "I don't see anything about God written up there."

Dean said, "Are you sure?" From memory, he recited Psalm 19:1: 'The heavens declare the glory of God; the skies proclaim the work of his hands.' " Then he asked, "If you heard a really great song on the radio, would you want to know who recorded it? And if you saw a beautiful picture, you'd probably want to find out who painted it. Great songs and paintings don't just happen by accident. Somebody has to make them. When you see the stars spreading across the sky, you wonder who made all of it," Dean said. "The stars talk about God without using words."

"What do they say about God?" Randy asked.

Dean answered, "The stars say, 'An awesome God made all of this!' "

Your Turn

1. What things in nature make you think of God?
2. Look around at what God made. What is the most amazing thing you see?

_____

_____

Prayer

God, I'm amazed at all You've made. Awesome! Amen.

Jesus Is Lord of All

[Jesus says,] "I am the Alpha and the Omega, the First and the Last, the Beginning and the End."
– Revelation 22:13

The Big Boss

"What's the brightest thing in the sky tonight?" asked Counselor Dean.

"The moon," Randy said, along with several other boys.

"Right," said Dean, "and the moon circles around the earth. What would happen if the moon got too close to the earth?"

"It might crash into us?" Randy guessed.

"Right," Dean said. "What would happen if the moon got too far away?"

"It would break loose and fly into space," Gerald guessed.

"Right again," Dean said. "The moon circles the earth, and the earth circles the sun. What would happen if the earth got too close to the sun?"

"We'd all burn up," said Gerald, "or if it was too far away, we'd freeze."

Dean said, "Now, find the second brightest thing in the sky."

After a few minutes, Randy pointed. "I think it's that star."

"That's the planet Venus," Dean said. "It circles the sun too. Most of those planets have moons traveling around them. Who is in charge of keeping all those worlds in place?"

"God!" yelled several boys at once.

"Yes!" Dean said. "Now, if God can handle all the stars and the planets, then He can surely handle anything you need."

Your Turn

1. Is God too busy taking care of the stars to watch over you?

_____

_____

_____

Prayer

God, I love the way You keep everything working. Amen.

Jesus Is Lord of All

*[Jesus says,] "I am the Alpha and the Omega, the
First and the Last, the Beginning and the End."*
– Revelation 22:13

Naming the Stars

"Bible-study time," announced Counselor Dean.

The boys in Cabin 8 rushed outside and plopped down on the grass.

"Let's count the stars tonight," suggested Woody.

"That might take a while," Dean said. "There are billions of stars. Did you know that God knows exactly how many stars there are? In fact, He calls each star by name."

"God gave names to all the stars?" Woody asked. "Why?"

"I think you can figure that out," Dean said. "Remember the minnows we saw in the lake today? Did you give names to them?"

"No," Woody said.

"What about your pets?" Dean asked. "Do they have names?"

"Sure," said Woody. "My dog is named Bailey and my cat is Gracie."

"I have a rabbit named Tools," Randy said.

"Randy, why did you name your pet rabbit, but not the rabbit you saw in the meadow today?" Counselor Dean asked.

Randy said, "I love my rabbit. I guess we name the things we love."

"That's right," Dean said. "So why did God name the stars?"

"Because God loves the stars," Woody said.

"Billions of stars," said Dean, "and God loves every one of them."

Your Turn

1. Every person has a name, too. How do you think God feels about each person?
2. How does God feel about you?

_____

_____

_____

Prayer

God, Your love is so big I can't imagine it—but I can sure feel it! Amen.

Jesus Is Lord of All

[Jesus says,] "I am the Alpha and the Omega, the
First and the Last, the Beginning and the End."
– Revelation 22:13

Rainy-Day God

"I'm tired of sitting in this cabin," Griffin said. "If God loves us so much, why did He send the rain to mess up this day?"

"The rain proves God loves us," Counselor Dean said. "Everybody get your rain gear on. We're taking a hike."

The boys followed Dean through the dripping woods and to the top of a grassy hill. They could see farms in the distance.

"Wet grass," Griffin said with a dull voice. "I'm impressed."

"Open your eyes," Dean said. "Something important is happening."

The boys gazed around the meadow then shrugged.

"The grass is growing!" Dean exclaimed.

"Big duh," Griffin said.

"God is saving the world right now," Dean said. "Without the rain, the grass would die. Without the grass, the mice and insects who live here would die, and then the birds who feed on them."

Dean pointed to cattle grazing in distant fields. "No grass, no cows. No cows means no hamburgers, no ice cream, no milk on cereal." He held out his hands to feel the rain on his palms. "Without rain the world ends. It's that simple. Every raindrop is a reminder that God is taking care of us."

Your Turn

1. Besides rain, how else does God take care of living things?
2. How does God take care of you?

_____

_____

Prayer

God, I love You whether the sun is shining or the rain is falling. Amen.

Jesus Is LORD of All

Awesome, Fantabulous, Amazing God!

God is awesome! God is incredible! God is… well, you understand. What words do you use to describe your glorious God? Help the stars declare God's glory. Fill in the blanks with words that tell how super God is. If you run out of blanks before you run out of words, draw more stars!

Prayer

God, when I look around and see Your beautiful creation, I realize again and again just how awesome You are. Amen.

Jesus Is Lord of All

A Whole Lotta Love

God loves everything in creation—and that includes you. If God had a refrigerator, your picture would be stuck up there with a magnet. If God had a wallet, your photograph would be in there. Is that hard for you to believe? Here are some Bible verses to convince you. Write your name in each blank. How great does this make you feel?

Then God said, "Let us make _____ in our image, in our likeness" (Genesis 1:26).

When I consider your heavens, the work of your fingers, the moon and the stars, which you have set in place, what is man that you are mindful of him, the son of man that you care for him? You made _____ a little lower than the heavenly beings and crowned _____ with glory and honor (Psalm 8:3-5).

_____ will call upon me, and I will answer him; I will be with _____ in trouble, I will deliver _____ and honor _____ (Psalm 91:15).

Who shall separate _____ from the love of Christ? Shall trouble or hardship or persecution or famine or nakedness or danger or sword? No, in all these things we are more than conquerors through him who loved us. For I am convinced that neither death nor life, neither angels nor demons, neither the present nor the future, nor any powers, neither height nor depth, nor anything else in all creation, will be able to separate _____ from the love of God that is in Christ Jesus our LORD (Romans 8:35, 37-39).

Do you not know that _____ is a temple of the Holy Spirit? (1 Corinthians 6:19)

Prayer

LORD, I'm glad nothing can separate me from Your love. Amen.

God Is Stronger

Praise [the Lord], sun and moon; praise him, all you shining stars.
– Psalm 148:3

Thunder and Lightning

Counselor Dean and the boys from Cabin 8 and watched the falling rain. Thunder rumbled and a jagged bolt of lightning tore across the sky. Thunder boomed again.

Dean rubbed his hands together in delight. "I love storms! Think about all that power in the sky." Lightning flickered miles away.

"I took a college class where we studied the weather," Dean said. "There are probably 4000 thunderstorms scattered around the world. Now count to ten slowly. In that ten seconds, about 1000 bolts of lightning burned across the sky. Who's good at math? Can you figure out how many bolts of lightning will happen today?"

Randy tried to multiply the numbers in his head, but he got lost.

Woody said, "That's more than 8 million lightning bolts!"

"Right. And one lightning bolt has enough energy to power a large city for a year."

Lightning struck closer, and thunder made the ground shake. "Okay, it's time to head for the cabin," Dean said.

"God sure is powerful," Randy said.

Your Turn

1. Name three times when God helped you.
2. What makes you aware of how powerful God is?

Prayer

God, You are awesome, mighty, and powerful! Amen.

God Is Stronger

Praise [the LORD], sun and moon; praise him, all you shining stars.
– Psalm 148:3

The World's Biggest Ribbon

"The rain has finally stopped!" Randy said to his friends in Cabin 8.

The campers tumbled out of the cabin, and Counselor Dean followed.

"Yea!" Gerald shouted. "That sunshine feels good!"

"Look," Woody said, "there's a rainbow."

"I know the story of the rainbow," Randy said. "At the end of the big flood, after Noah got off the ark, God put a rainbow in the sky."

"Do you know why?" Dean asked.

"Not exactly," Randy said.

"The rainbow is a reminder of God's promise to never again let a flood destroy the earth. That's what it says in Genesis 9."

"God made that promise to people and to all the animals. That's interesting," Woody said.

"So no matter how much it rains, we know God won't allow all life to drown on our planet," Gerald said.

"God is mighty in power. Let's not forget He is mighty in love," Dean said.

Your Turn

1. What would happen to life on Earth if God stopped caring?
2. What would happen if people stopped caring for the earth?

_____

_____

_____

_____

Prayer

God, thank You for always keeping Your promises. Amen.

God Is Stronger

Praise [the LORD], sun and moon; praise him, all you shining stars.
– Psalm 148:3

Sunrise, Sunset

Counselor Dean and the campers from Cabin 8 sat beside the lake watching the sun sink low in the sky. The red-and-orange sky reflected in the water, and a gentle breeze rippled the surface of the lake. A flock of geese landed on the lake, honking and splashing.

"When I see a beautiful sight like that," Dean said, "I praise God."

"I feel a little sad," Randy said. "I love camp, and another day is ending."

"Don't forget that another day is beginning too," Dean said. "The earth is a big ball turning in space," Dean said. "When the sun is going down here, it's coming up on the other side of the world."

"So, when we're saying our bedtime prayers tonight," Woody said, "somebody is saying their morning prayers."

"Awesome!" Griffin said. "That means God is worshipped 24/7!"

"Like a relay race," Randy said. "We all take turns praising God."

"That's exactly how it should be," Dean said. "Our God is so incredible that praising Him should never stop."

"That's why the Bible says we should praise God from the rising of the sun to the setting of the sun," Randy said.

Your Turn

1. Write down three wonderful things about God.
2. How often do you praise God?

_____

_____

_____

Prayer

God, I will praise You forever! Amen.

God Is Stronger

Praise [the LORD], sun and moon; praise him, all you shining stars.
— **Psalm 148:3**

Stars and Crickets

"How high is the sky?" Counselor Dean asked. Dean and the boys in Cabin 8 were on a night hike, moving along the path without flashlights. The tree branches were narrow at the top, and the starry sky was spread above them.

"The stars are millions and millions of miles away," Randy said, "so the sky must be even higher than that."

"Good thinking," Dean said. "Now tell me, what's higher than the sky?"

"The answer must be God," Griffin said.

Dean said. "The Bible teaches that God is the highest of all. He is lifted above the sky. The sun, moon, and stars praise Him."

"How do stars praise God?" Griffin asked. "Do stars sing?"

"Singing is one way to praise God," Dean said. "A star praises God by shining and following the right path through the sky."

"I don't get it," Woody said.

"Hear those crickets?" Dean said. "They rub their legs to make music in the night. That's how God made them. When crickets do what God made them for, they are praising God. When we do what God made us to do, then He is praised. He is praised."

"What did God create us to do?" asked Griffin.

"Think about that," said Dean. "We'll talk about it tomorrow night."

Your Turn

1. Think of one thing you can do today that gives praise to God.
2. Why do you think God created you?

Prayer

God, today I'm going to be the best me I can be in praise of You! Amen.

God Is Stronger

Praise [the LORD], sun and moon; praise him, all you shining stars.
– Psalm 148:3

The Simple Answer

The campers from Cabin 8 lay on their backs studying the stars. The night was noisy with crickets and frogs. An owl hooted nearby.

"So, have you guys figured out what God made us for?" Counselor Dean asked. "What does God want us to do with our lives?"

"We're here to make lots of money," Griffin said, and everybody laughed.

Randy said, "God put us here to watch television." There was more laughter.

"We're here to eat!" Woody said.

"No," Dean said, chuckling. "I think your purpose is to drive me crazy, and you're doing a great job!"

After the laughing stopped, Dean said, "Of all the things God does, the one thing He does best is love. The Bible says God's love is higher than the sky. God put us here," Dean said, "so He could love us and we could love Him and each other. The more we love, the more we become who God meant us to be. And the more we do that, the more we praise God."

"That's simple," Griffin said.

"Love is simple," Dean said, "but it's not always easy."

Your Turn

1. What does love mean to you?
2. Who do you love?

_____

_____

_____

Prayer

God, some people think love is mushy, but Your love is the strongest thing of all. Let me love like You do. Amen.

God Is Stronger

Hallelujah!

People all over the world are praising God right now, so they must be praising in many languages. Do you realize you already know how to say "Praise the LORD" in Hebrew? It's "Hallelujah"!

Here's your chance to learn some new ways to say "Praise the Lord." Read these aloud and see how they feel on your tongue. (The second lines help you pronounce the words.) If you have a globe or an atlas, find each country and point to it as you speak its language.

Holland (Dutch): Prijs de here! (prayz deh heer)

France (French): Louez l'eternel! (LOO-ay lay-ter-NEL)

Mexico (Spanish): ¡Alabado sea el señor!(ah-la-BAH-tho SAY-ah el say-NYOR)

Romania (Romanian): Laudati pe domnul! (LAW-dah-tee pay DOME-nool)

Germany (German): Lobt den herrn! (lohbt den hairn)

Haiti (Creole): Lwanj pou seyè a! (l'wahj poo SAY-yay ah)

Greece (Greek): ainete ton kurion (high-NAY-tay tahn KOO-ree-ahn)

USA (English): Praise the LORD!

Prayer

God, I am glad I get to praise You forever. You are a mighty and wonderful God. Amen.

God Is Stronger

The New Commandment

On His last night with the disciples before He was crucified, Jesus gave them a new commandment to follow forever. What was this new commandment? Decipher the code and find out!

! = A	@ = C	# = D	$ = E
% = H	^ = I	& = L	* = O
+ = R	< = S	> = T	? = U
[= V	] = Y		

———————————
& * [$

———————————
$! @ %

———————————
* > % $ +

———————————
! < I

———————————
% ! [$

———————————
& * [$ #

———————————
] * ?

Prayer

LORD, I know You told us that the greatest thing we can do is love You and love others. That's what I want to do. Amen.

God Loves and Creates

The whole earth is full of [the LORD's] glory.
– Isaiah 6:3

Pictures in the Sky

"See those three bright stars in a line?" Counselor Dean asked the campers from Cabin 8. "Those make Orion's belt."

Randy said, "I see them! And there's his arm and his bow."

"Close to Orion the Hunter is his faithful dog," Dean said. "Do you see the Dog Star?"

"I don't see a thing," said Griffin, "except a bunch of scattered stars."

"Let's try another one," Dean said. "Who can find the Little Dipper?"

"That's easy," Woody said as he pointed. "There it is."

"Good," Dean said. "And those two bright stars on the cup of the Dipper point straight to the North Star."

"I can't see the Dipper," Griffin complained. "The stars all look alike."

"Did God really put pictures in the sky?" asked Randy.

"Maybe God put so many stars in the sky so we could enjoy looking for pictures," Dean said. "After all, God didn't have to make the world so beautiful. He could have gotten by with just ten or fifteen stars, right?"

"I'd be able to find actual pictures," Griffin said.

"God made the world beautiful so we'd enjoy living here," Dean said. "What if God hadn't invented kangaroos? Or colors? Or fireflies? The world wouldn't be nearly as much fun."

Your Turn

1. This week, what reminded you of God's wonderful creativity?
2. Name three things you consider beautiful.

_____

_____

_____

Prayer

God, thanks for the wonderful things You created. Amen.

God Loves and Creates

The whole earth is full of [the LORD's] glory.
– Isaiah 6:3

Look Up, Look Down

The group from Cabin 8 had hiked to the hilltop after dark for stargazing. This was their last night of camp. Tomorrow they'd be returning to their homes. Everyone felt sad knowing their week together was ending.

"I'll miss our night-sky Bible lessons," Randy said.

"Me too," Woody said. "I've learned a lot about God and the sky."

"When I look at the stars, I'm going to think of God now," said Griffin.

"That's great," Counselor Dean said. "But you can look anyplace to see God's work. What reminds you of God?"

After a few minutes, Randy said, "There's an oak tree that shades our whole backyard. Maybe that's a reminder of God watching over us."

"I miss my dog," Griffin said. "Boomer's always glad to see me. He loves me no matter what. That's how God loves me. Does He mind being compared to Boomer?"

"I don't think God minds at all," Dean said. "Dogs were God's idea."

Woody said, "I have a neighbor, Mr. Tyler, who is always doing something nice for somebody. He helped me get an 'A' on my science project. When I see Mr. Tyler's smile, I think I see some of God's glory."

"Reminders of God's goodness are everywhere if we'll open our eyes to find them," Dean said.

Your Turn

1. Name some people you know who remind you of God's love.
2. What's a way people might see God at work through you?

_____

_____

_____

Prayer

God, You are all around me. Give me eyes to see Your glory. Amen.

God Loves and Creates

The whole earth is full of [the Lᴏʀᴅ's] glory.
– Isaiah 6:3

Follow that Star

"Thanks for getting up so early," Counselor Dean told the boys. "On our last morning, I wanted to show you one more sky lesson."

"I always get up while it's still dark," Griffin grumbled.

"Is it time for breakfast yet?" Woody asked.

The sky in the east was just beginning to lighten from black to gray. Dean pointed in that direction. "See that bright star near the horizon?" he asked. "The Bible calls that the 'morning star.' Can you guess why?"

"Maybe it gets up early too," said Randy, yawning.

"When you see that star low in the eastern sky," Dean explained, "you know dawn is coming. The morning star is a promise of a new day."

The boys watched the morning star. Slowly the sky turned pink, then bright orange. As the sun rose and the sky grew blue, other stars faded from view.

"Jesus said, 'I am…the bright Morning Star,' " Dean told the boys. "That's because Jesus gives us new beginnings. With Jesus, every day is a fresh start. His love makes every day new."

Your Turn

1. Do you worry about things in the past? Like what?
2. What can you do stop worrying?

_____

_____

_____

Prayer

Lᴏʀᴅ, I'm glad You let me start over when I mess up. Each day is new. Amen.

God Loves and Creates

The whole earth is full of [the LORD's] glory.
— Isaiah 6:3

The Big Brother

Robbie bounced the basketball, glancing up and down the street. He looked at his watch. Frank would come soon. They'd been getting together through the "Big Brother" program." They went out for pizza, saw a movie, or played hoops. Robbie just loved spending time together. His dad had died a long time ago. Robbie's mother was great, but sometimes he wanted an older guy to hang with. There was some stuff he didn't want to talk about with his mom.

Robbie heard the rattle of Frank's car chugging up the street.

Frank pulled over. "Rob-o, let's have some fun."

As they drove toward the park, Robbie said, "I've been thinking."

"I thought I smelled something smoking," Frank said.

"Har-har!" Robbie said. "Do you think I could be a Big Brother when I get older?"

"Sure," Frank said. "You'd make a super big brother. Some kid would be lucky to have you for a friend. It's a blast, especially if you get a great little brother like I did."

"I'd like helping a kid without a dad," Robbie said.

Your Turn

1. Why do you think Robbie wanted to be a Big Brother?
2. Would you like to be a Big Brother someday? Why or why not?

_____

_____

_____

Prayer

God, thanks for people who care about me and love me. Amen.

God Loves and Creates

The whole earth is full of [the LORD's] glory.
— Isaiah 6:3

The Bus Buddy

Two women in the supermarket reached for the same bottle of soap. They laughed. One woman handed the soap to the other and said, "Aren't you Cameron Storm's mother?"

"Yes, I am," Mrs. Storm said.

"I'm Lilly Batson. My son rides the bus with Cameron."

"Cameron told me how much he likes Graham," Mrs. Storm said. "I think they swap jokes every morning."

Mrs. Batson smiled. "Graham goes to a special class at school, but he rides the bus with the other students. Graham just loves Cameron," Mrs. Batson said. "Cameron is a little older, but he often sits with Graham. Graham told me the kids on the bus used to pick on him. Now that Cameron is his friend, they don't."

"I didn't know about any of this," Mrs. Storm said.

Mrs. Batson laid one hand on Mrs. Storm's arm. "It means so much to us that Graham has a friend like Cameron. Your son is a wonderful person."

That afternoon, Mrs. Storm was putting away groceries when Cameron came in. She wrapped him in a long hug and kissed him on the forehead.

"What's that for?" Cameron asked.

"Because I'm proud of you!"

Your Turn

1. What do you look for in a friend?
2. Are you a good friend to people with special needs?

_____

_____

Prayer

God, I want to be thoughtful and kind like Cameron…and You. Amen.

God Loves and Creates

Holy Hunting

It's time for a treasure hunt in your house. Find something in each room that reminds you of God's love and goodness. Maybe the fridge reminds you of how God feeds you. Or the bathtub might make you think of how Jesus washed you clean of sin. Carry this book through your home and write down your ideas. Look at things in a new way, and look for God everywhere.

ROOM: _____

WHAT I FOUND: _____

HOW IT REMINDS ME OF GOD: _____

ROOM: _____

WHAT I FOUND: _____

HOW IT REMINDS ME OF GOD: _____

ROOM: _____

WHAT I FOUND: _____

HOW IT REMINDS ME OF GOD: _____

ROOM: _____

WHAT I FOUND: _____

HOW IT REMINDS ME OF GOD: _____

Prayer

LORD, please open my eyes and my heart to see You wherever I look. Amen.

God Loves and Creates

Friends: True or False?

God's prophet Jeremiah had a surprising friend named Ebed-Melek (Jeremiah 38). Jeremiah came from Judah, and Ebed-Melech was from Ethiopia. Ebed-Melech worked for the king, and Jeremiah was often in trouble with the king. In spite of their differences, Ebed-Melek was a good friend to Jeremiah. When Jewish leaders threw Jeremiah into a dry well to die, Ebed-Melek asked the king for permission to rescue Jeremiah. Ebed-Melek and some other men pulled Jeremiah out of the well with long ropes. Ebed-Melek had even brought old clothes so Jeremiah could pad the rope under his arms and not get rope burns.

What does it mean to be a true friend? Here are some true/false questions to help you think about friendship. Circle the answers that make the most sense to you.

True or False People can be friends even if they are quite different.

True or False Friends help each other out.

True or False Friends only come around for fun times.

True or False A friend ignores you when you're in trouble.

True or False A friend shares his life with you.

True or False People can be friends even if they disagree and fight sometimes.

True or False A friend sticks by you when other people turn against you.

True or False A friend cares about your feelings.

True or False A friend will like you only if you always do what he wants to do.

True or False A true friend is a precious treasure.

True or False I know how to be a true friend to others.

Prayer

Heavenly Father, help me be a true friend to others. Amen.

Enjoy People Who Are Different

[Jesus said,] I was a stranger and you invited me in.
– Matthew 25:35

The Time Machine

"I'm going to visit Mr. Dibny at the nursing home," Iniko told his mother.

"I thought you said old people were boring," Mom said.

"I was wrong," Iniko said. "After my youth group went Christmas caroling at the nursing home, we had hot chocolate and cookies with some of the people who live there. That's when I met Mr. Dibny. He's awesome."

Mom smiled. "What do you do when you visit?"

"Sometimes we watch TV or play checkers. Mr. Dibny is in a wheelchair, and I push him around the nursing home. "Mostly we just talk," Iniko said. "I tell him about school, and he tells me stories about the old days."

"The old days?"

"Mr. Dibny talks about World War II. He was just a kid then," Iniko said. "He remembers before television! He went all over the world in the Navy."

"I guess Mr. Dibny is like a time machine for you," Iniko's mother said. "When he tells you those stories, you get to go back in time."

"Mr. Dibny isn't my time machine—he's my friend."

Your Turn

1. Do you have friends who have lived a long time?
2. Who can you talk to this week who is older than your parents? Ask how much things have changed since he or she was a child.

_____

_____

Prayer

God, help me find friends who are older. They know a lot! Amen.

Enjoy People Who Are Different

[Jesus said,] I was a stranger and you invited me in.
– Matthew 25:35

The Four-Legged Visitor

Iniko got Scruffy into a metal tub filled with soapy water. The spaniel stood very still while Iniko scrubbed. When Scruffy was clean, he jumped out, and Iniko rinsed away the suds.

Iniko's mother came outside. "Iniko, we've had Scruffy for six years. Every time he needs a bath, I have to make you do it. This is the first time you've done it voluntarily. What's up?"

Iniko said, "I'm taking Scruffy to visit Mr. Dibny today."

"At the nursing home?" Iniko's mother asked. "Is that allowed?"

"Yes," Iniko said. "The people at the nursing home love it when pets visit them. Last week a lady brought a rabbit and everybody petted it."

"Scruffy is so big," Iniko's mother said.

"He's very gentle," Iniko said. "He doesn't bark, and he likes strangers. I asked one of the nurses, and she said I could bring Scruffy today. I'm going to use the pretty red leash," Iniko said. "Mr. Dibny can hold the leash while I push his wheelchair. Everybody will meet Scruffy."

Iniko's mother laughed. She rubbed the dog's head and said, "Scruffy, have a good time today. Try to get Iniko home in time for dinner."

Your Turn

1. Do you think older people like to have fun?
2. What can you share with an older person to start a conversation?

_____

_____

_____

_____

Prayer

God, I'm going to help somebody have a happier day. Amen.

Enjoy People Who Are Different

[Jesus said,] I was a stranger and you invited me in.
– Matthew 25:35

The New Kid

"Here comes the new kid," Conner said. Mark and Conner were standing in line at the cafeteria.

"Naoko is a weird name," Mark said.

"Shhh!" Conner whispered. "Here he comes."

"It doesn't matter," Mark said. "He doesn't understand us."

Conner thought the Japanese boy looked lonely and a little scared. *How would I feel in a foreign country where I didn't speak the language?* He pointed at his chest. "Conner." He pointed at Mark: "Mark."

Naoko smiled. "Conner. Mark. Hel-lo. My name is Naoko."

"Hi, Naoko," Conner said. He looked hard at his friend.

"Oh, all right," Mark said. "Hello, Naoko."

Once again Naoko said, "Hel-lo."

"Look," Mark said, "if you're going to learn English, let's cover the important stuff." He pointed to a serving tray and made a face. "Cabbage. Yuck."

Naoko repeated it.

Conner, Mark, and Naoko laughed together.

Conner pointed to another tray. "Pizza." He rubbed his belly. "Good!"

Naoko said, "Pete-sah…good. Ex-tra cheese."

Conner said, "Naoko is going to get along fine here."

"Yep," Mark said. "He just needed a couple of friends."

Your Turn

1. How can you help a new kid in school? In church?

_____

_____

Prayer

God, when I meet new people, help me welcome them. Amen.

Enjoy People Who Are Different

[Jesus said,] I was a stranger and you invited me in.
– Matthew 25:35

The Outsider

"Are you going to marry that guy?" Ethan asked.

Ethan's mother stirred bubbling liquid in a pot on the stove. "I wish you wouldn't call him 'that guy.' His name is Trevor. He's been kind to you."

"So, are you going to marry him?" Ethan persisted. "Even if you do, he's never going to be my father."

"Trevor's not trying to be your father. He'd like to be your friend."

"I've already have plenty of friends," Ethan said.

"Yes," said Mrs. Troy. "And when they come here, I make them feel welcome. You should do the same for my friends. I know you miss your dad. So do I. But everything changes, Ethan. I don't know if Trevor and I will marry, but I like him. Can't you make room for him around here?"

Ethan stared at the floor.

His mother sighed. "I'm going to change clothes for dinner."

After his mother went upstairs, Ethan heard a car door slam. He looked outside and saw Trevor climbing the front steps. The doorbell rang. Ethan usually pretended he didn't hear it. The bell rang again.

Maybe Mom is right and I should give Trevor a chance. Ethan hesitated.

Your Turn

1. What should Trevor do? Why?
2. Have new people come into your family? How did you feel?

_____

_____

_____

Prayer

God, You've put plenty of room in my heart for people. Amen.

Enjoy People Who Are Different

[Jesus said,] I was a stranger and you invited me in.
– Matthew 25:35

Visiting Yard Sales

Craig coasted his bike to a stop and got off. He propped it on the kickstand and walked up the driveway. A woman sat in a lawn chair in the open garage. She was surrounded by tables filled with household items for sale.

"Hi. I'm Craig Walton. I live two blocks over."

"Hi, Craig," the woman said. "Are you shopping today?"

"Not really," Craig said. He handed her a card with the name of his church and a phone number. "When you finish your garage sale, if you have leftover stuff you don't want, you can call that number and somebody from my church will come and get it."

"What will your church do with it?" asked the woman.

"We sort it and put it on shelves in the basement," Craig explained. "When people ask for help, we let them take anything they can use."

"What a good thing to do," the woman said. "I'd love for your church to haul away whatever's left.."

"That would be great," Craig said.

"So, Craig, this is your job? To visit yard sales?" the woman asked.

"Our pastor says Christians should help make the world a better place," Craig said. "I decided I can do this, and it might help a little."

"Craig, your church sounds like a good place. I'd like to visit sometime!"

Your Turn

1. Do you know any kids who are helping others? What do they do?
2. What will you do this week to help someone?

_____

_____

Prayer

God, show me what I can do to make a difference in people's lives. Amen.

Enjoy People Who Are Different

Gray-Haired Heroes

Can you identify these wise and faithful people from the Bible. (If you need help, look up the Bible references.) Write their names on the lines.

1. I was 75 years old when God called me to go to a new land (Genesis 12:1-4).

2. I was content to die after I met baby Jesus (Luke 2:25-32).

3. I was 600 years old when God sent a flood and I saved my family in an ark (Genesis 7:6-10).

4. I led the people of Israel through the wilderness and brought them to the land of God's promise (Exodus 34:5-8).

5. I was an old woman when I gave birth to a baby named Isaac (Genesis 18:10-15).

6. I was a prophetess who saw baby Jesus in the temple and told everyone about God's plan for saving Israel (Luke 2:36-38).

7. I am the oldest man in the Bible. I lived 969 years (Genesis 5:27)!

1. _____   2. _____   3. _____

4. _____   5. _____   6. _____

7. _____

Prayer

LORD, help me show kindness and respect to the elderly. Amen.

Enjoy People Who Are Different

Sharing Your Stuff

Your house is probably filled with stuff you don't want or need anymore. Did you know that your stuff can help other people? There are probably groups in your town who will take your things and either give them to people who can use them or sell them and use the money to help families in need.

Ask your mom or dad to help you fill a box with unwanted-but-still-usable stuff from around your house. When the box is full, give it away. If you don't know who to give it to, ask your parents. Here's a checklist to help you fill your box.

Here's a checklist to help you fill that box quickly. Look for:

_____ Books you've read

_____ Music and movies you're tired of

_____ Toys, games and puzzles you no longer play with

_____ Towels, sheets and blankets in good shape

_____ Clothes you've outgrown

_____ Coats you don't need

_____ Items you no longer need or want

_____ TVs and radios that need a little repair

_____ Old furniture

_____ Kitchen stuff your parents don't use

_____ Tools no one uses

_____ Stuff in storage

Prayer

LORD, I want to make a difference in the lives of those who are in need. Amen.

Helping Out

Love your neighbor as yourself.
– Mark 12:31

The Youth Group Project

Diego didn't like speaking in front of people, but he stood. "I have an idea." He held up a small box. "Does everybody know what this is?"

"Sure," said Basilio. "That's an ink cartridge from a printer."

"An *empty* ink cartridge," Diego said. "Throw it away, right? Wrong! Recycling companies will pay money for this."

"That's cool," Xavier said.

"I know a church group that collects and sells them," Diego said. "They use the money to set up programs to help kids avoid gangs and drugs."

"Kids in my school could use that kind of help," Xavier said.

"We've got a printer," Basilio said. "I could bring in cartridges."

"My mom works in an office with a ton of printers," someone said. "I'll bet she could get a bunch."

"Everybody in church can bring their old ink cases," Danny said.

"I'll mail them whenever we get a boxful," Diego said.

"I'll make posters to hang around the church," Sarah said.

"I can decorate a collection box for the hallway," offered a boy.

"Let's set a goal of 300 cartridges this year," said Basilio.

Diego didn't like talking in front of a group, but he did like helping people.

Your Turn

1. Why help people you've never met?
2. How can you help other kids?

_____

_____

Prayer

Jesus, You helped everyone You could. I want to be a helper like You. Amen.

Helping Out

Love your neighbor as yourself.
– Mark 12:31

The Thirsty Dog

Zach walked toward home. The street was deserted because it was so hot. He saw a dog panting. It was tied to a stake, and its water bowl was empty. Zach knocked on the front door. After a time, a very thin woman opened the door.

"Hi, Mrs. Rogers," Zach said. "I think your dog is thirsty."

"I can't remember when I checked," she said. "I've been sick."

"Maybe I can help," Zach said. "I live just up the street. I don't have a dog of my own, so I'd like to come and see yours every day."

"His name is Bruno. His food is in the shed behind the house," Mrs. Rogers said. "I can't pay you."

"Leave it to me," Zach said. "I'll take care of Bruno for you."

Mrs. Rogers said thank you and closed the door.

Zach filled Bruno's water bowl from the hose. When Zach returned with dog food, Bruno's water bowl was empty. Zach filled it again, and Bruno lapped quickly.

"Don't worry, Bruno," Zach said. "You won't be thirsty anymore."

Your Turn

1. Why should you be kind to animals?

_____

_____

_____

_____

_____

Prayer

God, You made me and You made animals. Thank You! Amen.

Helping Out

Love your neighbor as yourself.
– Mark 12:31

Going to the Mall

"Dad, will you drive me to the mall?" Alex asked. "I want to go to the bookstore."

"Your sister has a gymnastics class near the mall tomorrow. Let's do both things on one trip," said Mr. Nelson.

"Why do I have to wait for her dumb gym class?" Alex said.

Alex's father lowered his newspaper. "Alex, every time we drive the car we put pollution into the air. The mall is 10 miles away. We drive 20 miles back and forth when we go to the mall. I could drive you to the mall today. Then I could go back tomorrow morning to shop for groceries. Then take your sister to her class tomorrow afternoon. That's three trips to the mall—60 miles."

"Or we could do all three things in one trip," Alex said. "Less air pollution," Alex said.

"When we drive less, we're taking better care of God's world," Alex's dad said. "So how about that book? Can it wait until tomorrow?"

"Sure, Dad," Alex said. "No problem."

Your Turn

1. Make a list of things your family can do to help take care of our world.
2. What will you do this week to help the planet?

Prayer

God, help me be wise when it comes to caring for Your world. Amen.

Helping Out

Love your neighbor as yourself.
– Mark 12:31

Spring Cleaning

"Look at all this trash," Emilio said. Emilio and his friend Kwame were helping with River Sweep, a Saturday project to pick up litter along the river.

"Some people think the world is their garbage can," Kwame said. He carried a stick with a nail in the end. He stabbed a paper cup and put it into his trash bag.

"And it's not even our world," Emilio said. "It's God's world."

Kwame speared a fast-food bag, "Yeah, but we take care of it."

Emilio leaned over the water to snag a plastic six-pack ring. "I'll bet it makes God sad to see what a mess people have made."

The boys leaned on their sticks and rested. A group of teenagers got up from a picnic table and piled into their car. They left behind empty bottles and food wrappers. The wind blew a paper napkin along the ground.

"I'll get the trash on the picnic table," Emilio said.

"I'll help," Kwame said. "Then we need new trash bags. These are full."

Your Turn

1. What do you do when you see a piece of trash on the ground?
2. What could you say to people you know when they litter?

_____

_____

_____

_____

Prayer

God, this world is beautiful, and I want to help keep it that way. Amen.

Helping Out

Love your neighbor as yourself.
– Mark 12:31

Partners with God

"Mom, do we have room to plant more trees in our yard?" Ben asked.

"I think so," his mom answered. "Do we need more trees?"

Ben answered, "We've been studying trees in science class. Did you know trees make oxygen for us to breathe? And trees give homes and food to animals. Tree roots keep rain from washing away soil. Shade makes houses cooler in summer. Leaves can be used as compost."

"Trees take work," Ben's mother said. "Who's going to do that?"

"I'll water them," Ben said. "While the trees are small, I'll pull the weeds around them. When they get big, I'll rake the leaves that fall."

Ben's mother laughed. "All right," she said. "You've convinced me."

"Let's go buy some trees right now," Ben said.

"We don't have to buy trees," Ben's mom said. "We can plant acorns and maple seeds this fall. By next spring they'll be growing."

"But they'll be tiny," Ben said.

"If you take care of them, God will make them grow. In four or five years, they'll be taller than you."

Your Turn

1. Do you think God wants your help in taking care of the world?
2. What would you like to plant: trees, flowers, or vegetables?

_____

_____

_____

_____

Prayer

God, I love working with You to take care of Your world. Amen.

Helping Out

Making Old Things New

Recycling means taking old things and reusing them, making them useful again, or transforming them into something new. Old cans and bottles get melted and made into new containers. Old batteries get recharged. Old ink cartridges get refilled and restored.

Did you know God is a recycler? Yep! In Revelation 21:5, God sits on the throne of heaven and says, "I am a recycler!" Well, those aren't the exact words. To find out what God really says, hold this page up to a mirror. Write down what it says.

Prayer

LORD, I want to make a difference in this world by using resources wisely. Amen.

Helping Out

What a Wonderful World

Do you want to find out how God feels about the world? Read the message wheel. Start with the circled letter at the top of the wheel and move to the right. Skip the second letter, read the next one, skip the next one, and so on, reading every other letter all the way around the wheel. When you've gone around the wheel twice and you end up at the period, you'll have the whole message. (You can check your answer with Genesis 1:31.)

Prayer

God, I love the world almost much as You do. Please help me take care of it and encourage others to do the same. Amen.

The Bible—God's Word

Your word is a lamp for my feet, a light on my path.
– Psalm 119:105

The Big Deal Book

"Everybody's always talking about how important the Bible is," Wesley complained as he and his friend Calvin walked home from youth group. "I don't get it. It's just an old book, and it's hard to read."

Calvin said, "Not all of it is hard. Besides, some versions of the Bible are especially made for kids, so they're easier to read."

""What's the big deal about the Bible?" Wesley asked.

"That's easy," Calvin said. "The Bible tells us about the most important Person in the whole universe: Jesus."

"I'd rather read about Jesus in a comic book," Wesley said.

"I've got some comic books about Jesus," Calvin said. "I'll loan them to you. What we know about Jesus is from the Bible."

"Now I see why the Bible is a big deal," Wesley said. "In the Bible, where are the stories about Jesus?"

"Look in the New Testament, in the books of Matthew, Mark, Luke, and John," said Calvin. They stopped under a streetlight and Calvin showed Wesley where to find those books.

Your Turn

1. What do you like about the Bible?
2. Is there someone you can introduce to the Bible?

_____

_____

_____

_____

Prayer

Jesus, I love to read about You in the Bible. The more I know about You, the more I love You. Amen.

The Bible—God's Word

Your word is a lamp for my feet, a light on my path.
– Psalm 119:105

Learning the Rules

"This stinks," David said. He had a board game open, pieces and cards spread before him. He turned the box upside down and shook it.

"What's the matter?" asked his older sister, Bethany.

"I bought this game at the flea market," David explained. "It looked like a lot of fun. The board is a battlefield, and the pieces are little soldiers."

"So what's the problem?"

"The rules aren't in the box," David said. "How am I supposed to know how the game works without the rules?"

"So you've got a board, dice, a spinner, and a bunch of pieces," Bethany said, "but you don't know how to play?"

"I only paid a dollar for the game," David said, "but I still got ripped off. Without the rules none of this stuff makes sense."

"Life is that way too," Bethany said.

"Duh," said David. "Life doesn't have rules."

"It does," Bethany said. "God created life and gave us the Bible so we'd know how to live. Without the Bible, life just wouldn't make much sense."

Your Turn

1. How can the Bible help you in life?

_____

_____

_____

Prayer

God, the more Bible I read, the more I understand You. Amen.

The Bible—God's Word

Your word is a lamp for my feet, a light on my path.
– Psalm 119:105

The Letter

Brad took the frame off the wall and handed it carefully to his friend. "My dad is really proud of it," Brad said. In the frame was a letter signed by President Clinton on White House stationery. "When dad was a boy, he wrote to President Clinton, and the president wrote back."

Brad's dad walked in. "I was so excited that for weeks I carried that letter everywhere I went."

"No wonder," James said. "A letter from a real, live president!"

"I've got something even better than that, James," said Mr. Danvers. He lifted a black book from his desk. Handing it to James, he asked, "Do you have one of these?"

"Sure," James said. "But it's not as cool as a letter from a president."

"This is much better. This is a letter from God!"

James looked at the Bible. He'd never thought of it that way.

"The Bible is filled with personal messages to you and me. Every time we read it, we find fresh insights from God."

"A letter from God is awesome," James said. "Too bad He didn't sign it."

Your Turn

1. How is the Bible like a letter from God?

_____

_____

_____

_____

Prayer

God, when I read the Bible, help me understand what You're saying. Amen.

The Bible—God's Word

Your word is a lamp for my feet, a light on my path.
– **Psalm 119:105**

Verses to God

Gilbert joined his brother at the bus stop. Justin was mumbling.

Gilbert said, "I always knew you'd crack up."

"I'm not talking to myself," Justin said.

"Your mouth was making words, and you were the only one out here," Gilbert said. "I call that talking to yourself."

"I'm practicing my Bible verses," Justin explained. "Saying the verses out loud helps me remember them."

"Why do you memorize verses?" Gilbert asked.

"I don't always carry my Bible. When I memorize verses, I'm putting wisdom in my heart permanently. Look," said Justin. "What if you were a soldier in the middle of a battle? You can't read the Bible in a battle, but you can recall verses if you've memorized them."

"That makes sense," Gilbert said.

"Last week I had that big math test, remember?" asked Justin. "I was really nervous, but I remembered, 'I can do everything through Christ, who gives me strength.' That's Philippians 4:13."

"Will you help me learn some verses?" Gilbert asked.

"Sure." Justin grinned. "But don't practice them out loud or people will think you're cracking up."

Your Turn

1. Name some situations when knowing Bible verses by heart helps.
2. Memorize your a Bible verse, and say it out loud to someone today.

_____

_____

Prayer

God, help me memorize Your word. I need it always. Amen.

The Bible—God's Word

Your word is a lamp for my feet, a light on my path.
– **Psalm 119:105**

Helping Michael

"Mom, it's terrible," Dylan said. "Michael's parents are getting divorced."

"The Cranstons are splitting up?" Dylan's mom said. "Poor Michael."

"He was crying when he told me," Dylan said. "I feel awful for him. I wish there was something I could do for him."

"You can be his friend," Mom said. "Michael's going to need someone to talk to, someone who will be there for him. You can do that."

"That doesn't seem like much," Dylan said.

"You can pray for him too," Mom reminded.

"If I pray hard enough, maybe God will have Michael's parents stay together," Dylan said with excitement.

Mom hesitated. "God can do anything. He might help the Cranstons find a way to stay together. Or He might answer your prayers in a different way. He could give Michael extra strength to get through this. If the divorce occurs, God might help them work through their anger and hurt."

"That makes sense," I guess," Dylan said.

""Praying for each other is always a good idea," Mom said.

"I'm going to tell Michael I'm praying for him every day," Dylan said. "He might feel better just knowing that."

"I think he will," Dylan's mother said. "You'll feel better too because you'll be helping your friend."

Your Turn

1. Who do you know that needs prayer?
2. What is one thing you can pray for each friend today?

_____

_____

Prayer

LORD, open my heart to know what to pray regarding my friends. Amen.

The Bible—God's Word

The Big Two

God gave Moses ten rules for living to share with God's people. We call them the Ten Commandments. From memory, fill in the blanks for the Ten Commandments. If you need help, read Exodus 20:1-17.

1. You shall have no other _____ before me.

2. You shall not make or worship an _____.

3. You shall not misuse God's _____.

4. Keep the _____ day holy.

5. Honor your _____ and _____.

6. You shall not _____.

7. You shall not commit _____.

8. You shall not _____.

9. You shall not give false _____.

10. You shall not _____.

One day a man asked Jesus about the most important rules for living. Jesus gave the man two rules. Jesus said these two rules are big enough to cover all the others. Fill in the blanks. If you need help, you can read the whole story in Mark 12:28-34.

Rule 1: Love the LORD your God with all your _____ and with

all your _____ and with all your _____ and with all your

_____.

Rule 2: Love your _____ as _____.

Prayer

LORD, Your Word is filled with great advice for living right. Help me memorize these two rules so I can carry Your Word in my heart everywhere I go. Amen.

The Bible—God's Word

Exercising Your Head

Have you ever memorized a whole chapter of the Bible. Would you like to? Don't worry, it's easier than it sounds. Psalm 117 is the shortest chapter in the Bible. It's only two verses long! Are you ready? Writing helps your mind remember, so write these verses down three times. Then say these verses three times out loud every day until you have them down pat.

Praise the LORD, all you nations;

extol him, all you peoples.

For great is his love toward us, and the

faithfulness of the LORD endures forever.

Praise the LORD.

Trusting God

*I will praise the LORD all my life; I will sing
praise to my God as long as I live.*
– Psalm 146:2

The Secret Prayer Word

"I don't know how to pray," Donovan said.

"You know how to talk," said his friend Rachel. "Prayer is just talking to God." She laid down in the fluffy snow and made a snow angel.

"Yeah, that's what everybody says, but I never know what to say. I try to pray and my brain goes blank," Donovan explained.

"Relax," Rachel said, brushing the snow from her clothes. "There's nothing to it. I can teach you to pray with just two secret words. The first word is 'bad.' "

"You want me to use a bad word when I pray?" Donovan asked.

Rachel looked at the sky and sighed. "No! Just start your prayer by telling God everything that's making you feel bad. He loves you and wants to hear about everything going on in your life."

"That sounds easy," Donovan said.

"Yep!" said Rachel. "And you'll feel so much better after you tell God all the stuff that makes you feel bad."

Your Turn

1. If God knows everything, why should you talk to Him?
2. What do you think Rachel's second word will be?

_____

_____

_____

_____

_____

Prayer

God, I'm not going to keep secrets. Thank You for listening. Amen.

Trusting God

*I will praise the L*ORD *all my life; I will sing*
praise to my God as long as I live.
– Psalm 146:2

The Second Secret Prayer Word

"Praying is easy," Rachel said, "if you know the two secret prayer words. The first word is 'bad.' " She pitched a snowball at icicles hanging from the roof of her house. Two broke and fell.

"Right," Donovan said. "I tell God all the stuff that makes me feel bad." Donovan threw a snowball and knocked off three icicles. "So what's the second secret prayer word?"

"The second word is 'glad.' First you tell God what's making you feel bad, and then you tell Him what is making you glad."

"I get it," Donovan said. "It's saying thank You to God for all the good stuff in life. "Getting an 'A.' Hitting a home run."

"Stuff like snow," Rachel added. "Dogs. Friends. Ice cream. Books."

"The bad stuff and the glad stuff," Donovan said. "That makes it easy to pray. I'll never run out of stuff to talk about if I tell God about all that."

"God will listen to *every* word you say," Rachel said. "He will help you with the bad stuff and be pleased by the glad stuff."

Your Turn

1. Why would God enjoy hearing about the good things in your life?
2. Why is He interested in the not-so-good things?

_____

_____

_____

_____

_____

Prayer

God, help me notice all the blessings You give me. Amen.

Trusting God

*I will praise the LORD all my life; I will sing
praise to my God as long as I live.*
– Psalm 146:2

Prayer with a Beat

On the drive home from church, Nick asked his brother, "What's your favorite part of the worship service?"

"I love the prayers," Ian said, drumming on his knee with both hands.

Nick rolled his eyes. "The prayers? My neck hurts from bowing my head so long. I almost dozed off during the prayer today."

"Not those prayers," Ian said. He shifted the drumming to the Bible resting on the backseat beside him. "I love the prayers we sing."

"You mean the hymns?" Nick asked. "Those aren't prayers."

"Sure they are!" Ian said. "We're singing to God, aren't we? What's the difference between talking to God and singing to God?"

"Singing is definitely more fun," Nick said.

"Talking to God with music is more fun for me too. Sometimes people see me walking, and singing, and playing air guitar. They don't know I'm really praying."

"Hey, I like that," Nick said.

"Sometimes I just talk to God," Ian said, "and that's cool. But when I add music, my heart really gets into the prayer."

Your Turn

1. Why do you think Christians sing so much?
2. What's a prayer you like to sing to God?

_____

_____

_____

Prayer

God, You make me so happy that I can't keep it inside. Amen.

Trusting God

*I will praise the LORD all my life; I will sing
praise to my God as long as I live.*
– Psalm 146:2

Making the Team

Brent straightened his tie and brushed his hair. He picked up his Bible and walked into the family room. "Dad, I'll wait in the car."

"All right. I'll try to hurry the girls along," Brent's father said.

Brent loved going to church. His dad said it was hard to be a Christian on your own. The church was like belonging to a team. That made sense. On a team, people worked together, took care of each other, and celebrated victories.

If the church was a team, then the worship songs were cheers for God. The sermon was like getting together in a huddle to hear the game plan. The preacher was the coach.

Sunday school and youth group were practices between games. It was the time and place to ask questions and make sure you knew what was going on. And like a real practice session, sometimes there was kidding around.

Brent's family came out the front door. Just for fun, Brent reached over the front seat and blew the horn. Caroline made a face, but then she laughed. In fact, everyone was smiling. Brent decided he wasn't the only one who liked going to church.

Your Turn

1. What do you like best about going to church?
2. Do you have a friend you could invite to church?

_____

_____

_____

Prayer

God, thanks for choosing me for Your team. Amen.

Trusting God

I will praise the LORD all my life; I will sing praise to my God as long as I live.
– Psalm 146:2

Delivery Boy

Austin propped his bike on the kickstand. He went through the door into the church office. Mrs. Sage, the church secretary, smiled as he came in.

"You're always on time," she said. "Every Monday, right on schedule."

Austin said, "My friends would worry if I ran late."

Austin's friends were five elderly members of his church. They couldn't come to worship because of health limitations. Each Sunday the worship service was recorded. Every Monday after school, Austin picked up copies and delivered them. His friends loved listening to the services. They said it kept them close to their church family even though they couldn't attend in person. They also loved getting visitors. Austin always made time to talk.

"It's nice of you to do this every week, Austin," Mrs. Sage said.

"I love having a church job." Austin said. "I thought I was too young to do anything here, but this job is perfect."

"It's not just a job," Mrs. Sage said. "It's *ministry.* Every Christian ought to have a ministry. I'm glad you've found yours."

"Me too!" Austin said. "I'd better go. Mrs. Magnus will have milk and cookies waiting for me. I guess that's her ministry."

Your Turn

1. How is doing good work a "ministry"?
2. What ministry can you get involved in?

_____

_____

_____

Prayer

Jesus, help me find ways to work for You in my church. Amen.

Trusting God

Bad and Glad

Make up a prayer using the two "secret" prayer words. It's easy! Just fill in the blanks. When you're finished, read the prayer out loud to God. You could even sing it!

God, here are three things that sometimes make me feel bad:

1. _____

_____

2. _____

_____

3. _____

Please help me handle these things. And, God, here are five things that make me feel glad:

1. _____
2. _____
3. _____
4. _____
5. _____

In Jesus' name, I thank You for these good things! Amen!

Trusting God

Go Team!

Here's your chance to be super-creative! Design the front and back of a jersey for your congregation—your church team. Should your church name be on the shirt? The person's name? Some symbols? What colors will you choose?

Now, create a cheer for your team? Something like:

We like music! We like song!
We can sing out loud and strong!

_____

_____

_____

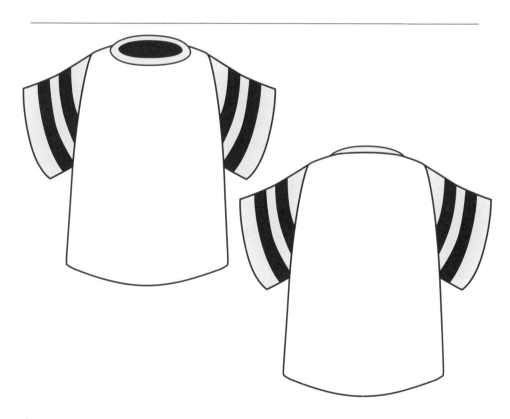

Prayer

Dear Lord, help me get active in Your church. Amen.

God Is in Charge

[Jesus said,] "I am with you always, to the very end of the age."
– Matthew 28:20

A Gigantic God

Earth, shining like a giant jewel in space, appeared on the classroom screen. "Planet Earth," Mr. Wylie said. "Has anybody visited there?"

Tyler chuckled. He loved science class.

Mr. Wylie continued. "If we could find a bathroom scale big enough to lay the planet on, we would find that Earth weighs over 6 billion trillion tons. That's a 6 followed by 21 zeroes! The Earth is one of eight planets circling the sun. There used to be nine planets, but poor Pluto was relegated to "dwarf planet" status. The screen showed a cartoon planet with arms and legs. It held a sign that read, "I am too a planet!" Mr. Wylie pretended to wipe away a tear before continuing, "The sun is a star big enough to swallow one million Earths. In our galaxy, there are roughly 100 billion stars." The Milky Way flashed on the screen.

"Are there other galaxies?" asked a girl near Tyler.

"Absolutely," said Mr. Wylie. "Using telescopes, scientists have spotted billions of galaxies, and there are probably more. It's a big, big universe."

"And a gigantic God!" Tyler whispered.

Your Turn

1. Of all the animals God has made, which is your favorite?
2. What is your favorite weather? Why?

_____

_____

_____

Prayer

God, You are totally amazing! Amen.

God Is in Charge

[Jesus said,] "I am with you always, to the very end of the age."
– **Matthew 28:20**

The Cookie Tray

Randy and Travis were in the lunch line at Camp Red Lake. Randy pointed at a tray of cookies and a sign that read, "One Cookie Per Camper. God Is Watching!" "That's funny!" He took a chocolate chip cookie.

Travis picked an oatmeal cookie. "About this morning…If God is everywhere, He sees everything I do."

Randy nodded as they settled at a table. "So?"

Travis lowered his voice. "God saw me when I put toothpaste in Counselor Stan's sock. And I put sugar in the salt shaker at table seven. Will God turn me in?"

Randy chuckled. "God isn't a principal in the sky waiting to punish us."

"But God's everywhere!" Travis insisted.

"Yep. Like at the pool when you did that crazy dive," Randy said.

"The lifeguard made me sit out the rest of pool time," Travis grumped.

"Your head barely missed the side," Randy said. "You could've died."

"But I didn't," Travis said.

"Maybe because God was keeping an eye on you," Randy said. "After all, He saw the dive. Maybe He kept you from conking your head."

"You think so?" Travis asked.

"God doesn't just watch. He lovingly interacts with us."

The camp cook announced, "Extra cookies if you want seconds!"

"Wow!" Travis said. "God really is helping us!"

Your Turn

1. How do you feel knowing God is always watching you?

_____

_____

Prayer

God, I like to be on the move. Thanks for keeping up with me. Amen.

God Is in Charge

[Jesus said,] "I am with you always, to the very end of the age."
– Matthew 28:20

The Lost Book

"That book has to be here," Braden said. He studied the piles of clothing, comic books, and toys that filled his bedroom. "If I can't find it, I have to pay the library seventeen bucks."

Ned shook his head. "You could lose a school bus in this mess. You go to church. Ask God to help you."

Braden frowned. He didn't like it when Ned made fun of his beliefs.

"You told me God likes to help people," Ned continued.

Braden thought, *God is helping me to not lose my temper.* He said, "I don't think it works that way."

"Why not?" Ned asked.

"How would you feel if your mom still hand fed you lunch?"

"I'd hide under the table," Ned said.

"What if your dad showed up at practice to tie your shoes?"

"I'd feel stupid if I couldn't do that stuff for myself," Ned said.

"Growing up means learning to do things on our own. If God found every lost book or gave me test answers, I'd never learn."

"So God won't help you find your library book?" Ned asked.

Braden smiled. "Maybe God sent you to help me!"

"Okay," Ned said with a sigh. "What's the name of the book?"

"How to Get Organized," Braden said.

Your Turn

1. Why do you think people don't always get what they pray for?
2. What prayer do you believe God hasn't answered yet?

_____

_____

Prayer

God, when I ask for Your help, I trust You to do what's best. Amen.

God Is in Charge

[Jesus said,] "I am with you always, to the very end of the age."
– Matthew 28:20

Chocolate Danger

Drake sat on the floor, staring at Charles with pleading brown eyes.

Charles nibbled the brownie. "No, Drake. No people food."

Drake whined, watching every bite that entered Charles' mouth.

Charles shook his head. "Drake, remember that time you gobbled down my meatballs in curry sauce? You threw up and felt awful." Charles reached into his pocket and took out a doggy treat. "Here's a chewie stick!" Drake took it from his hand and quickly hid it under the sofa. He returned to sit near Charles, again staring at the brownie.

"Chocolate is bad for dogs," Charles said. "I love you too much to give you this brownie. You don't know what's good for you." Charles took another bite and washed it down with milk. "I don't always get what I want, either. That doesn't mean God doesn't love me. He knows what will be good for me and what won't. I trust Him to decide."

Charles finished the brownie and scooped Drake onto his lap. "I love you, scruffy dog." The puppy rolled on his back, and Charles rubbed his belly. Drake wriggled in pleasure. "A belly rub is better than a brownie!" Charles declared.

Your Turn

1. What have you asked God for that didn't happen? Did God answer?
2. If you don't get what you ask God for, what do you do?

_____

_____

_____

Prayer

God, thanks for saying no when my request isn't what's best for me. Amen.

God Is in Charge

[Jesus said,] "I am with you always, to the very end of the age."
– Matthew 28:20

The Vocabulary Test

Bryce frowned at the weekly list of vocabulary words. *What a waste of time. These were words nobody would ever use. Maybe on a quiz show or something, but never in real life.* "Immutable." He glanced at the meaning: "Never changing. Always the same."

How was he supposed to use that in a sentence? "The Earth is immutable." *Not true. The Earth changes all the time.* "The sky is immutable." *Wrong again.* "Maybe the sun?" *Nah. Stars might shine for billions of years, but eventually they burn out. Everything changes; nothing lasts. Nothing can be counted on in this world.*

Bryce started feeling angry about "immutable." Why would somebody invent a word that couldn't be used? He could imagine that goofy girl in English class saying, "Love lasts forever. Love is immutable." *Barf!* That was fine for pretend, but not the real world. His mom and dad had stopped loving each other. *Love isn't immutable, and neither are families.*

Then he remembered something his pastor had said. "God's love for us never changes. It's always been here, and it will be here forever." Bryce grinned. *God's love is immutable!*

Your Turn

1. Does God ever change? Explain your reasoning.

_____

_____

_____

_____

Prayer

God, I can always count on You. You are immutable! Amen.

God Is in Charge

Here, There, Everywhere!

God is with you no matter where you go. Here are some places near and far that you could go and God would still be with you. Fill in the blanks, using the clues after each sentence. You might also need to look up the verse in the Bible for help.

GOD IS WITH ME IN THE DARKEST _____
Clue #1 - This is a place where it's always cool.
Clue #2 – Joshua 10:16

GOD IS WITH ME ABOVE THE _____
Clue #1 – You'd better wear a rain coat and a parachute.
Clue #2 – Psalm 68:4

GOD IS WITH ME IF I FLY TO THE _____
Clue #1 - This is a place very few men—and no women—have visited.
Clue #2 – Psalm 89:37

GOD IS WITH ME IN A _____
Clue #1 – I hope your kite doesn't end up here.
Clue #2 – 1 Samuel 10:3

GOD IS WITH ME IN THE _____
Clue #1 - This is a wild and lonely place.
Clue #2 – Isaiah 35:6

GOD IS WITH ME ON A _____
Clue #1 – There might be snow on top.
Clue #2 – Ezekiel 17:22

GOD IS WITH ME ON THE _____
Clue #1 – This place is fishy.
Clue #2 – Job 9:8

Prayer

God, I know You are everywhere at all times, which means You are always with me. Amen.

God Is in Charge

Immutable

God will never change His mind about loving you. He will never take back His guarantee to have a place for you in heaven. He will never break a promise. Here is something from Psalm 102:27 you can pray. To break the code:

- **cross out every P, and B, and C.**
- **change every X to E.**
- **change every Z to Y.**
- **change every Q to R**

Write the message in the word balloon and praise God.

Zbocpu qxmcpabin tpchx sapcbmx, abcnd
zobcuq zxacqs wbiclpl nxpcbvxq xncbpd.

Getting to Know God

God is greater than our hearts, and he knows everything.
– 1 John 3:20

What's Your Name?

Principal Robeson talked about the new Spanish Club. "Any questions?" The principal saw Connor's raised his hand. "Yes—you in the back row."

After class, Connor said, "The principal doesn't know my name. I've been here for three years, I run play ball, and I'm president of Chess Club."

"I don't think he knows anybody's name," Tim said. "I've helped in the office for two years. He sees me every day! It's like I'm a nobody."

Connor grinned at his friend. "We're just a pair of nobodies."

"God knows your name, and He's somebody," Tim said. "God is more important than Principal Robeson."

Connor laughed. "Way more important!"

"And God has more to watch over than the principal," Tim added.

"Way more," Connor agreed. "Animals and plants—and maybe even life on other planets."

"And yet He knows our names!" Tim said.

"Not just that," Connor said. "He knows my grade point average, my shoe size, and my favorite drinking fountain."

"You have a favorite drinking fountain?" Tim asked.

"Sure," Connor said.

"I didn't know that," Tim said.

Your Turn

1. When people forget your name, how do you feel?
2. Do you remember people's names?

_____

_____

Prayer

God, I know I'm important to You. That makes me feel great! Amen.

Getting to Know God

God is greater than our hearts, and he knows everything.
– 1 John 3:20

The Ear Killer

Aaaarroooaaahhh!

Max covered his ears with his hands. "What is that horrible sound?"

Austin looked up. They were doing homework in his room. "My little sister, Hayley, practicing her trumpet. She's only been taking lessons about a month."

"It's scrambling my brain," Max said. "Sounds like a hurt elephant."

"Or a dump truck running over garbage cans," Austin suggested.

"Or an angry cat fighting with a bagpipe," Max said.

"She'll get better with practice," said Austin.

"How can you be so patient?" Max asked.

"Remember how I used to be late for Sunday school?"

"You lived next to the church, but you were never on time," Max said.

"I'd show up ten minutes late still buttoning my shirt." Austin laughed. "Mr. Dent would smile and say, 'God is patient with me, so I can be patient with you. Maybe you'll make it on time next week.' "

"I get it," Max said. "God is patient with you and me when we're trying to get it right, so we should be patient with others."

Hayley's trumpet sounded like a train crashing into a glass bottle factory.

"Maybe we should be patient at my house for a while," Max suggested.

Your Turn

1. What are times God has been patient with you?

_____

_____

Prayer

God, thank You for being patient with me. Help me be patient with others. Amen.

Getting to Know God

God is greater than our hearts, and he knows everything.
– 1 John 3:20

The Riddle Game

Mason and his dad settled into their seats on the plane.

"This is a big plane," Mason said.

"This plane will carry 400 passengers," his dad said. "I know something that holds more."

"A cruise ship might hold 4500 people," Mason guessed.

"I'm thinking of something that holds a lot more than that."

The plane roared down the field and rose into the air. Mason' looked out the window. "New York City holds 8 million people."

"Nope. My answer is the universe. Top that, smart guy."

"What holds more than the universe?" Mason pointed at himself. "Me."

His dad's eyebrows went up. "Prove it."

"God has no limits, right?" Mason asked. "Even the whole universe isn't big enough to hold Him."

"Right," his dad agreed.

"The Bible says God lives in me," Mason said. "That means there's room inside me for the biggest God of all."

Mason's dad laughed. "I shouldn't play the riddle games with you."

Your Turn

1. God is so big that nothing can hold Him. How would you explain this idea to a friend?
2. How does it feel knowing God is inside you?

_____

_____

_____

Prayer

God, nothing can hold You or stop You. You're awesome! Amen.

Getting to Know God

God is greater than our hearts, and he knows everything.
– 1 John 3:20

Free Throws

"We lost the game by one stupid point!" Aaron said, stuffing his uniform into a gym bag.

"We're not going to the finals," Greg said.

The boys left the locker room and stepped into the cool night air.

"It's my fault," Aaron said. "I missed two free throws."

"Everybody misses sometimes," Greg sympathized.

"I was praying so hard!" Aaron admitted. "God wasn't listening. How hard could it be for Him to nudge a basketball?"

Greg said, "Wouldn't that be cheating?"

"What do you mean?" Aaron asked.

"They were your free throws. Could Coach shoot them for you?"

"That's against the rules," Aaron said.

"When Coach prays with us, He asks God to keep everyone safe and to give us a good game," Greg said. "He doesn't ask God to help us win."

"I see what you mean," Aaron said. "God loves both teams. It wouldn't be fair for God to help one team win and make the other lose."

"It's a sport," Greg said. "It's about practicing and playing well."

"So I guess it's not God's fault we lost," Aaron said.

"Nope," Greg said. "It's your fault."

"Hey!" Aaron said. "What about that shot you missed third quarter?"

"Nope," Greg said. "It's your fault. You said so yourself."

Laughing together, the boys ran the rest of the way home.

Your Turn

1. Can you think of things you shouldn't ask from God?

_____

_____

Prayer

God, I'm glad You're fair and just —and merciful! Amen.

Getting to Know God

God is greater than our hearts, and he knows everything.
– 1 John 3:20

Kitchen Talk

Corbin's mom pulled out a chair at the table. "Sit down, Corbin."

Oh no! Corbin thought. *A kitchen talk.* "What have I done now?"

"I've heard some of your friends using God's name," his mom said.

"Is that bad?" Corbin asked.

"It's fine when people are praying or studying the Bible," Mom said. "But it's a bad habit to use God's name disrespectfully. God is holy."

"Does that mean God is special?" Corbin asked.

"Very special," Mom said. "Okay, you have play clothes to wear when playing ball. If they get dirty, no big deal."

Corbin remembered sliding into third and ripping his jeans. His mom had laughed and sewn them up.

"You also have dress-up clothes for special occasions. Would you grease your bike in your good clothes? Or paint one of your models?"

"No way," Corbin said. "Those clothes are too special for dirty work."

"God is too special—too holy—to throw His name around just to sound cool, or impress people, or let off steam."

Corbin said, "My friends do that a lot. I understand, Mom. I love God."

Your Turn

1. How would you feel if someone misused your name?

_____

_____

_____

_____

Prayer

God, I want my words and thoughts to show You are holy. Amen.

Getting to Know God

Housecleaning

If God were coming to live in your house, you'd probably wash the windows, run the sweeper, and get out the good dishes. What if God were coming to live in you? Here's the big news: He already is! What can you do to make sure you are a good place for God to live? Here are some ideas. Draw a square around the ones you already are doing. Draw a triangle around the ones you would like to do.

Be Kind to Others

Eat Healthy Food

Pray Every Day

Build Up My Mind
With Learning

Tell The Truth

Worship God

Take Care Of
My Teeth

Practice Forgiveness

Read The Bible

Be Generous

Be Physically Fit

Make Sure My Talking
Is Clean

Treat My Body
With Respect

Prayer

When I think about You living inside me, I want to "clean house" and make sure I take care of myself. Amen.

Getting to Know God

God's Justice

God is fair, and He wants you to be fair. In each of the sentences below, underline any part you think seems unfair or like something God wouldn't want you to do. Then rewrite each sentence so it describes the way God wants you to treat others.

- Cory slipped and fell in the mud. Then Cory tripped Mack and made him fall in the mud, too.

_____

_____

- Brandon's sister had to stay home with Brandon while his parents went out to dinner. Brandon's sister said he wasn't allowed to ask a friend over to play because she didn't get to go out with her friends.

_____

_____

- On the way to school, Aidan told Zack about his great idea for a science project. When Aidan went to tell the teacher his plans for the project, she said he'd have to find another project because Zack had just told her his plans to do the same thing.

_____

_____

- Dylan ate all of his cookies, and then he ate the cookie his sister had saved from last night's dinner. Dylan pretended the dog ate the cookie.

_____

_____

Prayer

God, I want to be fair just like You are. I know You care about right and wrong, and I do too. Amen.

More Bible Truths

Your word is a lamp for my feet, a light on my path.
– Psalm 119:105

Listening Feet

Daniel climbed into the tree house the ABC boys used.

"Let's open the meeting," said Jacob, the ABC president.

The boys settled into a circle.

"Who are we?" Jacob asked.

"We are the Amazing Bible Club!" the boys chanted.

"What is our only rule?" Jacob asked.

"We will read the Bible every day!"

Jacob said, "I'll lead the prayer." The boys bowed their heads. "God, thanks for giving us the Bible so we can learn about You and how You want us to live. Your Word is a lamp for our feet. Amen."

"I've heard the 'Bible being a lamp' before. What does it mean?" Carlos asked.

Jacob said, "Imagine you are in a forest at midnight."

"I'd want a flashlight so I could see where I was going," Carlos said.

"God uses the Bible like a flashlight to guide us and keep us safe," Jacob said.

"I get it!" Carlos said.

"Cool," Mason said. "From now on, when I read the Bible, I'm going to make sure my feet are paying attention too!"

Your Turn

1. "The Bible only works when it is open." What does that mean?

_____

_____

_____

Prayer

God, when I read the Bible, help me hear what You're saying to me. Amen.

More Bible Truths

Your word is a lamp for my feet, a light on my path.
– Psalm 119:105

Biblical Pursuits

"It's sharing time," Jacob announced to the Amazing Bible Club.

"Me first!" Daniel exclaimed. "I found some great things this week." He cleared his throat. "What is the longest chapter in the Bible?"

After a moment of silence, he added, "It's almost the next-door neighbor of the shortest chapter in the Bible."

The ABC boys looked at one another and scratched their heads.

"Psalm 119 is the longest chapter in the Bible with 176 verses," Daniel said. "The shortest chapter is Psalm 117 with 2 verses."

"I'll memorize Psalm 117," Mason said to Daniel, "if you'll memorize Psalm 119."

"I've got another one," Daniel said. "Here's a riddle from the fourteenth chapter of Judges. 'Out of the eater came something to eat; out of the strong came something sweet.'"

Jacob shouted, "I know! After Samson killed a lion with his bare hands, a swarm of bees came and made a hive in the lion's body. The answer to the riddle is the honey that came from inside the dead lion."

The ABC boys cheered, and Jacob turned red.

"Here's a good one," Daniel said. "There are three books of the Bible that if you say their names in order it makes a sentence."

Every member of the ABC could name all 66 books of the Bible in order, so this riddle didn't take long to figure out.

In unison, Mason and Carlos chanted, "Joshua, Judges, Ruth!"

Your Turn

1. Does your family read the Bible?
2. Do you read the Bible every day?

_____

_____

Prayer

God, how did You squeeze so many cool things into one book? Wow! Amen.

More Bible Truths

Your word is a lamp for my feet, a light on my path.
– Psalm 119:105

Brain Burners

The members of the Amazing Bible Club sat in a circle in their tree house. Daniel said, "We know the first book of the Bible is Genesis and the last is Revelation. Can you list the first and last Bible books alphabetically?"

Several boys grabbed their Bibles.

"Acts is first," Carlos said.

"Zechariah is last," Mason added.

"So close," Daniel said. "The last book is Zephaniah."

"Who in the Bible needed the biggest pooper-scooper?" Jacob asked.

"Noah!" said Mason. "He had to clean up after all those animals."

"Besides Adam and Eve," Carlos said, "who had no parents?"

"Everybody has parents," Mason said.

"I give up," Daniel said.

Carlos grinned wickedly. "The answer is Joshua."

"The guy who took over after Moses?" Mason said. "Who led the Israelites into the promised land. What makes you think he didn't have parents?"

Carlos opened his Bible. "In the book of Joshua, it says that Joshua was the 'son of Nun.' Get it? The son of none."

A wad of paper flew through the air and bounced off Carlos' head.

"What a terrible joke," Daniel said with a grin and a groan.

Your Turn

1. Make up your own Bible riddle. Try to stump your family and friends.

_____

_____

Prayer

God, I know You like having fun. After all, You invented it! Amen.

More Bible Truths

Your word is a lamp for my feet, a light on my path.
– Psalm 119:105

The Invisible Bible

Daniel asked, "Why should I memorize verses from the Bible?"

"You don't *have* to," said Jacob, president of the Amazing Bible Club. "I do it because I like it."

"I can read the Bible anytime," Daniel said, "why learn parts by heart?"

"I can answer that," Mason said. "Last week in gym class, Mr. Wary yelled at me for being last in the 1000-meter run. He made me run an extra lap. I was mad and really tired. I wanted to quit running and walk, but I remembered one of my favorite memory verses: 'I can do everything through Christ, who gives me strength.' "

"That's Philippians 4:13, right?" asked Carlos.

"Right," Mason said. "I said that verse over and over to remember God would give me the perseverance I needed."

"I guess you didn't have a Bible with you on the track," Jacob joked.

"You'd look silly trying to read as you ran around the track," Carlos said.

"I carry an invisible Bible in the pocket of my heart," Mason said. "When I need encouragement or wisdom, I'm ready."

"I get it now," Daniel said. "I'm going to start memorizing today!"

Your Turn

1. When would you be glad to know some Bible verses by heart?
2. What verse will you memorize this week?

_____

_____

_____

Prayer

God, help me fill my head and my heart with Your wisdom. Amen.

More Bible Truths

Your word is a lamp for my feet, a light on my path.
– Psalm 119:105

The Tree House

"I love our tree house," Daniel said. "I feel close to God up here."

Mason cleared his throat nervously. "Can we talk about adding a new member to the ABC?"

"Do you know somebody who wants to join?" Jacob asked.

"Sort of," Mason said. "Devon goes to my church and reads the Bible. I mentioned our club, and he asked if he could come."

"Why didn't you bring him today?" Carlos asked.

"There's a problem," Mason said slowly. "Devon might not fit in."

"Why not?" Daniel asked. "He sounds great."

"He is," Mason agreed. "But he uses a wheelchair."

"So what's the prob…" Carlos began. "Oh, our tree house…"

"Maybe we could haul Devon up here somehow," Jacob said.

"Somebody would get hurt for sure," Carlos said.

"And we don't want him to feel like a suitcase," Mason said.

"That's too bad," Daniel said. "I guess there's no way he can join."

"Wait," Carlos said. "Remember the verse we learned about treating others the way we want to be treated? Should we give up so easily?"

"It's not our fault he can't climb a tree," Daniel said.

"Why doesn't he find a club that meets on the ground?" Daniel said.

"Are we learning the Bible," Carlos asked, "or are we *living* the Bible?"

"We should vote on this," Jacob said. "Everyone who wants to find a meeting place where Devon can join us, raise your hand."

Your Turn

1. How would you vote if you were in the ABC?

2. What do you think the Amazing Bible Club will do?

_____

_____

Prayer

God, it's easy to know what I want. Help me work on what other people need. Amen.

More Bible Truths

Never Lost

Most mazes are supposed to be tricky, but here is a maze that works differently. This is called a "labyrinth." Once you enter the labyrinth, you cannot get lost. As long as you keep going, you will always end up in the middle. Try out the labyrinth and see.

The labyrinth is like reading the Bible. As long as you keep following God's Word, you cannot get lost. He keeps you on the right path.

Prayer

Father God, I know that even when my path in life seems confusing, I can always count on You to lead me. Amen.

More Bible Truths

The Best Verse Ever?

Some people think that the best verse in the whole Bible is John 3:16. Many people can say it from memory. Have you memorized it? Here are some ways of saying John 3:16 from different translations of the Bible. Pick the one you like best and learn it by heart.

Tip Number One: Write the verse on a piece of paper, and study it when you have a few minutes on the school bus or while waiting in line at lunch.

Tip Number Two: If you already know John 3:16, pick a new verse to learn. Maybe you can memorize a verse from one of the other stories in this book.

■ For God so loved the world that he gave his one and only Son, that whoever believes in him shall not perish but have eternal life. (New International Version)

■ For God so loved the world, that he gave his only begotten Son, that whosoever believeth in him should not perish, but have everlasting life. (King James Version)

■ For God loved the world so much that he gave his one and only Son, so that everyone who believes in him will not perish but have eternal life. (New Living Translation)

■ De tal manera amó Dios al mundo, que ha dado a su Hijo unigénito, para que todo aquel que en él cree no se pierda, sino que tenga vida eterna.
(Reina-Valera 1995)

Prayer

God, I'm so thankful that You sent Your Son, Jesus Christ, to take away my sins. I want to follow You all the days of my life. Amen.

Giving and Receiving

[Jesus said,] "Freely you have received; freely give."
– Matthew 10:8

Better Than a Tree House?

"We're agreed," said Jacob, president of the ABC. "We'll invite Devon to join our club."

"Even though we won't meet in our tree house," Daniel said with a sigh.

"You guys can come over to hang out or pray in the tree house," Carlos said. "Even if I'm not around, you're always welcome."

"Thank you," Daniel said. "Still, it won't be the same."

"Why don't we turn it over to God?" Mason said. "Jesus said that if we ask in His name, God will give us what we need."

"Good idea," Jacob agreed. "Mason, will you lead us?"

"LORD, we're doing the right thing," Mason said, "but it means giving up our clubhouse. Do You have another place picked out for us? You said, 'Seek and you will find.' We're seeking a new clubhouse. Help us find one. Whatever You have in mind will be great with us. Amen."

Mason made a fist and rapped on the floor with his knuckles.

"What are you doing?" Jacob asked.

"I'm doing what Jesus told us to do," Mason said with a smile. "I'm knocking. Now it's God's turn to open the door to our new clubhouse."

Your Turn

1. Do you think God enjoys giving you good things?
2. What have you asked for that God answered in an amazing way?

_____

_____

_____

Prayer

God, I can ask You for anything, but You'll always do what's best. Amen.

Giving and Receiving

[Jesus said,] "Freely you have received; freely give."
– **Matthew 10:8**

Settling for a Shack

Carlos, Jacob, and Daniel followed Mason to Devon's front door. It was the first time most of the Amazing Bible Club would meet Devon. Mason rang the doorbell, and a voice called, "Come in!"

They entered the house and found a smiling, blond-haired boy waiting for them. He rolled forward in his wheelchair and said, "Hi, I'm Devon."

"Devon, we're glad to have you in the club. I'm Jacob, the current president. Mason says you're going to fit right in with our crazy bunch." Jacob introduced everyone.

Devon's mother came in. "Devon, there are chocolate chip cookies and lemonade in the kitchen. You can take them to the shack."

"The shack?" Mason asked.

"It used to be a workshop," Devon said. "My dad fixed it up for me. Grab the food, and I'll show you."

They followed a concrete walk that sloped downward.

"It must be hard to roll your wheelchair up this hill," Mason said.

"I've gotten used to it," Devon said. "My arms are strong."

They came around a curve and everyone stopped.

"That's the shack?" Jacob said.

Devon nodded. "What do you think?"

"It's awesome!" Daniel said, his eyes wide.

Your Turn

1. Should you only ask God for important things? Why or why not?

_____

_____

Prayer

Jesus, thank You that when I ask You to make the plans, You do more than I can imagine! Amen.

Giving and Receiving

[Jesus said,] "Freely you have received; freely give."
– **Matthew 10:8**

The New Clubhouse

The boys of the Amazing Bible Club stared in amazement at Devon's shack in the woods behind his house. "Pretty cool, isn't it?" Devon said.

"Cool?" Daniel echoed. "It's below zero!"

The shack stood beside a stream, water winding between moss-covered boulders. Ash trees and wildflowers surrounded the little building.

"That's not a shack," Jacob said. "It's a little house."

"Just one room," Devon said. "Lots of space, though. Come on in." He rolled into the shack, and the others followed.

"Wow!" Carlos said in a soft voice.

The building had a carpeted floor. Along two walls were shelves that held books and DVDs. Large windows faced the woods. A flat-screen TV was mounted on one wall. A refrigerator hummed in the corner.

"You've got electricity!" Mason said.

"Yes, but no running water in the shack," Devon said. "Sorry, no bathroom. We have to use the one in the house."

Jacob noticed a door on the back wall. "Closet?" he asked.

"Better than that," Devon said. The door opened onto a wooden deck with lawn chairs and a small table. Trees shaded it from the sun. Squirrel and bird feeders hung nearby.

"It's a good thing we asked God to find a clubhouse!" Mason said.

Your Turn

1. Is it hard for you to trust God to take care of you? Why or why not?
2. What do you want to ask God for this week?

Prayer

God when You tell me no, help me trust that You have a better plan. Amen.

Giving and Receiving

[Jesus said,] "Freely you have received; freely give."
– Matthew 10:8

Stick Tricks

"Moses' life is my favorite Bible reading," Devon said from his wheelchair. The Amazing Bible Club was meeting in their new clubhouse behind Devon's house. The other boys sat in lawn chairs on the deck in the afternoon sun.

"He brought God's people out of Egypt," Daniel said, "and led them to the promised land."

"I like Moses' staff," Devon said. "Think of the things he did with that walking stick."

"Let's see," Carlos said, thinking hard. "He threw it on the ground, and it became a snake to prove Moses was sent by God."

"Didn't Moses use his staff to bring punishments on Egypt?" Daniel said. "Stuff like locusts to eat the crops and the worst hail storm ever?"

"That's not all," Carlos added. "Moses raised his stick in the air, and the sea opened up so the people could walk across to the other side."

"I remember one," Jacob said. "When the people were thirsty in the desert, Moses hit a rock with his stick and water gushed out."

"That was a fantastic stick," Carlos said.

"Not really," Devon said. "God is fantastic. There was nothing special about the stick, but God did amazing things through it. Think about it," Devon said. "If God could overcome Egypt, save the Israelites, and part the sea with a stick, imagine what He can do through you and me!"

Your Turn

1. What talents do you have that God might want to use?

_____

_____

Prayer

Here I am, God. You created me, and I'm all Yours. Amen.

Giving and Receiving

[Jesus said,] "Freely you have received; freely give."
– Matthew 10:8

Heavy Lifting

"Behold this fantastic feat of strength," Jacob said to the Amazing Bible Club. "I will lift an entire library.." He took deep breaths, picked up his Bible, and lifted it over his head.

As Jacob took a bow, Daniel said, "I don't get it."

"The Bible is one book," Jacob explained, "but it's also a library of different books written by many authors inspired by God."

"There are two rooms in the library," Mason said. "The Old Testament has books about the Israelites, and the New Testament has books about Jesus and the Christian church."

"The Old Testament has stories about Abraham, Moses, Miriam, David, Ruth, and lots of others," Jacob said. "It also has poetry books."

"There are poems in the Bible?" Daniel asked.

"The book of Psalms is made up of poems and songs," said Carlos. "There are books about God's prophets too."

"I think I know what's in the New Testament library room," Mason said. "There are four 'gospels' about the life of Jesus, a book about the beginning of the Christian church, and letters between early Christians. There's Revelation too. The book with monsters and weird stuff about the end of the world."

Your Turn

1. Do you have favorite parts of the Bible? If so, what are they?

_____

_____

_____

Prayer

God, I could read the Bible my whole life and never get tired of it. Amen.

Giving and Receiving

Learning the Library

A library isn't much help if you don't know where to find the books you want. The same is true of the Bible. Did you know that stories about Jesus are found in the four Gospels? Did you know that the stories of the first Christians are found in the book of Acts?

Here's a chance for you to learn your way through the library. Your Bible probably has a contents page listing all the Bible books in order. Using that list, label these library books and you'll be on your way to learning how to use your Bible. Start with the first book in the Bible—Genesis—and write that on the first book on the top shelf of the library. Exodus comes next. Keep going until you reach Revelation. When you finish filling out this page, you can study how the Bible is put together.

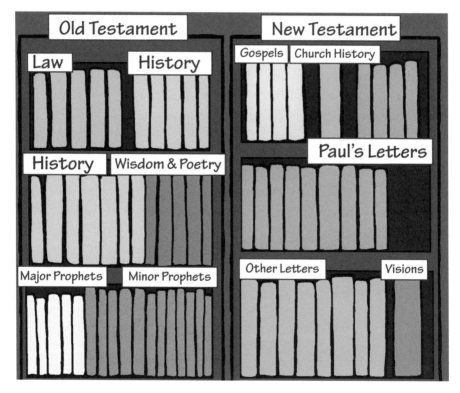

Prayer

God, I want to read the entire Bible. Please help me read some every day. I know You will always show me something new. Amen.

Giving and Receiving

What's in Your Hand?

Moses had a stick, and God used it in amazing ways. You have talents and skills God can use. Maybe it's something you own, something you're good at, or something you like to do. Draw your hand, and on each finger and your thumb write something in your life that God might use. If it's a hockey stick, okay. If it's your bug collection, or your allowance, or your ability to draw, that's okay too. You won't surprise God, but God might surprise you!

God, here is some stuff in my hand.
You can use it any way you want to.

Signed: _____

Prayer

God, I give You all my talents and possessions. Amen.

What God Wants

*Carry each other's burdens, and in this way
you will fulfill the law of Christ.*
– Galatians 6:2

The Scary River

Mr. Palmer said, "God has given us beautiful weather for our whitewater rafting adventure." The boys whistled and cheered.

Cass stared at the rushing river with wide eyes. As the leader explained what to do if someone fell from the raft, Cass felt knots of fear tangling in his stomach. Why had he come on this dangerous trip? Maybe if he pretended to be sick…

"On my first rafting trip, I was terrified of falling out," Mr. Palmer admitted.

Cass found it hard to believe Mr. Palmer was ever afraid of anything.

"I fell out of the raft three times in the first hour," Mr. Palmer said. "It didn't hurt a bit. Things we're afraid of are seldom as bad as we think."

Cass considered that. He remembered things he'd dreaded that turned out to be no big deal. Maybe rafting would turn out like that too.

"Pay attention," Mr. Palmer said. "Follow the rules. And remember God is watching over you. Is everybody ready?"

Cass took a deep breath and whispered, "Yes, God, I'm ready."

Your Turn

1. Can you think of something you feared that later turned out to be no big deal?

_____

_____

_____

Prayer

God, when I get scared, help me remember You're right here beside me. Amen.

What God Wants

*Carry each other's burdens, and in this way
you will fulfill the law of Christ.*
— **Galatians 6:2**

Overboard!

Elliot and Cass climbed into the inflatable raft with four other boys. Elliott grabbed the front seat, Mr. Palmer scrambled into the back where he could coach and guide. He surveyed the raft. "Elliot, you're new at this. I want you to trade places with Wayne."

"I can do anything Wayne can do," Elliot protested.

Mr. Palmer nodded. "I'll give you a chance. Just remember, when we get into rough water, you've got to keep paddling."

Elliot said, "You can count on me."

The first few miles on the river were gentle with a few easy patches of bumpy water. Elliot heard a roar ahead. The air vibrated with the thundering sound. Mr. Palmer called, "Boys, follow my directions, and we'll be fine." A rock loomed in their path, and the rushing water veered left. "Everybody paddle hard!" Mr. Palmer shouted. "Don't stop!"

Elliot dropped his paddle and grabbed the sides of the raft. "Paddle now!" someone shouted. The raft spun sideways, rose up, and then flipped, spilling everyone into the torrent.

Downstream, they righted the boat and gathered their paddles.

Mr. Palmer asked, "Everyone okay?" Everyone replied yes, and Mr. Palmer asked, "Did we learn anything from that?"

Elliot said, "Yes. I learned I wasn't ready to be in front."

Your Turn

1. Have you tried to do something that was too hard?
   How did it turn out?

_____

_____

Prayer

God, Jesus didn't put Himself first. Help me be like Him. Amen.

What God Wants

*Carry each other's burdens, and in this way
you will fulfill the law of Christ.*
— **Galatians 6:2**

Paddle Partners

The river was smooth, and the boys paddled lazily. "I let the whole group down," Elliot said miserably. "When we needed every paddle, I got scared and grabbed the sides of the raft."

Mark said, "This is your first time on whitewater, right?"

Elliot nodded.

"On my first raft trip," Mark shared, "we came into these rapids, and water was splashing into the raft. We were bouncing and rolling. Rocks were all around us. The guide was yelling at us to paddle. I freaked out and did exactly what you did."

Elliot grinned. "Did the raft turn over?"

Mark nodded. "That wasn't the worst of it. I lost my paddle."

"I guess you found it downstream," Elliot said.

"Nope," Mark said. "It must be on the bottom of the ocean by now. You've heard of being up the creek without a paddle? That was me."

Elliot laughed and slapped his knee.

"I found a long limb on the bank and tried paddling with that."

Elliot laughed again. "Everybody had a paddle, and you had a stick."

"So everybody messes up sometimes," Mark said. "Forget how you did on the last whitewater. What matters is how you do on the next."

"Thanks," Elliot said. "I'm feeling better."

Your Turn

1. When life is hard, does it help when someone encourages you?
2. How can you encourage someone who's made a mistake?

_____

_____

Prayer

God, when somebody is down, show me how to help them up. Amen.

What God Wants

*Carry each other's burdens, and in this way
you will fulfill the law of Christ.*
— **Galatians 6:2**

Every Paddle

Mr. Palmer shaded his eyes and stared ahead. "There's whitewater around the next bend," he said. "Let's get through this one right side up."

Elliot felt his face grow hot, remembering how he'd dropped his paddle and grabbed the raft. Partly because of him, the raft had flipped.

"We need every paddle," Mr. Palmer said. "We have to keep the raft moving forward or we can't steer. That means every paddle in the water. Nobody gets to goof off or coast. We're depending on each other. If one of us doesn't do his part, we'll all go swimming."

The sound of the river grew louder as they floated around the bend. Ahead they could see rocks larger than cars poking from the river with foaming water roaring and twisting around them. White spray filled the air.

Mr. Palmer looked around the raft, studying each boy. "If you see somebody going over the side, grab them and pull them back. I'm counting on Elliot, who's counting on Wayne, who's counting on Cass..." He continued on, naming every boy in the raft. "We do this together or we don't do it." He smiled. "Let's all paddle and have some fun!"

Your Turn

1. If you do chores, do you think it's fair you have to help?
2. Why is it important to do your part gladly—and completely?

_____

_____

_____

Prayer

God, I want to do my part in my family and church. Amen.

What God Wants

*Carry each other's burdens, and in this way
you will fulfill the law of Christ.*
— **Galatians 6:2**

And It Was Good!

Mr. Palmer poked the campfire. "In the beginning, God created heaven and earth. He created light to shine in the darkness. And it was good. On the second day, God created the sky, and it was good." The campfire popped, and a spark rose in the air. "On the third day, God created the land and the plants. And…"

After a moment of silence, Cass added, "And it was good."

"On the fourth day, God made the sun, moon, and stars, and…"

"It was good," the boys chanted.

"On the fifth day, God created swordfish, hummingbirds, whales, and hawks," Mr. Palmer said.

"And it was good!" the boys said loudly.

"On the sixth day, God made land animals and people. And…."

"It was good!" the boys shouted, their voices filling the air.

"God made you and me," Mr. Palmer said. "Does He ever do a bad job?"

"No way!" Elliot said.

"That's right," Mr. Palmer agreed. "God never messes up. Elliot, you are God's good work. *You* too, Wayne. And *you,* Cass." He worked his way around the circle, naming each boy. "When you feel bad about yourself, remember who made you. You are God's good work!"

Your Turn

1. List a few wonderful things about yourself.
2. List a few wonderful things about your parents. Let them know.

Prayer

God, You made me, and You don't make junk. Amen.

What God Wants

I've Got Your Back

Life is a lot easier when we pick each other up and help each other carry the load. Here's a trick you can try with a friend—but the only way this will work is if you carry each other's weight.

I. Sit back-to-back on the floor with a friend. Lean against each other.

2. Reach back and hook your arms through your friend's arms. Pull your feet close to you. With your arms hooked, each of you push against the other while rising to your feet. It might take a little practice, but you will get the hang of it. It works best if you and your friend are about the same size.

3. When you get good at this, try it with three people.

Prayer

Father God, when I notice that one of my friends seems down, help me lift him or her up. Amen.

What God Wants

God Doesn't Make Junk

If God made you, you must be pretty amazing. Nobody else is exactly like you, and nobody else could be you. Congratulations on being who you are! Maybe you don't think very much about how special you are. Try finishing each of these sentences. Don't be shy. Remember, God only makes the best.

Something that makes me special is...

A game I'm good at is...

My friends like me because...

A thing I like about myself is...

At school, I do well in...

God is proud of me because...

Made by God

Prayer

God, You made me so I want to take good care of myself. Amen.

Depending on God

Grow in the grace and knowledge of our LORD and Savior Jesus Christ.
– 2 Peter 3:18

Riding on the Wind

Elliot and Cass were on cleanup duty, washing dishes and pans in a small tub of soapy water. "This pan is hard to clean," Elliot moaned.

"The eggs were burned." Cass tossed a handful of sand and tiny pebbles into the cast-iron skillet. "Use the sand like a scrubber."

Elliot rubbed the rough sand into the pan, and the burned eggs peeled off. "Cool! That really works."

When they finished, they carried the water a few yards into the woods. They dug a hole about the size of a football and poured the water in. They kicked dirt back into the hole and covered it with dead leaves.

Exiting the woods, Elliot pointed to the sky. "Look! An eagle!"

Far overhead, a broad-winged bird moved in a slow, wide circle.

"He's not flapping his wings," Cass said. "How can he fly?"

"He's riding the wind," Elliot said. "When he's that high, he can glide for hours just holding his wings out while the wind does the work."

"Isn't there something in the Bible about God carrying us like an eagle?" Cass asked.

"I don't know," Elliot said, "but it makes sense. If we trust God the way the eagle trusts the wind, then God will carry us along."

Your Turn

1. Have you seen an eagle or hawk soar on the wind?
2. How is your faith in God like an eagle?

_____

_____

Prayer

God, no matter how far I go or how high I climb, You hold on to me. Thanks! Amen.

Depending on God

Grow in the grace and knowledge of our LORD *and Savior Jesus Christ.*
— **2 Peter 3:18**

Fierce Feathers

As Cass and Elliot watched the eagle soar, Mr. Palmer joined them. He scanned the hills, and then pointed. "See that tree by itself? That mess of sticks and branches in the top is an eagle's nest."

Cass said, "I guess nothing can bother the babies that high up."

"There are predators that climb that high," Mr. Palmer said. "And other birds would like to eat the eggs. Eagles keep a close eye on their nests."

"When there's danger," Elliot said, "the eagle sitting on the nest spreads its wings. Nobody's going to get past an eagle parent easily."

"That's the way God watches over us," Mr. Palmer said. "Like an eagle, He spreads His wings over us."

"God has wings?" Cass asked.

"No," Mr. Palmer said. "It's just a way to talk about God." He glanced at Cass. "You were a little scared when we started out. "How are you doing?"

"I'm having a great time. The next time I'm afraid, I'll remember that God's wings protect me."

"God's wings can even reach under water," Elliot teased. "Good thing, 'cause you spend half your time falling out of the raft."

Mr. Palmer and Cass laughed. "Load up!" Mr. Palmer announced. "Time to hit the river."

Your Turn

1. Think of a time you knew God was protecting you. How did you feel?

_____

_____

Prayer

Wow, God! You've got my back—and my front and sides too. Amen.

Depending on God

Grow in the grace and knowledge of our LORD and Savior Jesus Christ.
– 2 Peter 3:18

The Right Word

"We did it!" Wayne shouted. "All the way through those rapids!"

"Good job!" Mr. Palmer said. "I'm proud of you. Everyone followed orders; no one held back. We were there for each other."

"When that big wave hit us from the side," Elliot said, "if I hadn't grabbed Cass' life jacket, he'd have visited the fishies."

Cass said, "You're so full of hot air. I didn't need help."

"Hey, Elliot," Dylan said, "what about when you dropped your paddle? If I hadn't kicked it back, you'd have been no help."

"I could have reached it," Elliot snapped.

Mr. Palmer cut in. "Sometimes we're better at giving help than receiving it. Everybody needs help sometimes. When you get help, you can hide behind pride and deny it or you can use one powerful word. Anybody know the word?"

Cass thought for a moment and turned to Elliot. "Thanks."

Elliot nodded and turned to another boy. "Thanks, Dylan."

"That didn't hurt so much, did it?" asked Mr. Palmer.

Your Turn

1. Is it easier for you to give help or ask for help?
2. Why do you think you feel that way?

_____

_____

_____

_____

Prayer

God, when I need help, remind me that everyone does at times. Amen.

333

Depending on God

Grow in the grace and knowledge of our LORD *and Savior Jesus Christ.*
– 2 Peter 3:18

The Gopher Hole

After a full day of whitewater rafting, Mr. Palmer had steered the craft to a quiet shore where the boys swam, jumped from a tall rock into a deep pool, and had water fights. After the tents were set up, the leader declared an hour of free time. "You can rest or explore. Just don't leave camp without a buddy."

So what did Cass do? He went into the woods by himself to see what trees he could identify. He'd planned to go only a few yards into the woods, but he wandered quite far. When he decided to turn back, he stepped in a gopher hole and hurt his ankle. It had swollen like a balloon. Now he sat on the ground with his leg stretched out and his ankle throbbing.

Why didn't I follow the rules? he thought. *If I'd had a buddy, I wouldn't be in this mess.* Someone would come looking for him, he knew. But when? He brushed off the bugs that crawled over his body and watched the shadows grow longer. Cass heard movement in the dry leaves and voices yelling his name. "I'm here!" he yelled. "Over here!"

Your Turn

1. Why do people make rules?
2. Name two rules you follow that keep you safe.

_____

_____

_____

_____

Prayer

God, when I don't want to follow the rules, help me remember why I should.

Depending on God

Grow in the grace and knowledge of our Lord and Savior Jesus Christ.
– 2 Peter 3:18

Success

"Boys, you've done a great job," Mr. Palmer said as the raft bobbed lazily down a calm stretch of river. "We have one more stretch of whitewater before we reach the landing where our bus is waiting."

"We don't want to go home yet," Wayne said. "This is too much fun."

"Two days ago most of you had never been in a raft. Now you're paddling like experts," Mr. Palmer said. "To prove how much you've learned, I want you to steer the last whitewater."

"Whoa!" Elliot said. "We can't do that."

"I think you can," the leader said. "Wayne, you take my place here in the back and be the coach. I'll take your paddle and sit in the front."

Wayne carefully moved to the rear. Mr. Palmer described the upcoming rapids to him and made suggestions.

Mr. Palmer seated himself in the front as the water grew louder.

"Paddle right!" Wayne called. "Paddle left...hard left! Now!"

The raft slipped around rocks. A surge spun the boat backward. Watching the river over his shoulder, Wayne yelled, "Paddle backwards!"

After a stomach-grabbing drop and another spin, the raft emerged from the rapids pointed in the right direction. Shouts and high-fives filled the boat.

Your Turn

1. How are you different now than a year ago?
2. What success have you experienced lately?

_____

_____

Prayer

God, I hope I never stop growing in You. Amen.

Depending on God

Why Rules?

Most people don't like rules very much. They forget that most rules are meant to help them live better lives. You'll know some good reasons for following rules if you can find the safety words in this word search. Words are horizontal and vertical.

Share • Obey • Safe • Fair • Learn

```
T C P W F B L
E N S H A R E
L U A R I Z A
S T F P R U R
O B E Y N E N
```

Prayer

Heavenly Father, Sometimes I'm not very happy about having to follow rules, so please help me remember they are for my own good. Amen.

Depending on God

Bigger and Bigger

Jesus grew the same way we do. The Bible says that He grew in four ways: in wisdom, in body, in His relationship with God, and in His relationships with people. Write some things that show how you are growing in each of those four ways. Here are some examples to get you started. Put check marks in the right category. Come up with your own ideas too. Remember, some signs of growth might fit in more than one category.

ACTIVITY	BODY	MIND	GOD	OTHER
Getting taller				
Learning about the Bible				
Moving to a new city				
Doing more chores at home				

Prayer

God, it's easy to see that I'm growing on the outside. But even more, I want to grow on the inside and become more like You. Amen.

337

Caution!

All hard work brings profit, but mere talk leads only to poverty.
– Proverbs 14:23

Worthy Words

Coach said, "Good game, guys. Batting practice on Monday. Shawn, will you give me a hand?"

"Sure, Coach," Shawn said.

As they slid equipment into the canvas bag, Coach said, "Shawn, I heard some language in the outfield today that I don't approve of."

Shawn's face turned red. "I didn't mean to, Coach. It just slipped out when I dropped that fly ball."

Coach held up his hand. "Some boys use rough language to show they're cool or tough, but there's nothing tough about it."

"Everybody talks that way," Shawn said.

"I don't," Coach said. "I say what I have to say, and I don't throw in a bunch of bad words. If you use proper language, people will pay more attention to what you say. They'll respect you."

Shawn retrieved a ball near the backstop. "It's kind of a habit."

"Any habit you make," Coach said, "is a habit you can break. I expect the best from my players. Their best effort and their best behavior."

"Yes, sir," Shawn said.

"I'll be paying attention," Coach said, "to make sure you're doing your best on and off the field. "Now, some of the guys are going for ice cream. You have time for a double-dip?"

"For sure!" Shawn said.

Your Turn

1. Do you say things to impress others? Does it work?
2. Why is it good to not swear or use coarse words?

Prayer

God, my words show what's in my heart. Help me stay clean in thought and speech. Amen.

Caution!

All hard work brings profit, but mere talk leads only to poverty.
– Proverbs 14:23

Big Spender

"Let's go to the arcade," Cameron said. "We've got time."

"Okay, but I'll just watch," Noah said. "I'm a little short on money."

Cameron drove a race car and shot tigers in Wild Safari, and tried out a climbing wall. "I'm thirsty!'" At the food court, he ordered a triple-chocolate malt.

"We'd better go," Noah said. "We don't want to miss the movie."

"Crimson Spider Meets the Earth-Wrecker!" Cameron said. "Crimson Spider is the greatest superhero of all time."

In a store window, Cameron spotted a Crimson Spider baseball cap. "I've gotta have one!" He pulled Noah into the store. "I like the black one with the red spider-web." He paid and said, "I don't need a bag. I'll wear it!"

At the theater, the two boys lined up for tickets.

"Movies are expensive," Noah said, "I saved up for this."

Cameron pulled two dollars from his pocket. "Oh, no! I don't have enough money! "Will you loan me enough to get in?"

"I don't have enough for two tickets," Noah said.

"What are we going to do?" Cameron asked with a moan.

"I don't know about you," Noah said, "but I'm going to see the movie."

Your Turn

1. When Cameron bought the hat, did he think ahead?
2. Why does it help to have a plan for spending money?

_____

_____

_____

Prayer

God, help me be careful with money and other things You provide. Amen.

Caution!

All hard work brings profit, but mere talk leads only to poverty.
– Proverbs 14:23

Eighty-Nine Cents

Shane winked at Ian as they carried their trays to the table in Jumbo Burger Hut. They set down the trays containing fries, burgers, and Ian's drink cup. Shane reached into his jacket pocket and drew out a Jumbo Burger Hut drink cup. "I've used this cup like eight times."

Ian frowned. "What do you mean?"

"I bought a drink here last month," Shane explained. "I kept the cup. I sneak it in so I get free drinks when I eat here. Pretty cool, huh?"

"But that's stealing," Ian protested.

"I paid for it," Shane said. "And there's no limit on refills."

"Look, you know it's wrong," Ian said. "Don't try to twist this around. If it wasn't wrong, you wouldn't hide the cup in your pocket."

"It's hardly costing Jumbo Burger anything. Everybody knows they overcharge for soft drinks. So I'm bending the rules a little," Shane admitted.

"Call it what it is," Ian said. "It's not bending the rules. It's stealing."

"You're mad because I thought of it and you didn't," Shane said. "If you're smart, you'll bring your cup back next time."

"I am smart," Ian said. "Smart enough to know I don't want to be a thief."

Your Turn

1. When Cameron bought the hat, did he think ahead?
2. Why does it help to have a plan for spending money?

_____

_____

Prayer

God, I want to honor You by being honest. Stealing is wrong. Amen.

Caution!

All hard work brings profit, but mere talk leads only to poverty.
– Proverbs 14:23

Maybe Tomorrow

Cole stood on the porch and watched his family head to the state fair. He'd thought his dad would change his mind. No such luck. They had made a deal, and Cole hadn't done his part.

A month ago, everybody had been given chores to finish before the fair. Cole's younger sister had to clean out her closet. His older sister agreed to sort through the bookshelf and put the books in order. Mom would wallpaper the bathroom, and Dad would replace missing roof shingles. Cole's job was scrubbing the oil stains on the garage floor and then painting it.

It isn't such a big job, Cole had thought. Washing off the oil would be a pain, but painting the floor with a long-handled roller might be fun. But it was summer vacation, and Cole liked to take things easy.

He slept late every day, spent time with his friends, and played summer sports. The weather was hot, so Cole put off the sweaty garage work. He did start one day, but scrubbing the oil stains made him tired, so he went swimming instead.

So, here he was—left behind. He stood before the open garage and considered the job. *Maybe tomorrow.*

Your Turn

1. Did Cole learn anything?
2. Some people get right to work, and some put it off. What do you do?

_____

_____

_____

Prayer

God, help me be responsible and get my work done first. Amen.

Caution!

All hard work brings profit, but mere talk leads only to poverty.
– Proverbs 14:23

Chocolate-Covered Love

As soon as the door opened, Philip said, "Hi, I'm selling chocolate bars to raise money for new uniforms for our school's marching band."

"You're the boy who shoveled snow off my sidewalk," Mrs. Colan said. "I'll buy five chocolate bars."

At the next house, Philip gave his sales pitch to a boy who said, "Wait a sec." Philip heard him say, "Mom, Phil's selling candy bars…Yeah, the guy who helped me with math." The boy returned. "We'll buy two."

At the next house, Philip said, "Hi, Dr. Romita. Has your dog turned up?"

"Not yet. Thanks for helping me look for him."

"I'm selling chocolate for the band. Will you buy some?"

Dr. Romita pulled a wallet from his pocket and took out a ten-dollar bill. "I'm allergic to chocolate, but I'll make a donation."

At home, Philip said, "Mom, people in our neighborhood are so kind."

His mom smiled. "Philip, our neighbors are kind to you because you rake leaves, walk dogs, and run errands for them."

"I like being a good neighbor," Philip said.

"When you're kind to people, they'll be nice to you," his mom said.

"Not always," Philip said. "Mrs. Buscema said to never bother her again." He smiled. "Most of our neighbors are kind."

Your Turn

1. If you are kind to people, will they usually be kind to you?

_____

_____

Prayer

God, sometimes kindness comes back. What a great way to live. Amen.

Caution!

Making a Money Plan

Cameron's Aunt Bertha gave him twenty-five dollars for his birthday. Cameron wants to save fifteen dollars to buy the soundtrack from *Crimson Spider Meets the Earth-Wrecker* when it comes out next week. Can you help him plan his spending so he'll have at least fifteen dollars when the music is released? Start at the top and circle the things Cameron can spend money on and put an X through the things he shouldn't buy if he wants the music. Be careful! Make sure he has fifteen dollars left at the end.

Total Spent _____   Total Saved _____

Prayer

God, I want to be more careful with my money. Help me find guidance in the Bible and when I pray. Amen.

Caution!

Super Kindness

Make up names for these superheroes of kindness. Be creative! For instance, the first one might be Helpatronic or Handy-Boy. After you've named each hero, put a number on the scale from 1 to 10 to show how much you are like (or not like) that hero.

_____ is always willing to help when someone needs a hand opening a door, carrying a big stack of books, or figuring out the instructions on a math work sheet.

This describes me:

1_____10
    Not at all   Sometimes   Always

_____ does things that need doing before he is asked to do them. People at his house are always wondering: Who folded the clothes for me? Who packed a lunch for me? Who fed the dog? Who found my missing glove?

This describes me:

1_____10
    Not at all   Sometimes   Always

_____ wants everyone to know whenever he does something nice. He makes sure other people see it or hear about it whenever he is kind to someone. He always wants credit for his efforts and good deeds.

This describes me:

1_____10
    Not at all   Sometimes   Always

Prayer

Father God, help me see what needs to be done and then do it before I'm asked. Amen.

What's Important?

*Let someone else praise you, and not your own mouth;
an outsider, and not your own lips.*
– Proverbs 27:2

The Big Dinner

"Ryan invited me to dinner at his house tonight," Jared told his mom.

"I'll phone his mother to make sure it's okay," Mom said.

"Ryan lives in a huge house," Jared said. "They have servants."

"So do you," his mother said with a wink. "Her name is Mom."

"What are you cooking tonight?" Jared asked.

"Meat loaf," Mom said.

"Hah! We'll have something better at Ryan's house," Jared said.

"Let me know if you decide to move in with him," Mom said, smiling.

Dinner was as good as Jared had hoped—salad, steak, and mashed potatoes with cheese and bacon bits. They used fancy glasses and had a table too big to fit into Jared's house.

Better food than at home, Jared decided, *but not as much fun.* Hardly anyone said a word. No joking. No messing around. No laughing. Jared thought about the laughing and joking that went on during dinner at home. Dad kidded Mom about her cooking. Jared and his brothers told funny stories from school. It wasn't unusual for Jared to laugh so hard that milk squeezed from his nose.

"How was dinner?" his mother asked when she picked him up.

"Okay, I guess," Jared said. "Hey, is there any leftover meat loaf?"

Your Turn

1. What's a way you can thank your parents for all they do for you?

_____

_____

_____

Prayer

God, I don't have everything, but I have enough. Thank You. Amen.

What's Important?

*Let someone else praise you, and not your own mouth;
an outsider, and not your own lips.*
                                          – Proverbs 27:2

The Captain

The members of the academic debate team stood on the stage during a school assembly. The had won the award for first place in "rapid recall."

"I'm very proud to accept this trophy," Hunter said. "As captain, I worked hard to take our academic team to the championship."

"He built our team?" Sophia whispered to Sam. "He missed half our practice debates, and he goofed off when he did show up."

"You answered twice as many questions as he did!" Sam said.

"I decided that running drills in different subjects would get us ready," Hunter said. "My strategy helped us make it to the championship."

Sophia turned red. "Hey, that was my idea," she said under her breath.

The principal leaned toward Hunter and whispered, "Remember, the championship was a team victory."

"Absolutely," Hunter said, beaming. "I was too sick to attend one match. The team somehow managed to win even without my presence."

The principal said, "Hunter, maybe you'd like to demonstrate how you led the team to victory? Tell us the speed of light."

"Sure," Hunter said. He turned to the team. "Who knows the answer?"

Your Turn

1. Have you shown off? Did you feel important? What happened?
2. How do you feel about people who praise themselves?

_____

_____

_____

Prayer

God, help me to do my best and remember to put others first. Amen.

What's Important?

Let someone else praise you, and not your own mouth;
an outsider, and not your own lips.
– **Proverbs 27:2**

The Red Truck

The Scout Master, Mr. Starlin, turned to Dan. "Could your father bring his truck to help us with the grocery drive?"

"His truck?" Dan asked.

"The red truck with the racing stripes," Jake said, nudging Dan. "Double cab, extra-long bed. It's all you've been talking about."

"Sure," Dan said nervously. "Yeah, I'll ask Dad if he will help."

Later, waiting in the church parking lot for their parents, Jake said, "Maybe your Dad will pick you up in the truck. I'd love to see it."

"I don't think he will," Dan said. "Dad sold the truck."

Jake looked at his friend "Dan, you made the whole thing up! Your dad never bought a truck, did he?"

"I thought it would be cool if my dad had a big, red truck," Dan said. "Then I kind of told some people that he did."

"What are you going to tell Mr. Starlin?" Jake asked.

Dan said, "I'll tell him dad is going to be out of town."

"And what if Mr. Starlin bumps into your dad at the bowling alley and brings up the truck?" Jake asked.

"I'll tell Dad Mr. Starlin must have me confused with another kid."

Jake shook his head. "Lies to cover up lies. Why not just tell the truth?"

Your Turn

1. Have you told a lie? Did it make things better or worse?
2. What would you do if your friend told a lie?

_____

_____

_____

Prayer

God, lying is easy, but telling the truth is *always* better. Amen.

What's Important?

Let someone else praise you, and not your own mouth;
an outsider, and not your own lips.

– Proverbs 27:2

Get Well Soon

On the bus ride home after school, Rob told Kevin, "I don't think I'll make it to choir practice tonight. I've got a stomachache."

Walking home from the bus stop, Kevin bumped into BJ, and said, "Rob is pretty sick. I think he has food poisoning."

When BJ got home, he told his sister, "You know that kid Rob? He got food poisoning in the school cafeteria. I'm glad I took my lunch."

Rob's sister called her friend Kim. "Did you hear that BJ's friend Rob is in the hospital with food poisoning? They're pumping his stomach."

Kim told her mother, "Remember that boy Rob who sings in the church choir? I heard he's having surgery."

Kim's mom drove to Rob's house. When Rob's mother opened the door, Kim's mom said, "Joyce, I heard about Rob. Is there anything I can do?"

Just then Rob joined his mother at the door. "Hi, Mrs. Allard," he said. Then he said to his mom, "Stomachache is gone. I'm going to choir practice." He trotted down the walk, humming.

Rob's mother turned to Mrs. Allard. "What did you hear about Rob?"

Mrs. Allard looked embarrassed. "That he was very sick. I guess not."

Your Turn

1. Have you repeated a story that wasn't true?
   How do you think those stories get started?
2. What is "gossip"?

_____

_____

_____

Prayer

God, I want to say only things that are true and helpful. Amen.

What's Important?

*Let someone else praise you, and not your own mouth;
an outsider, and not your own lips.*
— **Proverbs 27:2**

The Hot Head

"You're the worst captain in the whole world!" Rico shouted.

"I make some mistakes," Juan admitted, "but I'm doing my best."

"You shouldn't have benched me," Rico said.

"Rico, you were limping after you slid into third," Juan explained. "I decided you should stay off that foot for a while."

Rico held up his fists. "I'll show you how hurt I am. Come on!"

The players gathered around Rico and Juan. They chanted, "Fight! Fight!"

"Knock it off," Juan said loudly. "Rico, go home. We'll talk later."

"You're afraid to fight me," Rico said.

"Think what you want to," Juan said. "Go home now."

Rico walked away, making chicken noises in his throat. The other boys laughed and drifted away, leaving only Juan and his best friend, Chuck.

"Man, you should have knocked him on his can," Chuck said.

Juan took a deep breath. "I won the fight that mattered."

"What do you mean?" Chuck asked.

"The fight inside of me," Juan said. "Rico really made me mad. I wanted to punch his lights out. But then we'd both be kicked off the team. Nobody wins then."

Your Turn

1. Have you done something in anger? How did it turn out?
2. What are some things you can do when you get mad?

_____

_____

_____

Prayer

God, help me use my head and stay out of trouble. Amen.

What's Important?

My House

Pretend that this is a picture of your house or apartment. Inside, draw the members of your family and other people that you care about. If there's any extra room, draw some of your favorite things.

God, thank you for...

Prayer

God, I am thankful for the people and things in my life. Help me be content. Amen.

What's Important?

Crazy Talk

Ask some friends or family members to help you. Without reading the sentence aloud, ask someone to give you a word to fill in the blank. For instance, ask someone to say a person's name. Put that name in the first blank. When you finish, read the story to your friends. Notice that changing just one or two words can make a big difference in what you say about another person.

_____ is a _____ friend.
(name of person)   (describing word)

He acts like a/an _____ whenever
(name of an animal)

we go out to eat. His favorite food is

_____. In the lunch room, he
(name of a vegetable)

always eats pudding with his _____.
(name of a body part)

Sometimes he carries _____ in his
(a squishy food)

pocket as a snack. Maybe he

belongs in a _____.
(place where people go
with their families)

Prayer

Lord, sometimes I want to share what I know about people, but I know gossiping and spreading rumors are wrong. Please help me hold my tongue. Amen.

What Is Coming

Cast your cares on the LORD and he will sustain you.
– Psalm 55:22

Television Tension

Ted sat in the family room reading his Bible while his father watched the evening news. Ted glanced up and saw a clip of bombs falling on a city in the Middle East. A newscaster explained that one missile destroyed a school and killed four children.

The coverage shifted to a different country. People were in the streets protesting against their government. The protesters threw rocks and bottles, and soldiers shot into the crowd. Protesters and soldiers moaned or lay dead on the pavement.

During the commercials, Ted read, but the news caught his attention again. Two African tribes wanted to destroy each other.

Suddenly the TV went blank and silent. His father, holding the remote, said, "Nothing but bad news on television." He waved at the Bible in Ted's lap. "Any good news in there?"

"It says that someday God will bring peace to the whole world," Ted said. "No more killing or hurting. Even the animals will be at peace. Little kids will play with snakes. Wolves and lambs will nap together. Cows and bears will be buddies. 'They will neither harm nor destroy on all my holy mountain for the earth will be filled with the knowledge of the LORD.' That's in Isaiah 11."

His father closed his eyes. "Read more. I can use some good news."

Your Turn

1. Why do you think there is so much violence in the world?
2. Should you try to change the world? If yes, how?

Prayer

God, life gets scary. I'm glad I know You are in charge. Amen.

What Is Coming

Cast your cares on the LORD and he will sustain you.
– Psalm 55:22

Rocks in the Stream

"We might have to move," Neil said. "Dad might lose his job."

"That stinks," Josh said. "Are you scared?" Josh said.

"A little scared, I guess," Neil admitted. "Mom says I shouldn't worry."

"Because your dad can find another job?" Josh asked.

"No, because God will take care of us," Neil said.

"Cool," Josh said. "So you won't have to move."

"I don't think it works that way," Neil lifted a rock, and a snake darted away.

Watching the snake, Josh said, "My family doesn't go to church. I don't know much about God. Will He take care of you or not?"

Neil considered. "God will take care of us, but we still might move. God doesn't always keep our family from having trouble, but He always gets us through the trouble."

Josh hoisted up a large rock with both hands and threw it into the middle of the stream. A huge crash threw water into the air.

"Maybe it's like this stream," Neil said. "Big rocks and dead trees get in the way of the stream. The water changes course and pushes stuff, but it still gets where it's going. Things get bumpy, but God keeps us moving forward."

Your Turn

1. Do you worry about potential problems? Does it help?
2. Instead of worrying, what can you do?

_____

_____

_____

Prayer

God, I trust You to get me through hard times. Amen.

What Is Coming

Cast your cares on the LORD and he will sustain you.
– Psalm 55:22

The Stronghold

"Dad, a tornado might be coming," Riley said. "Doesn't that scare you?"

"It's scary, but we'll be okay." Dad led Riley through the kitchen and down into the basement. He opened a door to a small room with shelves packed with tools and boxes.

"Your work room," Riley said. "So what?"

"This is our stronghold," Dad said. "If the storm gets scary, we'll come down here."

Riley entered the room. He knocked on a wall. "Concrete."

"So is the ceiling," Dad pointed out. "We're under the side porch."

"No windows in here," Riley said. "So the storm can't get in."

"A tornado won't hurt us in here," his father assured him. "We're underground. We're surrounded by concrete. We're safe."

"Even if the house blew away?" Riley asked.

His dad nodded. "Even if the house went flying like a kite."

"What did you call it?" Riley asked.

"Our stronghold," Dad replied. "Tell you what. We can come down here right now. You get the checkerboard and set it up on the workbench. I'll get a couple of chairs."

A few minutes later, as they played checkers, Riley said, "I like having a stronghold. I'm not scared anymore."

Your Turn

1. Where is the safest place in your home?
2. Where is the safest place for your heart?

_____

_____

Prayer

God, I don't know what's coming, but You're my stronghold. Amen.

What Is Coming

Cast your cares on the LORD and he will sustain you.
— **Psalm 55:22**

Heart Trouble

Nick sat in bed wearing a hospital gown. A wall-mounted television was on, and a dinner tray sat beside the bed. Jose and Will walked in uncertainly.

"How's it going?" Will asked.

"I'm feeling fine," Nick said. "I'll be well before midterms."

"Then it's not too bad," Jose said. He sounded relieved.

"Oh, it's pretty bad," Nick said. "My heart is messed up. It's a problem I was born with. But I'm still getting well. Cable TV, Dinner in bed. Totally cute Nurse Gwen. It's not so bad."

"Maybe we should come back when she's on duty," Jose said.

"How about your doctor?" Jose asked.

"She's going to put a pig valve in my heart," Nick said. "Maybe I'll grow a curly tail and start oinking."

"That's too weird," Will said.

Nick took a Bible from a drawer. He opened it to a marked page and handed it to Jose. "Read aloud the part that's underlined, please."

Jose said, "Matthew 19:26. 'What is impossible with man is possible with God.'"

"So God will fix your heart if that is His plan," said Will.

"And why wouldn't He? You guys won't pass math without me."

Your Turn

1. God can do anything. What are some times you need to remember this?

_____

_____

Prayer

God, remind me that what seems impossible to me is easy for You. Amen.

What Is Coming

Cast your cares on the LORD and he will sustain you.
– Psalm 55:22

Worrying About Wayne

Chase set his tray on the table and said, "You know that guy Wayne, the one my mom has been dating?"

"Sure," Adam said. "He's always telling your mom she's too easy on you, that you need more discipline, blah blah blah."

"He proposed to Mom yesterday," Chase said. "I'm praying a lot."

"Praying for your mom not to marry Wayne?" Adam asked.

"I might have mentioned that to God," Chase said, grinning. "Mostly I'm asking God to settle me down and help me through whatever comes."

Adam said, "Maybe your mom will decide Wayne isn't the right guy."

"Or maybe Wayne will ease up," Chase suggested. "Or I might learn to like him more. I feel better about it when I talk to God."

"Really?" Adam asked. "I don't pray much. How does it work?"

"At first, I'm all upset so I tell God how Wayne bugs me and I wish it was just Mom and me again. I guess I throw my junk on God and let Him carry it. After a while I feel calmer. Just knowing God cares and understands makes me feel safe. Does that sound dorky?"

"It sounds great," Adam told him. "I think I'll try it."

Your Turn

1. Does telling God your problems make you feel better?
2. When you tell God your problems, do you ask Him to guide you?

Prayer

God, when things are hard, You say to give them to You. Thanks! Amen.

What Is Coming

On a Stormy Day

In Luke 8:22-25 there is a story about Jesus protecting the disciples on a dangerous day. Below, the story has gotten messed up. Can you fix it? Wherever you find a wrong word, scratch it out and put in the right word. You can look the story up if you get stuck.

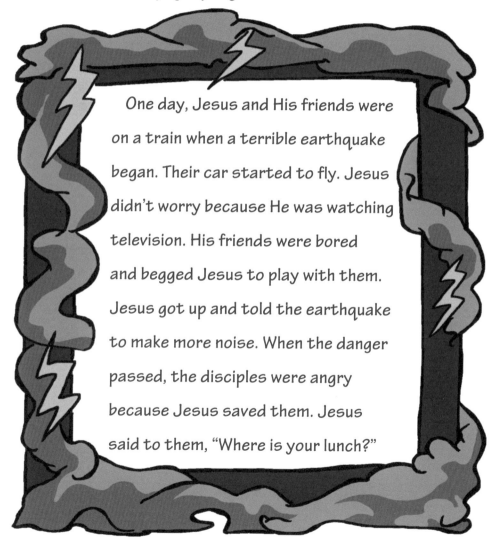

One day, Jesus and His friends were on a train when a terrible earthquake began. Their car started to fly. Jesus didn't worry because He was watching television. His friends were bored and begged Jesus to play with them. Jesus got up and told the earthquake to make more noise. When the danger passed, the disciples were angry because Jesus saved them. Jesus said to them, "Where is your lunch?"

Prayer

LORD Jesus, I'm going to remember this story so when I'm scared I will remember to ask You for help. Amen.

What Is Coming

Two Things

You don't have to carry your problems by yourself. There are two things you can always turn over to God and ask Him to carry them for you. To find out the two things, use the clues to find the letter that goes in each blank.

_____ THE BEST GRADE YOU CAN GET

_____ THE OPPOSITE OF OUT

_____ THIS LETTER IS A QUESTION

_____ SOMETHING YOU CAN DRINK HOT OR COLD

_____ LOOKS LIKE A FOOTBALL GOAL POST

_____ DO YOU HAVE TWO OF THESE IN YOUR FACE?

_____ A Z KNOCKED ON ITS SIDE

_____ THE SEVENTH LETTER IN THE ALPHABET

AND

_____ A BACKWARDS 3

_____ LOOKS LIKE A TWO-FINGER PEACE SIGN

_____ ANOTHER BACKWARDS 3

_____ I AM. HE IS. THEY _____ .

_____ POR QUE?

_____ SOMETHING TO SET A GOLF BALL ON

_____ THE LETTER YOU CAN'T HEAR IN "HONEST"

_____ ME, MYSELF, AND _____.

_____ THIS LETTER IS ALMOST AN M

_____ THE FIRST OR LAST SYLLABLE OF "GEOLOGY"

Prayer

God, I know that anything and everything that happens in my life never takes You by surprise. Amen.

Be Thankful

Give thanks in all circumstances.
–1 Thessalonians 5:18

The Crummiest Summer

Jeremy and his brother, Reese, were watching TV. Jeremy was on the sofa, his left ankle in a heavy cast was propped on a pillow.

"What a rotten time to break my ankle," Jeremy grumbled. "No swimming, no soccer, no fun. What a terrible summer ahead."

"Your complaining is driving me crazy," Reese said.

"I've got plenty to complain about," Jeremy shot back.

"You've got even more to be thankful for," Reese said. "One, when you fell off your skateboard, you broke your ankle instead of your neck. Two, it's a clean break and will heal up fine."

"Three, my brother is a pain in the neck," groused Jeremy.

"I'm not finished," Reese said. "Three, you live in a country with great doctors. Four, your family took you to the doctor. Five, you'll be walking in a few weeks. Six, you've got books to read, movies to watch, and food to eat."

In a gentle voice, Reese continued. "I'm sorry you got hurt. But if you have a lousy summer, blame your attitude. You choose to complain or you choose to be thankful." He saw Jeremy's frown. "Maybe a root beer float will help," Reese said.

"Maybe it would," agreed Jeremy.

Your Turn

1. When you complain, do you feel better?
2. How do you feel when you think about good things?

_____

_____

_____

Prayer

God, there are so many good things in my life. Thank You! Amen.

Be Thankful

Give thanks in all circumstances.
–1 Thessalonians 5:18

Rolling

Jeremy's brother punched the television remote and changed channels. A sporting event replaced a cartoon.

"Hey!" Jeremy said. "Who made you boss of the television?"

"You've got to see this," Reese said.

Jeremy shifted his leg on the pillow, adjusting the cast on his broken ankle. "If I weren't stuck in this recliner..."

"I'm shaking with fear," Reese said. He nodded at the TV.

On the screen two teams raced across a basketball court. The action was fast, the passing smooth, and the shooting excellent. It was like many games Jeremy had seen, except every player was in a wheelchair and moving at dizzying speeds.

The players rolled across the floor, interweaving but never crashing. "A couple of these guys are marathoners," Reese said.

"Twenty-six miles at top speed in a wheelchair?" Jeremy asked. "Wow. They must have arm muscles like Superman."

"Believe it, little brother," Reese said. "You won't find better athletes than these, and their determination is even bigger than their biceps."

"You want me to watch this and stop feeling sorry for myself," Jeremy said.

"Is it working?" his brother asked.

"Absolutely!"

Your Turn

1. Can you think of people who have overcome great problems?
2. What can you do to keep your attitude positive?

_____

_____

Prayer

God, it's so easy to feel sorry for myself. Show me how much strength I have in You. Amen.

Be Thankful

Give thanks in all circumstances.
–1 Thessalonians 5:18

Black, White, and Gray

"It's time for chess," Grandpa said. He unfolded the black-and-white board on the table beside Jeremy's recliner.

Jeremy chose white and set up his side of the board. He liked the look and feel of the pieces, especially the knights, which were horse heads.

Grandpa shook a finger and corrected, "Remember, queen on her own color."He paused. "Today I'm going to teach you how to 'castle,' " Grandpa said. He explained the move and let Jeremy try it out.

"You've got it," Grandpa said. "Let's play."

Jeremy moved a pawn; Grandpa brought out a knight.

"How did you learn to play chess, Grandpa?"

"My grandfather taught me," he said. "We lived on a farm, so wintertime was slow. Opa came here from Germany. He didn't speak good English, but he was a fine chess player."

Jeremy liked playing chess, but, even more, he enjoyed his Grandpa. This extra time with him was a wonderful blessing brought about by Jeremy's broken ankle. Jeremy moved another pawn forward.

"You sure about that?" Grandpa asked.

"Umm, maybe not," Jeremy said. He chose a different pawn to move.

"Much better," Grandpa said.

"So you learned chess from your grandfather the way I'm learning from you?" Jeremy asked.

"I guess it's up to you to teach *your* grandson," Grandpa said.

Your Turn

1. What have you learned from people older than you?

Prayer

God, thank You for my parents, grandparents, and older people who share their love and learning. Amen.

Be Thankful

Give thanks in all circumstances.
–1 Thessalonians 5:18

Who Knew?

Pastor Chris accepted the coffee mug from Jeremy's mother and settled it on his knee. He turned to Jeremy. "I heard you were banged up. Did you really break something or are you just faking it for sympathy?" Pastor Chris had a sparkle in his eye.

When Jeremy said it was a skateboard accident, the minister nodded knowingly. "When I was about your age, I took a spill on my board and ended up with a broken arm."

Jeremy stared in amazement. "*You* used to skateboard?"

"Sure," Pastor Chris said. "Do you think I walked around singing hymns all day when I was a boy? I was probably as crazy as you." Pastor Chris chuckled. "At the hospital they'd say, 'Here comes Chris again.' Sometime I'll tell you about my tree house and zip line."

"You're like a regular person," Jeremy said.

"Jeremy, there's no reason Christians can't have fun," Pastor Chris said. "God invented fun!"

Who knew spending time with the preacher could be fun? Jeremy thought.

Your Turn

1. Why do some people think being a pastor is stuffy and boring?
2. What would you say to someone who thinks this way?

_____

_____

_____

Prayer

God, I'm Your kid and You love me! That keeps me smiling. Amen.

Be Thankful

Give thanks in all circumstances.
–1 Thessalonians 5:18

The List

"Jeremy, I need to be on my way," Pastor Chris said. "I want to leave this with you." He handed a piece of paper to Jeremy. "It's this week's prayer list."

"I don't know these people," Jeremy said.

"You don't have to know them to pray for them," Pastor Chris told him. "You have time on your hands right now, and every person on that list needs God's help."

Jeremy felt confused. "I don't know how to do that."

"Easy as pie," Pastor Chris said. He glanced at the paper. "Mattie Close has a broken hip. If you want to pray for her, you just talk to God and say, 'LORD, please heal Mattie's hip.' "

"That's all I have to do?"

"Yes. And only if you want to," Pastor Chris said. "No pressure."

After Pastor Chris left, Jeremy asked his mother, "Do we have a directory of church members with pictures?"

"Yes, I'll get it for you," she said.

Jeremy leafed through the book and found the photo of Mattie Close. She had white hair and a pleasant smile. "God, please bless Mattie Close and help her get well. Amen." *That wasn't so bad,* he thought. *It even felt good.*

Your Turn

1. Who are people you pray for every day?
2. Who do you pray for that is not in your family? Not in your church?

_____

_____

Prayer

God, people need Your love and healing. Please be with them. Amen.

Be Thankful

Learning About Living

Older people have lived many years and learned a lot of things. That's why you can learn so much from your parents, aunts, uncles, and grandparents. The Bible gives great respect to people who have lived a long time. To learn one thing the Bible says about older people, solve the puzzle.

You'll need your Bible. Use the clues to fill in the correct letters. For instance, if the clue says SECOND BOOK, SECOND LETTER, look up the second book of the Bible (Exodus) and fill in the blank with the second letter of that book's name (X). If you need help, look up Proverbs 16:31.

FIRST BOOK, FIRST LETTER   _____

EIGHTH BOOK, FIRST LETTER   _____

SIXTH BOOK, LAST LETTER   _____

FIFTH BOOK, LAST LETTER   _____

SIXTEENTH BOOK, LAST LETTER   _____

FIFTEENTH BOOK, LAST LETTER   _____

THIRD BOOK, FOURTH LETTER   _____

FIFTEENTH BOOK, THIRD LETTER   _____

FIRST BOOK, LAST TWO LETTERS   _____

THIRTIETH BOOK, FIRST LETTER   _____

THIRD BOOK, SEVENTH LETTER   _____

EIGHTH BOOK, FIRST LETTER   _____

EIGHTEENTH BOOK, SECOND LETTER   _____

FORTIETH BOOK, LAST LETTER   _____

LAST BOOK, LAST LETTER   _____

Prayer

LORD, thank You for the godly older folks in my life. Amen.

Be Thankful

Prayer List

Make a list of people to pray for and identify something specific to pray about each person. Complete the list and start praying.

Monday - I will pray for
_____,
_____
that God will _____.
_____

Tuesday - I will pray for
_____,
_____
that God will _____.
_____

Wednesday - I will pray for
_____,
_____
that God will _____.
_____

Thursday - I will pray for
_____,
_____
that God will _____.

Friday - I will pray for
_____,
_____
that God will _____.

Saturday - I will pray for
_____,
_____
that God will _____.

Prayer

God, I want to get in the habit of praying daily for people because I know You always hear me and always answer. Amen.

Making a Difference

[Jesus said,] "Whoever serves me must follow me."
– John 12:26

Meeting in Math

"How was therapy today?" Dad asked.

"Lily is a slave driver," Jeremy said. "She's working me really hard, but I'm getting better. I did stuff today I couldn't do last week."

"Who's Lily?" Dad asked, holding the door for his son.

"The physical therapist," Jeremy said. "She moved here from Florida last year. Her son goes to my school, but I've never met him."

They moved slowly across the parking lot because of Jeremy's cast.

"Do Lily and her son like it here?" Dad asked, unlocking the car.

Jeremy settled into the seat and fastened his seat belt. "Her son misses his old friends. His grades have tanked, and now he's hanging with some kids Lily doesn't like. "She's worried his new friends might be into drugs."

"Bad business," Dad said. "Lily and her son must be having a hard time."

"I guess so. I let Lily look at my class schedule. It turns out that her son and I will be in the same math class," Jeremy said. "I told her I'd introduce him to some of my friends. If he gets with some good kids, maybe it will keep him out of trouble."

"That would be great," his father said. "It's a kind thing for you to do."

"Wouldn't it be cool if God used my broken ankle to help Lily's son?"

Your Turn

1. Do you think listening to someone with problems helps the person?
2. Do you know someone who could use a listening ear this week?

_____

_____

Prayer

God, when I help people, my problems don't seem so big. Amen.

Making a Difference

[Jesus said,] "Whoever serves me must follow me."
– John 12:26

When I Grow Up

Jeremy studied the chessboard. "Are you ever going to let me win?"

"Nope," Grandpa said. He captured Jeremy's rook with a bishop. "Keep your eyes open."

"I might like to be a physical therapist someday."

"Yes?" Grandpa said, raising his gaze from the board. "Tell me more."

"Physical therapists help people get better after accidents and surgery," Jeremy said. "They exercise people and give massages and stuff."

"You're good with people," Grandpa said. "You would do well in work like that. Physical therapy pays well and makes the world better. Making money is fine," Grandpa said, "but you want work worth doing. Let God help you decide. Some people pick a job because of what it pays or because it's easy. As Christians, we represent Jesus at work too."

"If I hadn't broken my ankle," Jeremy said, "I wouldn't even know there was such a thing as physical therapy."

"It takes a lot of schooling to become a physical therapist."

Jeremy moved his queen to protect his other rook. "I can do it. I get good grades."

"You can do anything you really want to do," Grandpa said. He moved his queen. "Checkmate."

"Except beat you at chess," Jeremy said with a groan.

Your Turn

1. Have you thought about what work you might do someday?
2. What do you look for when thinking about work?

_____

_____

Prayer

God, please help me find the right work now and when I grow up. Amen.

Making a Difference

[Jesus said,] "Whoever serves me must follow me."
– John 12:26

Mad Dogs and Spooky Guys

Jeremy's ankle hurt. He shifted the heavy cast then clicked through TV stations.

His mother laid three books on the table at his side. "I called the school to find out what you'll be reading in English this fall. You can get a head start."

"You expect me to spend summer vacation reading schoolbooks?"

Mom picked up one of the books. "I read *To Kill a Mockingbird* when I was your age. I loved it."

Jeremy returned to surfing channels and ignored the books.

His mother said, "I'll leave them in case you get bored."

Jeremy turned off TV. Idly picked up the top book. Leafing through it, there was some kid named Scout—a cool name. Then a man shot a mad dog. That was different. He flipped back to the first page. When his mother brought his lunch on a tray, he'd read twenty-five pages.

"What about the creepy guy in the old house?" Jeremy asked. "Is he a going to be a bad guy or a good guy?"

"Keep reading and you'll find out," his mother said.

"I didn't know reading could be so much fun," Jeremy said. "This might be the year I get an 'A' in English."

Your Turn

1. Why aren't we born knowing everything we need to know?
2. Do you enjoy learning? What can you do to make learning more fun?

_____

_____

Prayer

God, the more I learn, the more I see what an amazing world You made. Amen.

Making a Difference

[Jesus said,] "Whoever serves me must follow me."
– John 12:26

Blazing Six Guns

"My turn to pick the movie," Jeremy's father said. "*Blazing Six Guns.* Outlaws, bounty hunters—this movie has it all."

"Ooh, I can hardly wait," Mom said. "I'll make the popcorn."

"While I clear the table and load the dishwasher," Dad said.

"I'll set up the movie," Jeremy's brother, Reese, volunteered.

Jeremy got up from the table. Thanks to his broken ankle, he was released from chores. He hobbled into the living room.

"Wednesday night family movies," Jeremy said. "It's really corny."

Reese said, "Mom and Dad are doing this to keep you company. Dad always picks goofy westerns, and Mom does chick flicks."

"Even if the movie is lame," Jeremy said, "I like being together."

"And the popcorn," Reese said. "Parmesan popcorn at that!"

A few minutes later their parents joined them. Mom carried a heaping bowl of popcorn and four bowls.

"When my ankle heals," Jeremy asked, "will we have movie nights?"

"Would you like to?" Dad asked.

"Sure, it would be okay, I guess," Jeremy said.

His mother hugged him. "It would be okay with me too."

Your Turn

1. What fun things do you enjoy with your family?

_____

_____

_____

Prayer

God, my family isn't perfect, but I love them. Amen.

Making a Difference

[Jesus said,] "Whoever serves me must follow me."
– John 12:26

The Greatest Summer

The doctor turned off the saw and pulled apart Jeremy's cast. The skin underneath was shiny and pink. "Yuck!" Jeremy said. "That stinks!"

"Soap and water will take care of the smell," the doctor said. He turned Jeremy's foot, examining his ankle. "The bone has healed very well."

"I'm glad to get out of that cast before school starts."

"Not much of a summer vacation being laid up," the doctor said.

"It was a great summer," Jeremy said. "I learned to play chess and spent time with my grandpa. We had family movie night every week with parmesan popcorn. My preacher showed me how to pray for sick people. I found out about physical therapy, and I think that might be my job someday. I read some great books."

"Are you saying the broken ankle was a good thing?" the doctor asked.

"No way!" Jeremy said. "But God used it to bless me. He took a bad accident and used it for something really great!"

The doctor grinned. "You've learned a lot this summer. I wish all my patients were as savvy as you."

Your Turn

1. Can you think of a bad thing in your life that God turned into a good thing?
2. If someone you know gets hurt, what can you do to help him or her?

_____

_____

_____

Prayer

God, when Jesus went to the cross, You took the worst thing of all and used it to save people. Amazing. Amen.

Making a Difference

Wheel of Careers

You can't think about becoming something you don't even know about. Use this exercise to find out about some careers. Ask three adults you don't know very well what type of work they do. Ask them why their jobs are good careers for them. Record their answers on the career wheel.

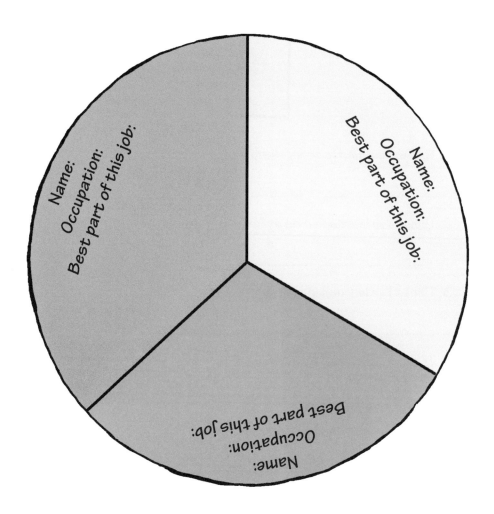

Prayer

God, I don't know what I want to do when I'm grown, but I know You will help me figure it out. Thanks. Amen.

Making a Difference

I'm Learning and Growing

Sometimes people don't realize how much they're learning and growing. Complete the chart about the things you've learned. Thank God for all these things and for the people who helped you.

1. Things I learned in school last year

_____

2. Things I've learned to do at home that help our family

_____

3. Things I've learned in church

_____

4. Things I've learned about myself

_____

5. Things I've learned to make or operate

_____

Prayer

God, thank You for this book. I've learned so much about You. Help me keep all I've learned in my thoughts and in my heart so I can be a light in this world. Amen.

ANSWER KEY

Page 15

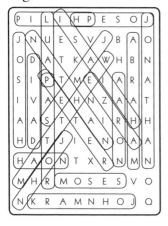

Page 22

Be fair
Be honest
Show mercy
Help others

Page 29

You are my friends if you do what I command. (John 15:14)

Page 42

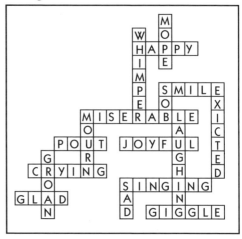

Page 43

Philippians 4:6-7 could be used for any of the worries.
Other choices:
The future: Matthew 6:34;
Death: John 11:25-26;
Divorce: Philippians 4:6-7;
Bad grades: Psalm 32:8

Page 70

Peter, Joseph, Lot, Paul, ruthless

Page 85

The apple tree has one orange; the bird is upside-down; the sun and the moon are out at the same time; the dog has only three legs; one boy has one pant leg up; one boy is missing a shoe; a plate and fork are on the grass; the boy is telling the other boy that he doesn't forgive him (this is the main thing that is wrong!). The one thing that could be changed is the boy's speech balloon to "I forgive you."

Page 92

- Gideon/Menace to a horde of Midianites.
- Deborah/Sacker of Sisera's army.
- Samson/The Philistine foe.

Page 98

sinners, taxmen, deaf, lame, lepers, blind, poor, sick, insane

Page 106

1. The temple; Solomon; Collect cedar...
2. The ark; Noah; Collect cypress...
3. The tabernacle; Moses; Aaron; Collect 11 curtains...

Page 119

love, joy, peace, patience, kindness, goodness, faithfulness, gentleness, self-control.
You'll need patience as God works.

Page 126

apple, cedars, wheat, dates, pomegranates, figs, barley, grapes, rose, olive, cucumbers, melons, onions, lilies, mustard

Page 134

sport teams, church members, employees, firefighters, army, orchestra, family, students

Page 140

1. The Christians. 2. They listened to the apostles' teaching, shared with each other, and worshipped together. 3. They sold their possessions and used the money to help each other. 4. They met together every day. 5. They cooperated because they believed in God. God helped them love each other.

Page 141

May God...help you live in complete harmony with each other. Romans 15:5

Page 147

1. D
2. A
3. C

Page 162

He will cover you with his feathers, and under his wings you will find refuge. (Psalm 91:4)

Page 169

Abraham: "I will give you a land of your own."
Sarah: "I will give you a child."
Moses: "I will bring my people out of Egypt."
Joshua: "I will not leave you or forsake you."
Gideon: "I will help you defeat the Midianites."
Jeremiah: "I will make you as strong as an iron pillar."
Solomon: "I will give you wisdom."

Page 182

1. C   2. B   3. A

Page 203

1. Barnabas welcomed Paul and told others Paul could be trusted. He also introduced him in person to the church leaders.
2. Barnabas went to help. He encouraged the new believers. He also sent for Paul so Paul could use his gifts to help the new Christians.
3. Barnabas disagreed with his friend Paul. When Paul wouldn't change his mind, Barnabas planned his own mission trip and took John Mark along.

Page 204

self-control
love
gentleness
kindness
joy
peace
patience
goodness
faithfulness

Page 218

He who has been stealing must steal no longer.   (Ephesians 4:28)

Page 224

police
bus-driver
teacher
doctor
firefighter
parents
principal
coach
minister

Page 231

Apply your heart to instruction and your ears to words of knowledge. (Proverbs 23:12)

Page 245

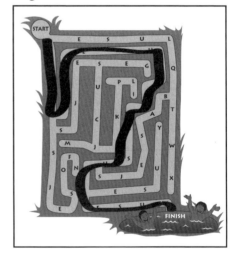

Page 246

- Boy with a sack lunch /Helped feed 5,000 people
- David/He killed a giant
- Jesus/Talked with the wise men in the temple
- Samuel/He heard God's voice in the night
- Miriam/She guarded her little brother on the river
- Joash /Became king when seven years old
- Children of Jerusalem/Sang praises to Jesus

Page 260

Love each other as I have loved you. (John 15:12)

Page 273

1. Abram
2. Simeon
3. Noah
4. Moses
5. Sarah
6. Anna
7. Methuselah

Page 280

I am making everything new!

Page 281

God saw all that he had made, and it was very good. (Genesis 1:31)

Page 301

God is with me...

in the darkest CAVE

above the CLOUDS

if I fly to the MOON

in a TREE

in the WILDERNESS

on a MOUNTAIN

on the SEA

Page 302

YOU REMAIN THE SAME, AND YOUR YEARS WILL NEVER END.

Page 322

OLD TESTAMENT

LAW

* Genesis

* Exodus

* Leviticus

* Numbers

* Deuteronomy

HISTORY

* Joshua

* Judges

* Ruth
* 1 Samuel
* 2 Samuel
* 1 Kings
* 2 Kings
* 1 Chronicles
* 2 Chronicles
* Ezra
* Nehemiah
* Esther

WISDOM AND POETRY
* Job
* Psalms
* Proverbs
* Ecclesiastes
* Song of Solomon

MAJOR PROPHETS
* Isaiah
* Jeremiah
* Lamentations
* Ezekiel
* Daniel

MINOR PROPHETS
* Hosea
* Joel
* Amos
* Obadiah
* Jonah

* Micah
* Nahum
* Habakkuk
* Zephaniah
* Haggai
* Zechariah
* Malachi

NEW TESTAMENT
GOSPELS
* Matthew
* Mark
* Luke
* John

CHURCH HISTORY
* Acts

PAUL'S LETTERS
* Romans
* 1 Corinthians
* 2 Corinthians
* Galatians
* Ephesians
* Philippians
* Colossians
* 1 Thessalonians
* 2 Thessalonians
* 1 Timothy
* 2 Timothy

Page 336

Page 357

One day, Jesus and his friends were on a BOAT when a terrible STORM began. Their BOAT started to SINK. Jesus didn't worry because he was SLEEPING. His friends were SCARED and begged Jesus to SAVE them. Jesus got up and told the STORM to STOP. When the danger passed, the disciples were GRATEFUL because Jesus saved them. Jesus said to them, "Where is your FAITH?"

Page 358

ANYTHING and EVERYTHING

Page 364

GRAY HAIR IS A CROWN.
Proverbs 16:31

Ages 6-9   **Ages 10-12**

Gotta Have God!
52 Week Devotional for Boys
380–388 pages, Softcover, Full Color Illustrations.

L46971   L46972

Gotta Have God!
232–248 pages, Softcover, Full Color Illustrations.

Jesus knows all about being a boy because He was one! Jesus knows all about being a boy because He was one! Gotta Have God helps young men learn how much He loves them and wants to be the model for their lives. Each age-based book, for boys ages 2–5, ages 6–9, and ages 10–12, includes devotions and activities designed to help boys understand how they can grow to be strong Christian men. Over 100 devotionals in each book.

L46961   L46962   L46963

L46964   L46965   L46966

L46967   L46968   L46969

Find more great stuff by visiting our website: www.Rose-Publishing.com